Laxmisha Rai
Programming in C++

Information and Computer Engineering

___

Volume 5

Already published in the series

Volume 4
Shuqin Lou, Chunling Yan, Digital Electronic Circuits, 2018
ISBN 978-3-11-061466-4, e-ISBN 978-3-11-061491-6, e-ISBN (EPUB) 978-3-11-061493-0

Volume 3
Baolong Guo, Signals and Systems, 2018
ISBN 978-3-11-059541-3, e-ISBN 978-3-11-059390-7, e-ISBN (EPUB) 978-3-11-059296-2

Volume 2
Jie Yang, Congfeng Liu, Random Signal Analysis, 2018
ISBN 978-3-11-059536-9, e-ISBN 978-3-11-059380-8, e-ISBN (EPUB) 978-3-11-059297-9

Volume 1
Beija Ning, Analog Electronic Circuit, 2018
ISBN 978-3-11-059540-6, e-ISBN 978-3-11-059386-0, e-ISBN (EPUB) 978-3-11-059319-8

Laxmisha Rai

Programming in C++

Object-Oriented Features

DE GRUYTER Science Press
Beijing

Author
Laxmisha Rai
College of Electronic and Information Engineering
Shandong University of Science and Technology,
Qingdao, China.

ISBN 978-3-11-059539-0
e-ISBN (PDF) 978-3-11-059384-6
e-ISBN (EPUB) 978-3-11-059295-5
ISSN 2570-1614

Library of Congress Control Number: 2018954463

Bibliographic information published by the Deutsche Nationalbibliothek
The Deutsche Nationalbibliothek lists this publication in the Deutsche Nationalbibliografie; detailed
bibliographic data are available on the Internet at http://dnb.dnb.de.

© 2019 Walter de Gruyter GmbH, Berlin/Boston, Science Press
Typesetting: Integra Software Services Pvt. Ltd.
Printing and binding: CPI books GmbH, Leck
Cover image: Prill/iStock/Getty Images Plus

www.degruyter.com

Preface

Today, use of computers and application of software can be seen everywhere. The rapid progress in information technology (IT) has changed our conventional ways of thinking. It is hard to imagine life without computers and software these days. Programming is an essential part of computing. Many programming languages were developed over the years, however, very few of them survived in the IT market. C++ is one such programming language that can rightly be called as a successor to C language. C++ is a general-purpose programming language with a rich set of object-oriented programming (OOP) and generic programming features. This language was created by Bjarne Stroustrup, a Danish computer scientist, in 1980s. Today, C++ is one of the most prominent and useful OOP languages. It is studied widely by students and programmers alike. C++ supports a number of features, such as classes, objects, inheritance, constructors, and polymorphism that make it so useful. This book covers all of these concepts along with the basics of programming, including selection statements, looping, arrays, strings, function sorting, and searching algorithms.

The book is written by focusing programmers, both experienced and inexperienced, who would like to learn C++ with or without any prior programming experience. The main objective of the book is to present an overview of C++ programming language with OOP concepts. The book is presented in simple English and easy examples. It can be used as a textbook for graduate or undergraduate programs. The book will provide every reader an idea to write and practice C++ programs as well as understanding various computers and programming terms in English. There are many features that will make this book unique among C++ textbooks. A large number of example programs and illustrations will be presented throughout the book. All of the programs are written with maximum care and attention. Many programming exercises are also provided, wherever necessary. We are sure that every reader will enjoy C++ programming while reading this book.

This book covers almost all of the necessary features of object-oriented programming with C++. There are a total of 18 chapters in the book. Each chapter starts with a brief introduction about its contents and scope. Each chapter has a set of questions for the reader to answer and think about possible answers as well. The book presents over 180 complete programs with their respective input and output details. We suggest every reader to go through all of the chapters starting from 1 to 18 in order to master C++ programming. This book can be divided into two parts. The first part is from Chapters 1 to 13, which covers the basics of C++ programming, or concepts which are not directly related OOP. Even though these chapters use the terms classes and objects here and there, there is no need of exclusive knowledge of OOP concepts. So, teachers who are willing to train their students in the basics of C++ may choose these chapters as introductory lessons on C++ programming. The second part is from Chapters 14 to 18. This part is about topics that are directly related to OOP. These chapters provide the readers the exclusive features of OOP in C++. So, the learners

https://doi.org/10.1515/9783110593846-201

who are familiar with the basics of C++ may start from Chapter 14 to understand the OOP concepts directly. However, the book is written in such a way that the reader can jump to any chapter to acquire exact information without following the sequence of chapters.

In addition to all these chapters, the book presents five appendices for supporting the materials presented in this book. Appendix A provides the list of C++ header files and library functions. It is provided as a quick reference for learners to locate several library functions provided by C++. The brief description of these header files and respective library functions are provided in multiple tables. Appendices B and C provide a list of non-OOP and OOP exercises of C++, respectively. The book provides two different sections, so that the instructors are able to divide the exercises on the basis of the students' ability and course requirements. In some universities or colleges, instructors prefer their students to learn object-oriented concepts of C++ only. In such cases, it is better to refer to the exercises shown in Appendix C. However, if the instructor is more focused on teaching fundamentals of programming concepts through C++, then programming exercises listed in Appendix B are preferable. In addition to these programming exercises, there are also some programming exercises presented at the end of each chapter in section "Review Questions."

Appendix D lists the Decimal-Binary-Octal-Hex ASCII (American Standard Code for Information Interchange) conversion chart. It is very useful while writing programs of especially related character data type. In addition, it is necessary for learners to understand how the numbers are represented in different formats. Appendix E provides Bibliography information.

The book uses different fonts such as **bold**, and `Inconsolata` , to identify the various concepts. For example, the **bold** text reminds the user that these words are important and commonly used terms in understanding concepts of C++ and OOP. All the programs shown in the book are in `Inconsolata`, so that the readers can easily identify them. Moreover, we have also used this font within the text for describing the concepts, to show the readers that these words may form a part of a program, or be closely related to a program. The outputs of example programs are also provided so that the readers can easily guess that the results obtained after the execution of program.

We hope that you find this book interesting, enjoyable, and informative. We wish all the readers every success in C++ programming.

Happy Programming!

Laxmisha Rai

Contents

About the Author

Laxmisha Rai received a bachelor's degree in computer engineering at Mangalore University and a master's degree in computer science and engineering at Manipal Institute of Technology of India. He received a PhD in electronics from Kyungpook National University, South Korea. He was also a postdoctoral researcher at Soongsil University, South Korea.

Since 2010, he has been working as a professor at Shandong University of Science and Technology, China. Dr. Rai has lectured at several conferences in the United States, the United Kingdom, and several countries of Asia. His research interests are software engineering, knowledge-based systems, real-time systems, embedded systems, mobile robots, wireless sensor networks, and massive open online courses. He is the author of two books including *Programming in Java with Object-Oriented Features*, two patents, and over 50 research papers in international journals and conferences. He is a senior member of IEEE. He is also a member of ACM.

In his spare time, he enjoys studying Chinese, and solving Rubik's cubes. He can be reached at *1229521415@qq.com.*

https://doi.org/10.1515/9783110593846-202

1 Introduction to Computers and Programming

Opportunities multiply as they are seized.
—Sun Tzu

1.1 History of computers

Computers are used everywhere in the world these days. History of computers goes back to *Abacus*, a simple calculating device, invented in China around second century BC. We can see this device in China and other countries till date. Many scientists agree that Abacus is the first computer of its kind. Later in 1614, John Napier from Scotland invented the *log* method that reduces multiplication and division to addition and subtraction, respectively. In 1642, Blaise Pascal, another famous French mathematician, built a mechanical calculator that had the capacity for eight digits. Later, Joseph-Marie Jacquard of France invented an automatic loom controlled by punched cards.

In 1820s, Charles Babbage, the famous English mathematician, invented Difference Engine, but he stopped his work and developed Analytical Engine later. The Analytical Engine is a mechanical computer that can solve mathematical problems by using punched cards. This revolutionary invention of Babbage led to the development of more advanced computers at that time. For his great contribution, Charles Babbage is widely known as the **Father of Computers**. Many years later, Konrad Zuse, a German engineer, developed the first general-purpose programmable calculator in 1941. In 1945, University of Pennsylvania's Moore School of Electrical Engineering completed the work of Electronic Numerical Integrator Analyzer and Computer (ENIAC). Later in 1947, Bell Telephone Laboratories developed the transistor. This facilitated a rapid development of computers with greater capability.

After the evolution of digital computing, the computer technology changed rapidly. Many improvements were made in internal organization of computers and computer programming languages. Later, many programming languages were developed to support various applications of computers.

1.2 Introduction to computer and computer science

Computer is a machine that is used to perform calculations. Computer can be programmed to perform many tasks. It can do repetitive tasks quickly and efficiently. It has a large capacity to store, retrieve, and manipulate data. The physical components of a computer are known as **hardware**. The main components of a computer are: Central Processing Unit (CPU), Input, Output, and Memory. The CPU acts as brain of the computer and executes a program (or **software**) that instructs the computer

https://doi.org/10.1515/9783110593846-001

about what is to be done. Input and output (I/O) devices allow the computer to communicate with the user and the outside world. Input device is used to receive data and output device is used to display or produce the information. Memory is used to store the data and information.

Sometimes, computer science is viewed as the study of algorithms. This study encompasses four distinct areas:
1. Machines for executing algorithms
2. Languages for describing algorithms
3. Foundations of algorithms
4. Analysis of algorithms

An **algorithm** is a finite set of instructions that, if followed, accomplish a particular task. Moreover, studying algorithms is fundamental to understand computing principles. If you study computing for many years, you will study algorithms of frequently used processes. A number of books have been written about the algorithms for common activities, such as storing and ordering data. Although it is easy to find standard algorithms for those parts of programs that do common activities, one may develop own algorithms for unique problems. Two commonly used tools help to document program logic (the *algorithm*): **flowcharts** and **pseudocode**. Generally, flowcharts work well for small problems, but pseudocode is used for larger problems. Algorithms are written in pseudocode that resembles programming languages such as C or Pascal. Every algorithm must satisfy the following criteria:
1. *Input*: zero or more externally supplied quantities should be there;
2. *Output*: at least one quantity should be produced;
3. *Definiteness*: each instruction must be clear and unambiguous;
4. *Finiteness*: if we trace out the instructions of an algorithm, then for all cases the algorithm will terminate after a finite number of steps; and
5. *Effectiveness*: every instruction must be sufficiently basic, so that it can, in principle, be carried out by a person using only pencil and paper. It is not necessary that each definite operation must also be feasible.

The term algorithm was originally derived from the phonetic pronunciation of the last name of Abu Ja'far Mohammed ibn Musa al-Khowarizmi, who was an Arabic mathematician and had invented a set of rules for performing the four basic arithmetic operations (addition, subtraction, multiplication, and division) on decimal numbers. An algorithm is the representation of a solution to a problem. One of the obstacles to overcome in using a computer to solve our problems is that of translating the idea of the algorithm to computer code (or program). Usually people cannot understand the actual machine code that the computer needs to run a program, so programs are written in a programming language such as C or Pascal, which is then converted into machine code for the computer to run. In the problem-solving phase of computer programming, programmers usually spend much of their time on designing algorithms. This means that students will have to be conscious of the strategies to solve problems in order to apply them to programming problems. These algorithms can be designed by the use of flowcharts or pseudocode.

A **flowchart** is a diagram made up of boxes, diamonds, and other shapes, connected by arrows, where each shape represents a step in the process, and the arrows show the order in which they occur. Flowcharting combines symbols and flowlines, to show figuratively the operation of an algorithm. From this common understanding, a number of interesting things may happen. For example, process-improvement ideas will often arise spontaneously during a flowcharting session. Moreover, after flowcharting, one may able to write a detailed procedure to solve a problem, which is a good way of documenting a process. Process improvement starts with an understanding of the process, and flowcharting is the first step toward process understanding. Flowcharting uses symbols that have been in use for a number of years to represent the type of operations and/or processes being performed. The standardized format provides a common method for people to visualize problems in the same manner. The use of standardized symbols makes the flowcharts easier to interpret; however, the sequence of activities that make up the process is more important. Note that the pseudocode also describes the essential steps to be taken, but without graphical enhancements. In the recent years, a general-purpose, developmental modeling language known as Unified Modeling Language (UML) was popularly used to visualize the design of a system.

A **program** is a set of quite a number of commands. It goes through many steps during its development. A typical program development may have the following steps:

1. *Requirement Analysis*: In this step, a programmer tries to understand what the program is supposed to do?
2. *Program Design*: After understanding the requirements, the programmer draws conclusions about how to do it. In this step, the programmer creates a strategy to achieve the goal. One of the techniques used during the design phase is drawing a flowchart of the program. In the flowchart, different shapes represent different kinds of steps, such as input and output, decisions, or calculations.
3. *Coding*: In this step, the programmer writes the program in a chosen language.
4. *Testing*: The programmer tests the program against the requirements of Step 1.
5. *Documentation*: An important part of any program development is documentation. It is a good practice to have documents for every program we write. The documents explain other readers *what* we did, *why* we did it, and *how* we did it.

1.3 Introduction to software

The computer hardware includes physical devices such as keyboard, mouse, monitor, etc. The software includes a set of programs. Software allows us to perform various tasks by using computer. These tasks include word processing, database computations, programming, etc. Two common software types are **system software** and **application software**. System software is responsible for controlling, integrating, and managing the individual hardware components of a computer system. The operating system is the most important system software that generally interacts with the computer hardware. The application software is used to perform some specific applications such as drawing software, imaging software, etc.

Software is developed by using programming languages. There are many types of programming languages such as, **interpreter** or **compiler**-based languages. Software can be developed by using any of these types of languages depending on the application. In general, software is a collection of programs and routines that work together to perform a specific operation. A program is simply a set of instructions written in a particular language.

Over the years, the development of software is becoming increasingly complex. To guide the software development process, a number of software-based tools are developed. In general, there are five main steps during the development of software, which become major part of Software Development Life Cycle (SDLC). The main goals of SDLC are to reduce and minimize the risks involved in development. The software project planning, organizing, and maintenance are based on SDLC models. Some of the important and popular SDLC models are waterfall model, iterative model, spiral model, fountain model, V-model, and big bang model.

The simplest, most straightforward, and oldest SDLC model is the waterfall model. In this model, a number of activities are organized in a sequential manner. As shown in Fig. 1.1, each activity is followed after completion of the previous activity:

1. Requirements gathering (or analysis)
2. Design
3. Coding (or implementation)
4. Testing
5. Delivery or maintenance

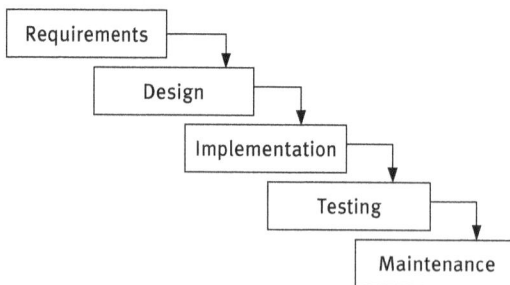

Fig. 1.1: Waterfall Model.

In software testing, verification and validation (V&V) is the process of checking that a software system meets the requirement specifications. The validation tests answer the question: *Are we building the right software?* On the other hand, the verification tests answer the following question: *Are we building the software right?*

Although waterfall model is simple, and easy to understand, it has a few disadvantages. For example:

1. Delays are highly probable in this model, because there is a little scope for revision once a phase is completed.
2. Moreover, any problems in the intermediate phases cannot be fixed until we reach the maintenance stage.

Logical improvement to the waterfall model resulted in the fountain model. In a fountain, water rises up to the middle and then falls back, either to the pool below or is re-entrained at an intermediate level. The same activities as those in the software development of the waterfall model are used in fountain model in the same sequence. However, there is an overlap and iteration of activities. The fountain model is a graphical representation to remind us that although some life cycle activities cannot start before others, there is a considerable overlap and merging of activities across the full life cycle.

Another flexible model in SDLC is the spiral model that emphasizes the need to revisit the earlier stages as many number of times as the project progresses. This allows multiple rounds of refinement. This takes the cues from iterative model and repetition of activities in the same. This model can also be viewed as a series of short waterfall cycles, where each cycle is producing an early prototype representing a part of the entire project. Main advantage of this model is that the customers are able to grasp the idea of entire project in the early part of the cycle.

In the recent years, software prototyping concept has also been very popular. In general, a **prototype** is a working model of software with some limited functionality. The software prototyping facilitates an understanding of the customer requirements at an early stage of development. With prototyping, the users have the chance to evaluate the software and try it before final implementation. This helps get valuable feedback from the customers. It also helps software designers and developers understand about what exactly is expected from the software under development.

Percentage of costs incurred during the different phases of SDLC is quite different from what software engineers can imagine. It can be observed that the maintenance of software is 60%, whereas all the other costs are only 40%. Hence, maintenance is an important factor to be considered in the software development process. Also, earlier programming languages did not support reusability. An existing program cannot be reused because of the dependence of the program on its environment. Thus, these two major problems demanded a new programming approach, **software maintenance** and **software reuse**.

1.4 Programming languages

A program is a means of instructing computer what to do. As we know, computers can understand only 0 and 1, that is, **binary code,** so there should be a means of translating the program code into 1's and 0's. A program is usually written in high-level language similar to English, instead of binary codes. A compiler is a program that translates the language's statements into 0's and 1's for the computer to understand. FORTRAN is one of the major languages developed in 1957. FORTRAN stands for FORmula TRANslation. This language was designed at IBM for scientific computing. Basically this language is used in numerical computations. Later, COBOL was developed to perform many business applications. The language makes it easy to handle large input and output applications. Its syntax is similar to English, and it is easy to learn. In 1958, LISP or LISt Processing was created for Artificial Intelligence (AI) applications. At the same time, ALGOL language was also developed. A major contribution of this programming language is that its features were used in the later generations of programming languages, such as Pascal, C, C++, and Java. The programming language Pascal was developed in 1968. It has many additional features as compared with earlier programming languages. It combined the best features of COBOL, FORTRAN, and ALGOL languages. The combination of features, input/output, and strong mathematical features made it a highly successful and widely popular language. Although Pascal has many good features, it has some shortcomings too. Later, Modula-2 was created as a successor to Pascal, but the same time C language was gaining popularity everywhere. The C language was developed in 1972 by Dennis Ritchie at Bell Laboratories. It has gained more popularity than all previous programming languages and is considered one of the best languages used till date. It has lot of similarities with Pascal. Table 1.1 provides an overview of the development of programming languages.

Table 1.1: Development of programming languages.

Year(s)	Programming Language	Developer(s)
1954–1957	FORTRAN (FORmula TRANslation)	John Backus and his team at IBM
1958–1960	LISP (LISt Processing)	John McCarthy at MIT
1959–1960	COBOL (COmmon Business Orientated Language)	IBM
1960	ALGOL (ALGOrithmic Language)	Committee of European and American Scientists
1961	APL (A Programming Language)	IBM
1964	PL/I (Programming Language I)	IBM
1965	BASIC (Beginners All Purpose Symbolic Instruction Code)	Thomas E. Kurtz and John Kemeny, Dartmouth College, USA

Table 1.1 (continued)

Year(s)	Programming Language	Developer(s)
1967–1971	PASCAL	Niklaus Wirth
1972	C	Dennis Ritche of Bell Laboratories, USA
1973	Prolog	University of Luminy-Marseilles in France by Alain Colmerauer.
1979	Ada	Jean Ichbiah and team at Honeywell
1983	C++	Bjarne Stroustroup
1991	Java	James Gosling and Team, Sun Microsystems

In the early 1980s, a new programming method that was known as object-oriented programming, or OOP, was being developed. OOP has a different approach to programming than all previous programming languages. C++ language was developed by Bjarne Stroustroup in 1983. It is an extension to C known as "**C with Classes.**" C++ was designed to write programs with the authority of C and additional OOP. Although C++ is an OOP language, it is not *purely object-oriented*. The C++ is not a pure object-oriented language because it does not obey all the rules of a typical object-oriented language. For example, we can write a program without creating a class in C++. Later, Sun-Microsystems developed Java programming language, which is purely an *object-oriented* language. It gained high popularity around the world, due to its simplicity and powerful GUI applications. Java has a rich set of libraries to perform many different tasks; a Java program can run on a web browser. Today, C++ is one of the most prominent and useful object-oriented programming language. Programmers and students have been continuously enjoying it. The language supports various features, such as classes, objects, inheritance, constructors, polymorphism, etc., which helps the learners understand the nuts and bolts of an object-oriented language in general.

1.5 Types of programming languages

Today, programming languages are classified into different types. Most of these types are based on their application and usage. However, programming languages are traditionally classified on the basis of programming paradigms, that is, ways in which programming languages are classified on the basis of their features. The common programming paradigms are imperative, functional, declarative, object-oriented, procedural, logical, structured, and symbolic. We will briefly summarize the features of procedural, structured, and object-oriented programing paradigms.

Procedural Programming Languages

Procedural programming specifies a list of operations that the program must complete to reach the desired state. Each program has a starting state, a list of operations to complete, and an ending point. This approach is also known as **imperative programming**. Integral to the idea of procedural programming is the concept of a procedure call.

Procedures, also known as functions, subroutines, or methods, are small sections of code that perform a particular function. A procedure is a list of computations to be carried out effectively. Procedural programming can be compared to unstructured programming, where the entire code resides in a single large block. By splitting the programmatic tasks into small pieces, procedural programming allows a section of code to be re-used in the program without making multiple copies. It also makes it easier for programmers to understand and maintain program structure. Two of the most popular procedural programming languages are FORTRAN and BASIC.

Structured Programming Languages

Structured programming is a special type of procedural programming. It provides additional tools to manage the problems created by larger programs. Structured programming requires that programmers break program structure into small pieces of code that are easily understood. It also opposes the use of global variables and instead uses variables local to each subroutine. One of the well-known features of structural programming is that it does not allow the use of the GOTO statement. It is often associated with a **"top-down"** approach to design. The top-down approach begins with an initial overview of the system that contains minimal details about the different parts. Subsequent design iterations then add detail to the components until the design is complete. The most popular structured programming languages include C, Ada, and Pascal.

Object-Oriented Programming Languages

Object-oriented programming is one the newest and most powerful paradigms. In object-oriented programs, the designer specifies both the data structures and the types of operations that can be applied to those data structures. This pairing of a piece of data with the operations that can be performed on it is known as an **object**. A program thus becomes a collection of cooperating objects, rather than a list of instructions. Objects can store state information and interact with other objects, but generally each object has a distinct and limited role.

There are several key concepts in object-oriented programming. A **class** is a template or prototype from which objects are created, so it describes a collection of variables and methods (methods are also called as functions). These methods can either be accessible to all other classes (public methods) or can have restricted access (private methods). New classes can be derived from a parent class. These derived classes inherit the attributes and behavior of the parent (**inheritance**), but they can also be extended with new data structures and methods. The list of available methods of an object represents all the possible interactions it can have with external objects, which means that it is a concise specification of what the object does. This makes OOP a flexible system, because an object can be modified or extended with no changes to its external interface. New classes can be added to a system that uses the interfaces of the existing classes. Objects typically communicate with each other by passing message. A message can send data to an object or request that it invoke a method. The objects can both send and receive messages. Another key characteristic of OOP is **encapsulation**, which refers to how the implementation details of a particular class are hidden from all objects outside of the class. Programmers specify what information in an object can be shared with other objects.

A final attribute of object-oriented programming languages is **polymorphism**, which means that objects of different types can receive the same message and still respond in different ways. The different objects need to have only the same interface (i.e., method definition). The calling object (the client) does not need to know exactly what type of object it is calling, only that is has a method of a specific name with defined arguments. Polymorphism is often applied to derived classes, which replace the methods of the parent class with different behaviors. Polymorphism and inheritance together make OOP flexible and easy to extend.

Object-oriented programming proponents claim several advantages. They maintain that OOP emphasizes modular code that is simple to develop and maintain. OOP is popular in larger software projects, because objects or groups of objects can be divided among teams and can be developed parallelly. It encourages careful upfront design that facilitates a disciplined development process. Object-oriented programming seems to provide a more manageable foundation for larger software projects. The most popular object-oriented programming languages include Java, Visual Basic, C#, C++, and Python.

1.6 Review questions

1. What is *Abacus*? How can calculations on numbers be performed by using Abacus? Explain.
2. Write a brief note on the history of computers.
3. What is a computer? List the benefits of a computer in everyday life.
4. What is an algorithm? What are the minimum satisfying criteria for algorithms?
5. Define flowchart and pseudocode. How they are useful in writing programs? Discuss.

6. Define the term *software*. What is difference between *system software* and *application software*? Classify the different softwares available in your computer as application and system software.
7. What is a programming Language? How it is different from languages such as Chinese, English, Hindi, French, etc.?
8. Describe briefly the history of development of programming languages.
9. What are the basic five steps of writing effective programs? Explain.
10. List the software development activities in the waterfall model by using a diagram.
11. List different SDLC models available today.
12. How is C language different from C++? Which features are unique to C++? Discuss.
13. Define programming paradigms. What are the common programming paradigms?
14. What is the meaning of the term object-oriented programming (OOP)? List some examples for OOP languages.
15. Write the full forms of these programming languages: FORTRAN, LISP, COBOL, ALGOL, APL, PL/I, BASIC.

2 Introduction to Object-Oriented Programming and C++

Life is a series of natural and spontaneous changes.
   Don't resist them – that only creates sorrow.
   Let reality be reality. Let things flow naturally forward in whatever way they like.
—Lao Tzu

2.1 Introduction

In Chapter 1, we have studied about the basic concepts of computers and programming languages. There are many types of programming languages, such as procedural, functional, and object oriented. Our main purpose in this chapter is to understand the main features of OOP languages and the ways of compiling and running a C++ program successfully. In object-oriented programming, writing a program is easier and more convenient than many other types of programming languages. Today, an OOP language, such as C++, is popular and widely used to develop many software applications. However, the OOP is a new paradigm among programming languages. The basic concepts of an OOP language revolve around topics such as objects, classes, data abstraction, encapsulation, inheritance, polymorphism, and dynamic binding. In this chapter, we will focus on some of the basic concepts of object-oriented programming and how to write a simple C++ program. In addition, we will also present the steps to compile a program using freely available online compilers, Visual Studio, VC++ compiler, and CodeBlocks.

2.2 Object-oriented concepts

Object-oriented programming has a number of advantages. It is simpler and easier to read and write programs. It can reuse the code more efficiently, and provide a robust and error-free code. In this section, we will try to understand various features of object-oriented programming languages briefly.

Objects and classes

In OOP, programs are written by using **objects** and **classes**. OOP concepts are different from other programming languages. All real-world objects are represented by objects. Every object has certain state and behavior. The state of the object is represented by variables and the behavior by methods. An object together with

https://doi.org/10.1515/9783110593846-002

variables and related methods is a software entity. Moreover, an object is an instance of a class. The class is similar to a model or blueprint for creating objects. One class may have multiple instances of objects. For example, Wang is a student. Here, Wang is an object and student is a class.

Modularity and information hiding

In OOP, the source code of an object can be written and maintained independently of the source code for other objects. This will greatly help us to use the object anywhere in the program. This property is called **modularity**. Also, an object has **private** and **public** interface. It will greatly help us to maintain the information and helps us to communicate with other objects.

Inheritance

Object-oriented programming allows us to define classes from other classes, which is called **inheritance**. It plays a major role in writing large programs. Inheritance property is highly useful when we deal with many similar classes with minor changes. Inheritance enables us to define a new class based on an existing class definition. For example, if a book is a **class** then a notebook is a **subclass**. We will see that many characteristics of a notebook are derived from the book class, such as size, pages, and cover, etc. Here, we call the book class as a **parent class** (or **super class** or **base class**) and the notebook class as a **child class** (or **subclass** or **derived class**).

Constructors

The constructors are one of the most powerful features of object-oriented languages. They are used for initializing objects during its creation. Initialization of data members is necessary when we deal with multiple objects of the same class. A constructor is a special method that is executed when the object of that class is created. The name of the constructor must be the same as that of the class name.

Polymorphism

Polymorphism is also important and one of the most essential features of an object-oriented programming. Polymorphism increases the ability of writing the programs simpler with reusability. The polymorphism means many forms (such as many faces). For example, a person may be a father at home, an officer at office, or a customer at restaurant. Here, a father, an officer, and a customer all refer to the same person. Earlier, we discussed about the book and the notebook. Here, the notebook is a subclass derived from the book class. It is also clear that notebook is also a book.

There are two types of polymorphism–(1) **compile time** and (2) **runtime**. The **operator** and **function overloading** are compile time or static polymorphism types. However, a **virtual function** is of **dynamic** or **runtime polymorphism** type. The **operator overloading** is an advanced feature of C++, where a programmer has the flexibility to overload the built-in operator for different purposes. Similarly, it is possible to use functions with the same name but with different arguments. This is called **function overloading**. These functions might have different implementation. When we overload a function or an operator, the compiler will select the most appropriate definition or implementation by comparing the arguments and their data types. This process of selecting the most appropriate overloaded function or an operator is called **overload resolution**.

2.3 Introduction to C++

History of C++

The widely known language C was developed at Bell Laboratories during 1970s. In the same organization, in the early 1980s, researchers created C++ language. This language was developed by Bjarne Stroustrup and named as C++. The special focus is to create a programming language, "**C with Classes**," with the objective of making the programmer to write a good program easily and friendly. The C++ is generally considered as a superset of C because a program written in C can also be executed in C++. So, the object-oriented features of C++ added the extra characteristics to the C component. However, over the years, there are significant changes added to the C++. The first edition of C++ was released in 1985.

What is C++?

C++ is a high-level and an object-oriented language, such as C, Java, Perl, and Smalltalk, etc. It can be used to write many computers' applications. C++ has a lot of similarity with languages, such as C and Java. To learn C++, one does not need to know C or Java. It is quite easy to learn C++ without any other programming background. If one has some knowledge of C language, it is easier to learn C++. C++ has a large set of libraries to support many functions. It is easy to write and read C++ programs. C++is also an excellent language for beginners to learn programming.

2.4 Versions of C++

So far, we can find four versions of C++ standardized by an ISO (International Organization for Standardization) working group known as JTC1/SC22/WG21:
– ISO/IEC 14882:1998 (C++ 98, released in 1998)
– ISO/IEC 14882:2003 (C++ 03, released in 2003)
– ISO/IEC 14882:2011 (C++ 11, released in 2011)
– ISO/IEC 14882:2014 (C++ 14, released in 2014)

The latest version is C++ 14 that was released on 15 December 2014. It is a major update to the previous versions of C++. Some of the unique features of this version are as follows:
– bug fixes and small features
– function return type deduction
– alternative type deduction on declaration
– relaxed constexpr restrictions
– variable template
– aggregate member initialization
– binary literals
– digit separators
– generic lambdas
– lambda capture expressions

Some of the new standard **library functions** in C++ version 2014 are as follows:
– shared mutexes and locking
– heterogeneous lookup in associative containers
– standard user-defined literals
– tuple addressing via type

2.5 Writing the first C++ program

Let us try to understand a simple C++ program. In this section, we will introduce a "Hello! Ni Hao!" program to display "Hello! Nihao!" on the computer screen.

```
// Program 2.1
// Program to display "Hello! Ni Hao" on the computer screen

#include <iostream>
using namespace std;

int main()
{
    cout << "Hello! Ni Hao";
```

```
    cout << endl;

    return 0;
}
```

As shown in Program 2.1, every C++ program contains the function `main()` and this is the function where execution of the program begins. The `main()` function in the example consists of the function header defining it as `main()` and everything from the first opening curly brace (`{`) to the corresponding closing curly brace (`}`). The braces enclose the executable statements in the function, which are collectively referred to as the **body** of the function.

The first two lines in the following program are **comments**. They are written along with two forward slashes (`//`). They are not executable statements of C++ program. They are used only for reader's convenience and understanding. All comments are ignored by the compiler. Comments can be used by two successive slashes (`//`) or we can also use an alternative form of a comment bounded by `/*` and `*/`. The comment using `//` covers only the portion of the line following the two successive slashes, whereas the `/*...*/` form defines whatever is enclosed between the `/*` and the `*/` as a comment, and this can span several lines. As a rule, one should always comment on your programs comprehensively. The comments should be sufficient for another programmer or you, on a later date, to understand the purpose of any particular piece of a code and how it works. It is always a good practice to write more comments in C++ program. A good program should have comments, including name of the program, purpose, input, output, name of the programmer, and his contact information as shown here:

```
// Program 2.1
// Program to display "Hello! Ni Hao" on the computer screen
// Name of the program: HelloNiHao.cpp
// Input: No Parameters
// Output: Display "Hello! NiHao!" on Computer Screen
// Programmer: Liu Shan, Date: November 18, 2017
// Contact E-mail: 1229521415@qq.com
```

Following the comments, we have an `#include` directive:

```
#include <iostream>
```

This is called a **directive** because it directs the compiler to perform something; in this case, the compiler is inserting the contents of file named `iostream`, identified between the angled brackets `<>`, into the program source code before compilation. The `iostream` file is called a **header file** because it gets invariably inserted in another source file by using directive. The `iostream` header file is a part of the standard C++ library and it contains definitions that are necessary for us to be able to use C++ input and output statements. So, without including the `iostream` in the program, the program would not be compiled. The name of the header file can also be written between double quotes, thus

```
#include "iostream"
```

The statement after #include <iostream> is related to namespace.

```
using namespace std;
```

This statement is a using directive and the effect of this is to import all the names from the std namespace into the source file so that we can refer to anything that is defined in this namespace without qualifying the name in our program. A **namespace** is a mechanism in C++ for avoiding problems that can arise when duplicate names are used in a program for different things, and it does this by associating a given set of names, such as those from the standard library, with a sort of family name, which is the namespace name. All the standard library facilities are defined within a namespace with the name std, so every item from this standard library that we can access in our program has its own name, plus the namespace name, std, as a qualifier. The names cout and endl are defined within the standard library so their full names are std::cout and std::endl. The using declaration tells the compiler that we intend to use the names cout and endl from the namespace std without specifying the namespace name.

The program statements making up the function body of main() are terminated with a semicolon. It is the semicolon that marks the end of a statement, not the end of a line. The first statement in the body of the main() function is

```
cout << "Hello! Ni Hao";
```

This is an output statement. In C++, a source of input or a destination for output is referred to as a **stream.** The name cout specifies the **standard** output stream and the operator << indicates that what appears on the right of the operator is to be sent to the output stream, cout. The meaning of the name cout and the operator << is defined in the standard library header file iostream. The second statement inside the main() block is

```
cout << endl;
```

This is another output statement that sends a newline character denoted by the word endl to the command line on the screen. The last statement in the program is

```
return 0;      // Exit the program
```

This terminates the execution of the main() function, which stops the execution of the program. The control returns to the operating system and the 0 is a return code that tells the operating system that the application terminated successfully after completing its task. The statements in a program are executed in the sequence in which they are written, unless a statement specifically causes the natural sequence to be altered. Moreover, we can enclose several statements between a pair of braces, in that case, they become a **block** or a **compound statement.** The body of a function is an example of a block. After the successful execution of this program, the following result (or output) is displayed on the computer screen.

```
Hello! Ni Hao
```

The standard output stream to the command line on the screen is referred to as cout. The complementary input stream from the keyboard is referred to as cin. Of course, both stream names are defined within the std namespace. To obtain input from the keyboard through the standard input stream cin we use the extraction operator for a stream ≫. The **extraction operator** ≫ "points" in the direction of data flow; in this case, from cin to each of the two variables in turn. To read two integer values from the keyboard into integer variables a and b, we can write this statement:

```
cin ≫ a ≫ b;
```

The standard output stream is called cout, which is used to send the output to the command line (Program 1.1). It uses the **insertion operator** << to transfer data to the output stream. This operator also "points" in the direction of data movement.

2.6 Compiling and running C++ Programs

After writing a C++ program in a file, we have to compile the program for errors. Once the program is compiled successfully, the next step is to execute the program (or run) to obtain the results. Here, we would like to summarize the meaning of compilation and execution of a program.

The source code of a C++ program is written in a text file, which is called **source file**. It is also possible that a large and complicated C++ program may include multiple source files. Keeping the programs in multiple files helps the programmers while debugging. As the code becomes bigger in a single source file, it becomes difficult for the programmers to debug the code during removal of errors. The source file of a C++ program has the extension **.cpp**. That means, if we write a C++ program to add two numbers, the program file with source code may be named as **myadd.cpp**. There are some header files that end with **.h**. However, the programs written by users are non-header files that end generally with **.cpp**.

The programing languages, such as C, C++, and Java, are English-like programming languages and are called **high-level languages**. In order for the computer to understand the code, they must be compiled and executed. That means, the source code written in English-like language needs to be translated into a language that computer understands. Generally, most of the high-level languages are either interpreted or compiled into a machine code. The C++ source code is compiled to generate the machine code. A **compiler** typically checks the source code for errors, usually for syntax or grammatical errors. Each programming language defines its own rules and regulations for writing the statements in a program. This is synonymous to writing a letter in English following the grammar rules. The user has the chance to correct the errors after the compilation and the program can be recompiled until it is error free. The objective of the compiler is to translate the program into a machine code and create an executable file to run on the host computer. The executable version of a source code is created if there are no serious syntax errors in the source code. However, there are also some warnings during compilation to guide the user to check for both syntactic and semantic errors in the program. The executable version of a source file is called **object file**, which includes the machine code translation of the source code. The object files usually end with **.o** and are binary files that are ready for execution. The complete executable program is then produced by linking all the object code files together. A **Linker** is another computer program similar to the compiler, where its main purpose is to take one or more object files generated by a compiler and combine them into a single executable file, a library file, or another object file.

There are several ways of compiling C++ programs. The easy available way is to compile online. However, it is not recommended while learning a programming language because the learner does not have the access to explore different tools or options available to understand the full capabilities of a compiler while compiling a C++ source code online. In this chapter, we would like to provide details of compiling C++ programs in multiple ways: online and offline. Initially, we will describe ways of compiling C++ programs using online environment.

2.7 Running C++ programs online

There are several websites that provide options to run C++ programs online. However, this option requires constant Internet connection. This option is preferred in those cases where the user is unable to download or able to obtain the C++ compiler in their computer. There are several websites that provide this option and most of them are able to execute the latest version C++14. Some of these websites provide facilities to the users, such as downloading the projects they have created, autosuggestion options, color coding, and screen settings. Table 2.1 lists some of the commonly used websites for online C++ compilation. Some basic details of these online compilers are also provided in this section.

Tutorialspoint: The www.tutorialspoint.com website provides online compiler for executing C++ source code through link https://www.tutorialspoint.com/compile_cpp_online.php/. As shown in Fig. 2.1, we can write the program in the window

Table 2.1: List of popular online C++ compilers and their URLs.

Online Compiler	URL
Tutorialspoint	https://www.tutorialspoint.com/compile_cpp_online.php
Codechef.com	https://www.codechef.com/ide/
C++ Shell	http://cpp.sh/
Rextester.com	http://rextester.com/l/cpp_online_compiler_clang
Codepad	http://codepad.org/
OnlineGDB	http://www.onlinegdb.com/

provided, and use the Execute option to check for errors and run the code. The screen on the right to the source code window displays the results or a program output. The source code executes successfully (Fig. 2.1). In Fig. 2.2, the source code is intentionally written with an error (missing semicolon in line 7) to show the display of errors.

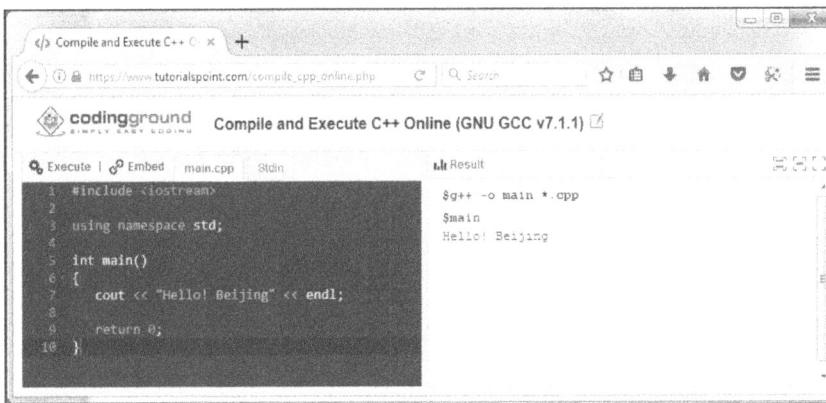

Fig. 2.1: Running a C++ program successfully in Tutorialspoint online compiler.

Codechef: The website, https://www.codechef.com/ide, supports all versions of C++ up to C++14 with various features such as color coding, error detection in source code, downloading, and autosuggestion. Fig. 2.3 shows the source code window for typing, and the results are shown in Fig. 2.4.

C++ Shell: C++ Shell is an online C++ compiler that supports all versions of C ++ up to C++14. It provides features such as color coding and error detection. This can be accessed using website http://cpp.sh/. The compilation of a source code with an error and the results after successful compilation are shown in Figs. 2.5 and 2.6, respectively.

Rextexter: This is an online C++ compiler that supports different versions of C++, such as C++ (**clang**), C++ (**gcc**), and C++ (**VC++**). Rextexter C++ compilers perform fast execution of the source code with features such as color coding, and pointing out the error in the source code. An example of writing a program in Rextester.com is shown in Fig. 2.7.

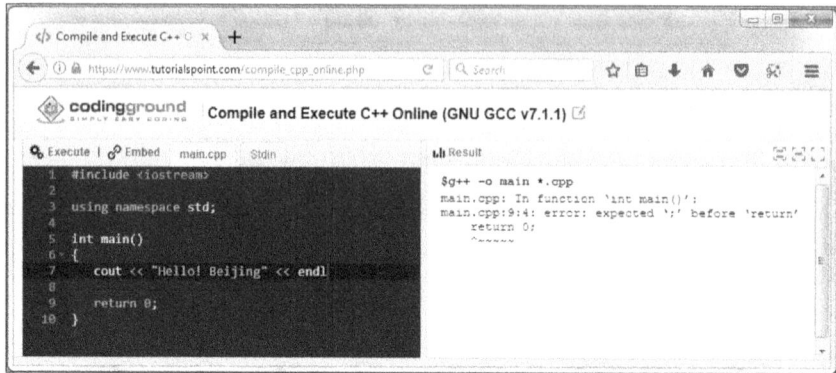

Fig. 2.2: Running a C++ program with errors in Tutorialspoint online compiler.

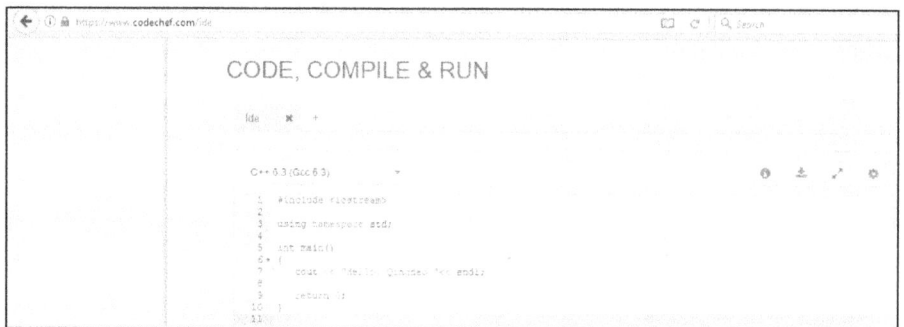

Fig. 2.3: Writing a C++ in Codechef online compiler.

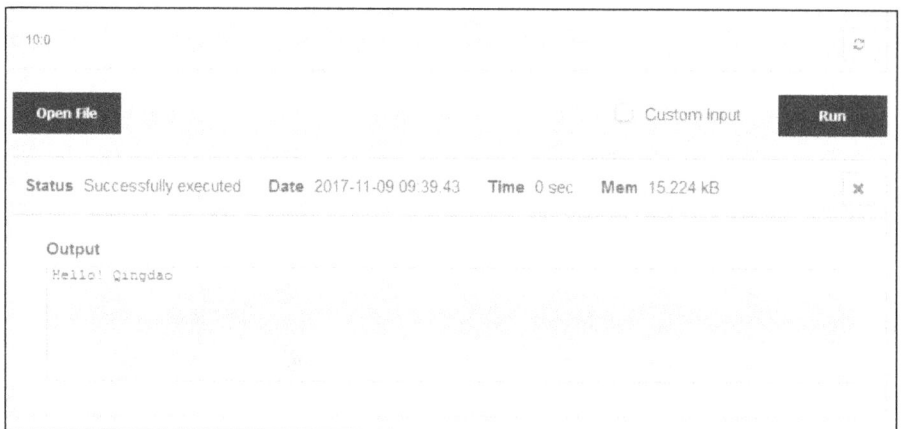

Fig. 2.4: Display of results in C++ in Codechef online compiler.

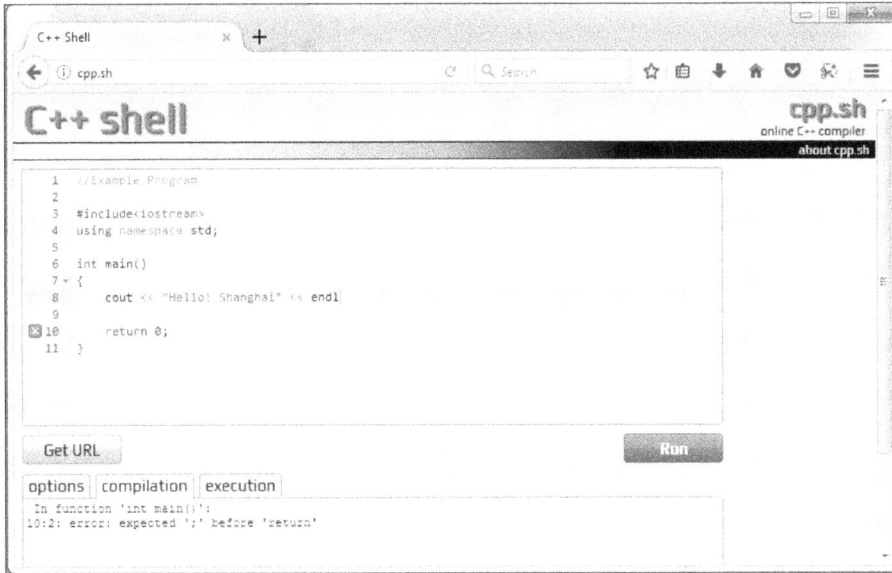

Fig. 2.5: Compiling a C++ program with errors in C++ Shell online compiler.

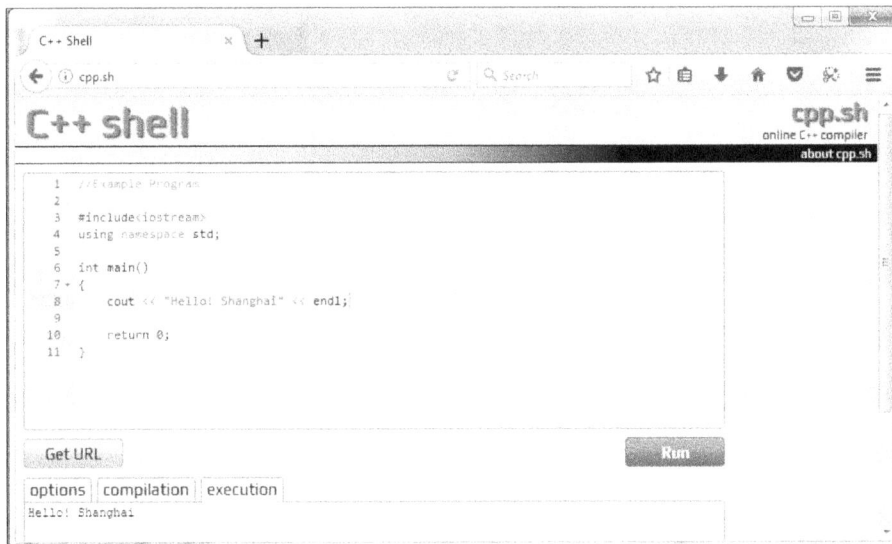

Fig. 2.6: Display of results in C++ Shell online compiler.

Codepad: This online compiler supports all versions of C++ up to C++14. This compiler provides a quick execution of C++ codes with the features such as error detection, downloading the raw code, and login with an account. However, there is

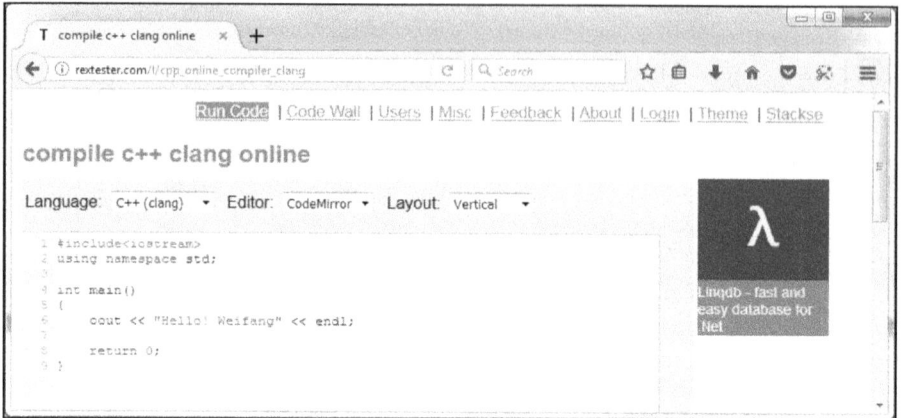

Fig. 2.7: Writing a C++ in Rextester online compiler.

one limitation that the output is displayed in another window. An example window with a program in Codepad is shown in Fig. 2.8.

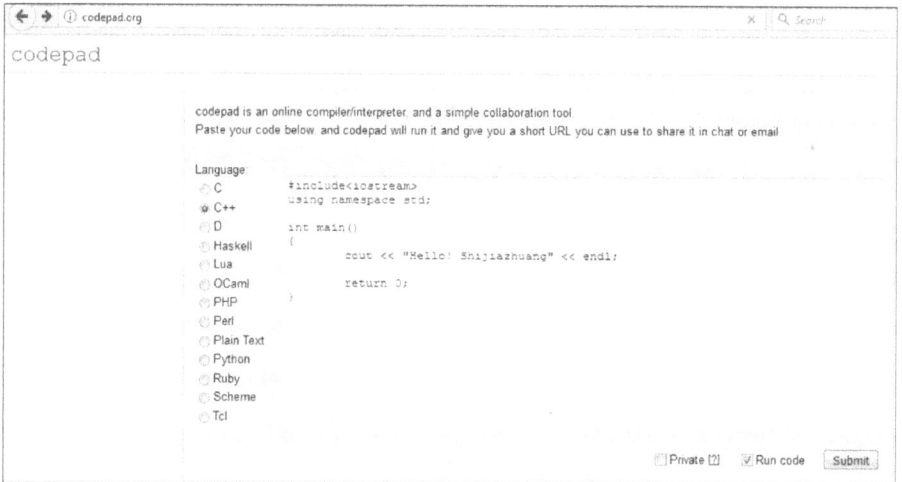

Fig. 2.8: Writing a C++ in Codepad online C++ compiler.

Online GDB: This compiler supports all C++ versions up to C++14. It provides fast execution with features such as color coding, error detection, the screen customization, creating project, and login with the account. An example window with a C++ program in Online GDB is shown in Fig. 2.9.

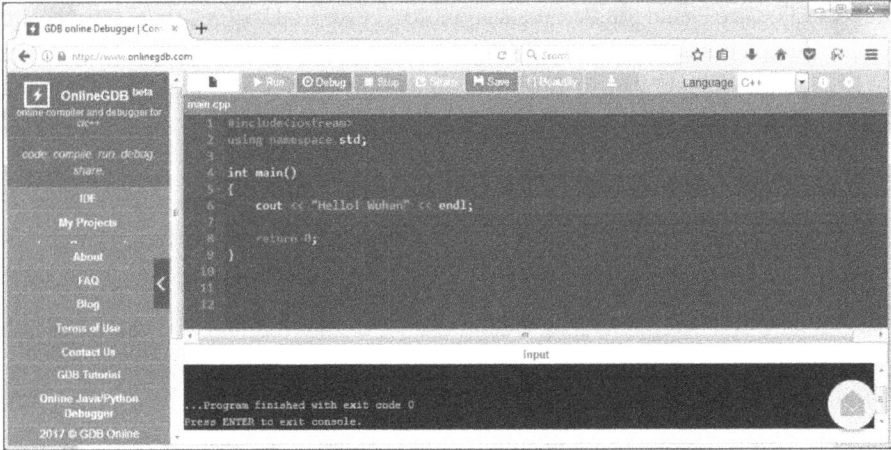

Fig. 2.9: Writing a C++ program in Online GDB compiler.

2.8 Running C++ programs in visual studio 2017

In this section, we will describe the steps involved in running a C++ program using Visual Studio. Today, it is a common practice to use Visual C++ to run C++ programs. The Visual Studio products provide the best IDE (integrated development environment) to develop applications easily. The www.visualstudio.com website provides free trial for users to download. The procedure from downloading to executing a sample C++ program is as follows:

Step 1: Download the latest and stable version from https://www.visualstudio.com/ downloads/, click on Visual Studio Professional free trail. Currently, the latest and stable version is Visual Studio Professional 2017.

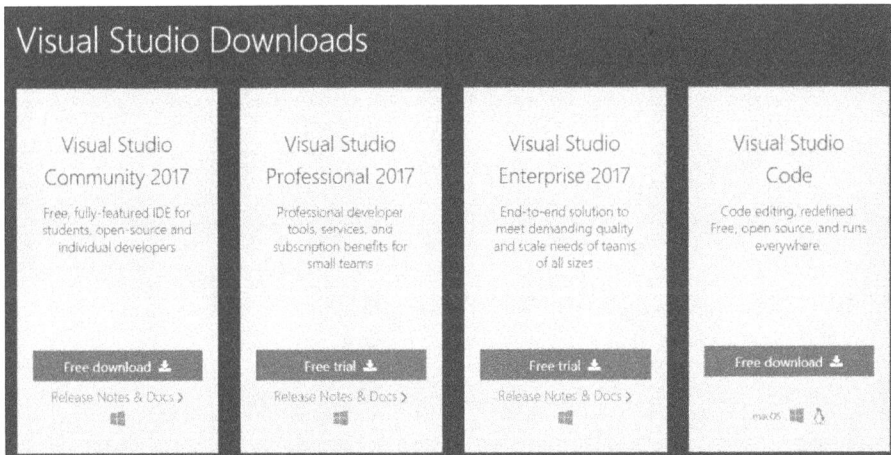

Step 2: Click the Visual Studio Professional 2017, Free trial button. Then, the website jumps to next page with the information as shown in the given screenshot, and it will allow us to download an **exe** file (vs_Professional.exe). Store the file in your computer.

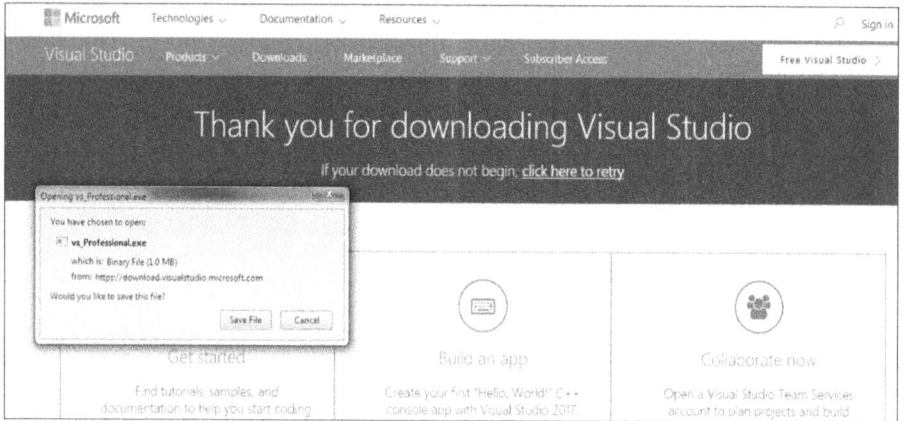

Step 3: After downloading the **.exe** file, identify the file in your computer and double click to install with administrative permission.

Step 4: For running C++ programs in Visual Studio, install the Desktop Development with C++ through the Visual Studio Installer, as shown in the following screenshot:

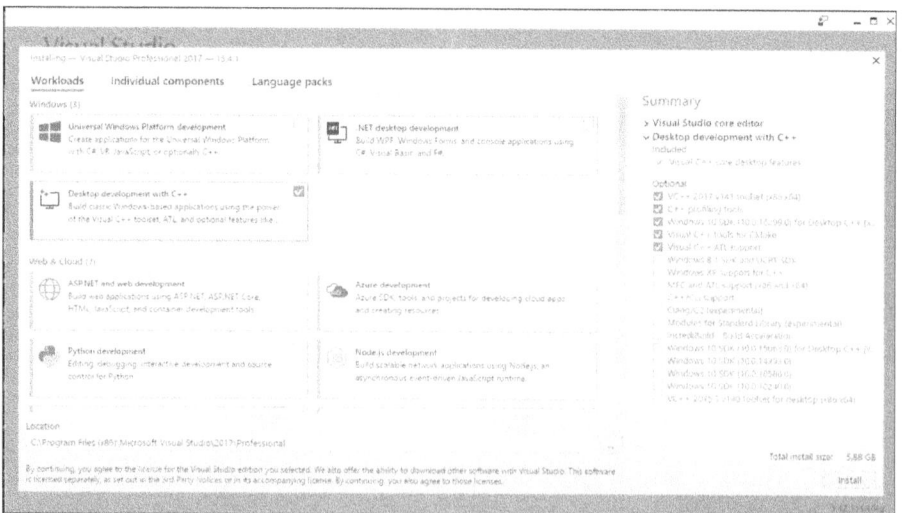

Step 5: Wait for complete installation, as shown in the following screenshot:

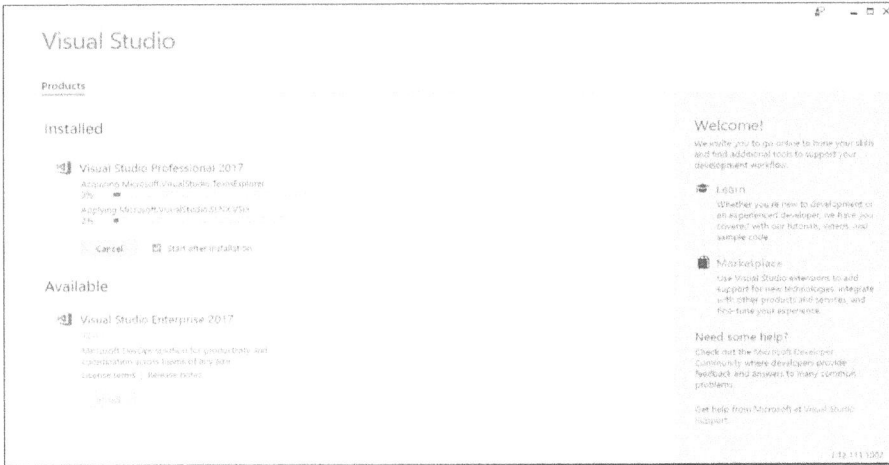

Step 6: Users may create an account or simply continue by pressing "Not now, may be later" to get started. Creating a Microsoft account is optional.

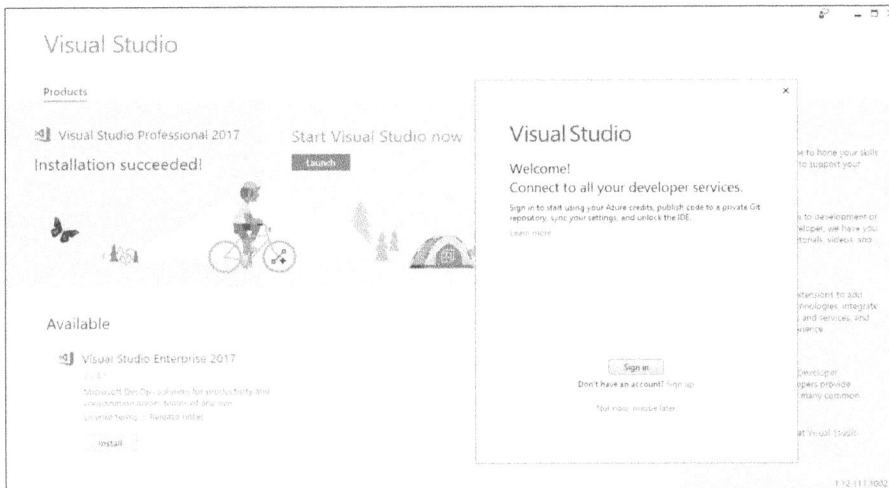

Step 7: After the successful installation, the Visual Studio 2017 can be found in your computer, and by clicking, one can see the following window:

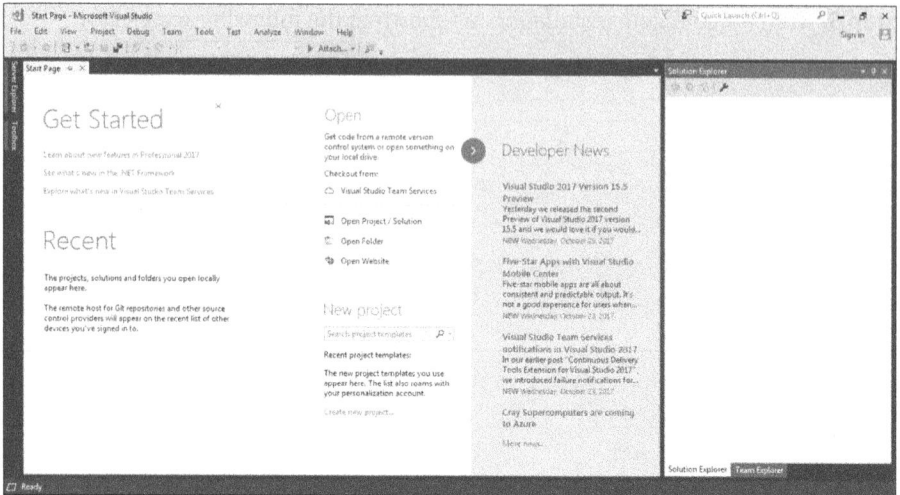

Step 8: From the top left, choose **File, New**, and then **Project**, select the highlighted Windows Console Application as shown in the given screenshot. You can also enter a new application name in the space provided. In this example, we have named the application as Example Application, and now press OK button.

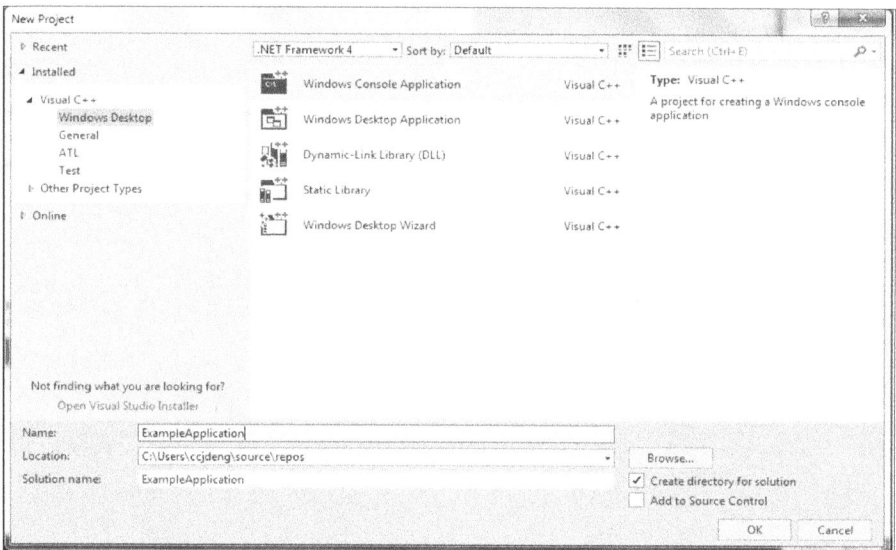

Step 9: After pressing OK, the following window appears. Now, one can start writing the program by keeping the statement, #include "stdafx.h"

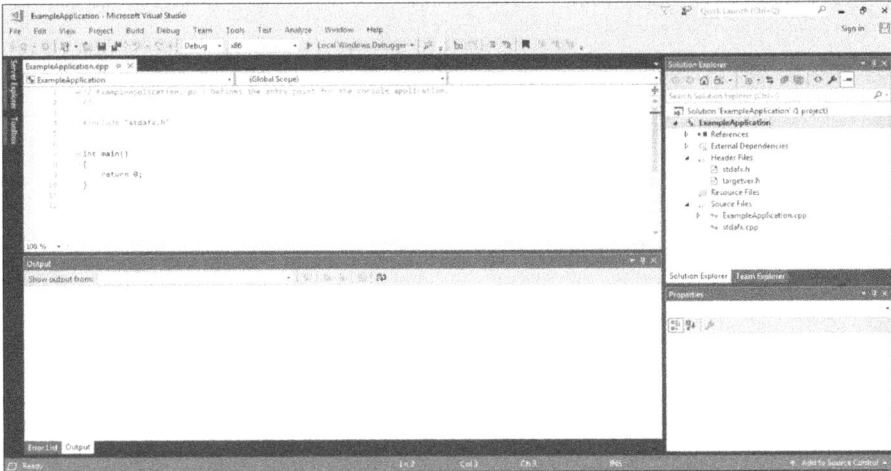

Step 10: In the following screen, a program to add two numbers and obtain their sum is written. To compile the program, we can use the **Compile** option from **Build** menu or press **Ctrl+F7**.

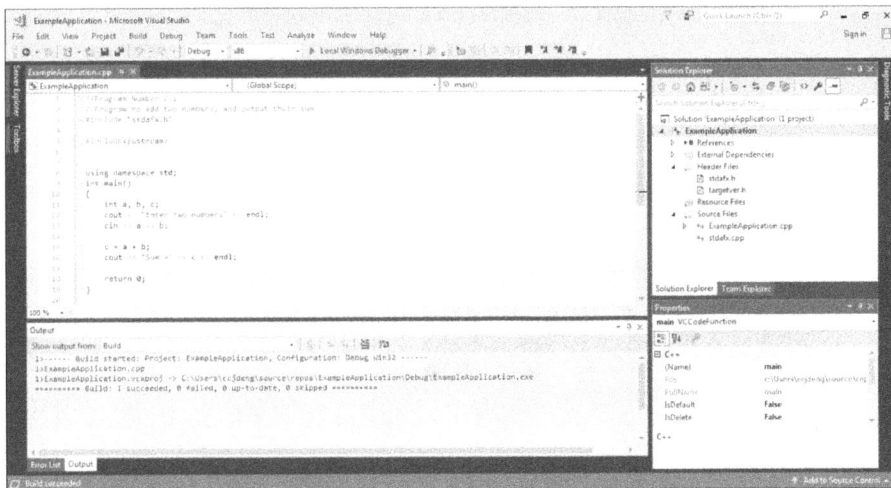

Step 11: Once the program compiles successfully, we can run the program by pressing a green triangle button (Local Windows Debugger) or press **F5**. Then a pop-up window appears asking the user a question "Would you like to build it?" Press Yes.

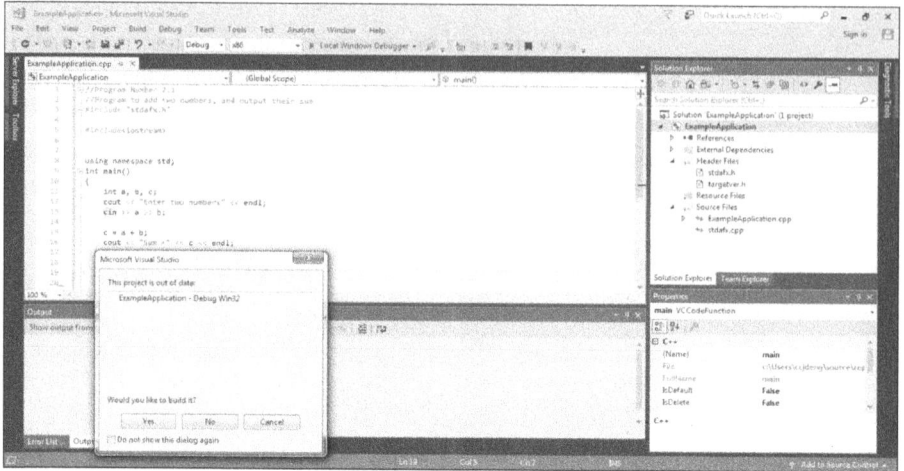

Step 12: The result is displayed as shown in the following screen. However, the output screen quickly disappears, so use breakpoint to see the results for longer periods of time.

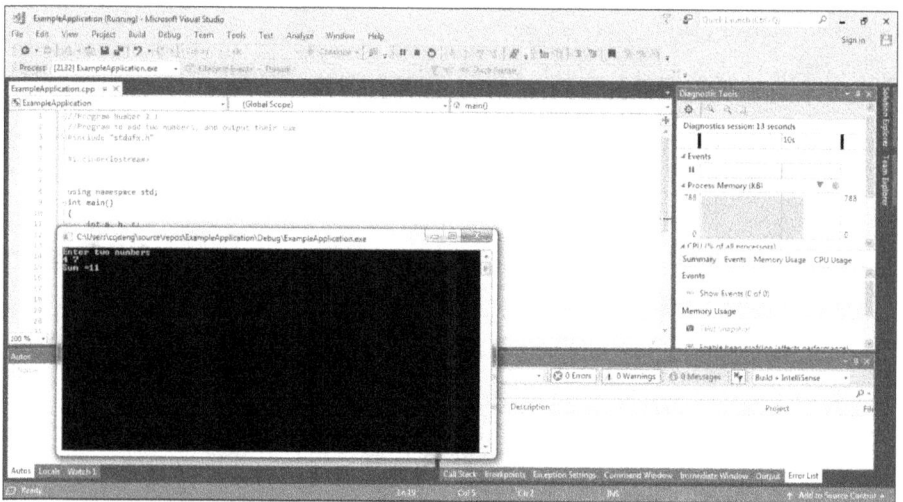

2.9 Running C++ programs in Microsoft visual C++

In the previous section, we have described the ways of installing the latest and stable version of Visual Studio 2017 and running a sample C++ program. However, it is a common practice in many universities and research laboratories that the students are advised to use Microsoft Visual C++. Here, we will briefly describe the ways of running a simple program using Microsoft Visual C+ 6.0. If the VC++ is already installed in a computer, the following window appears once we click it.

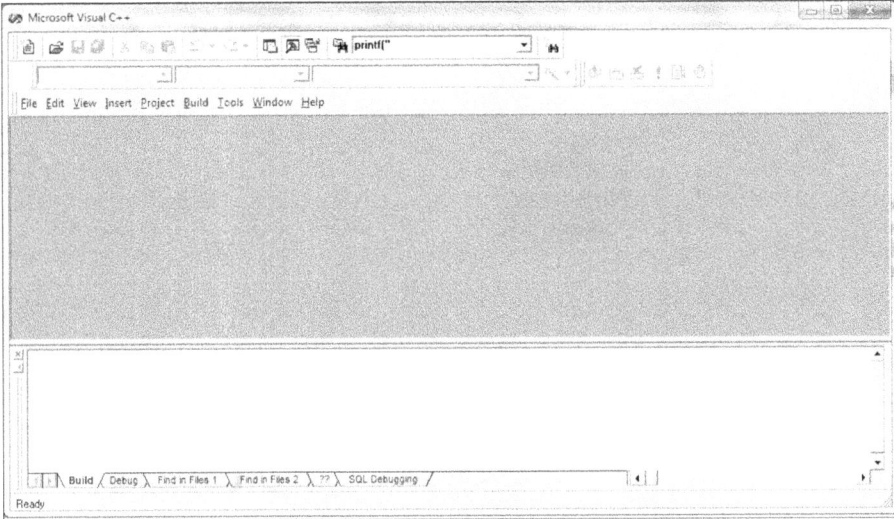

Step 1: Select **File, New**, and then under **Projects** tab, chose Win32 Console Application as shown in the following screen, and then provide a project name. In this case, it is myProject, and then click **OK** button.

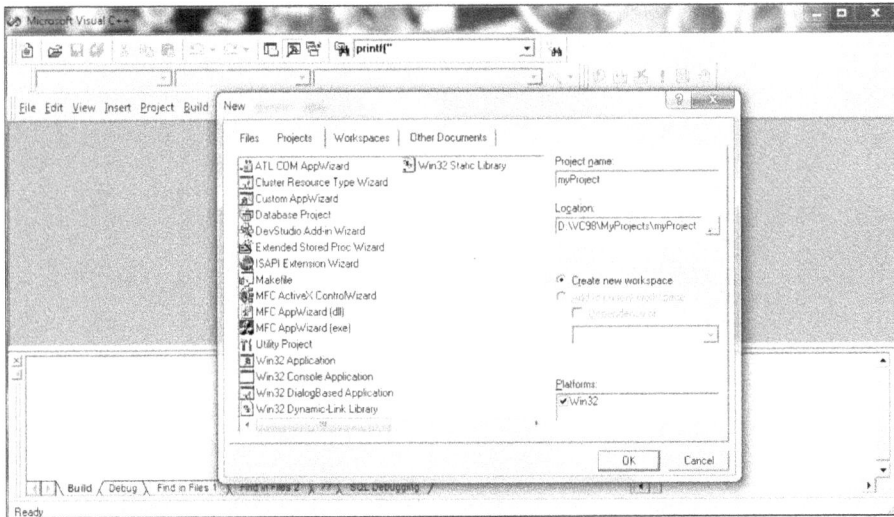

Step 2: The following window appears after completing step 1, just click on **Finish** button.

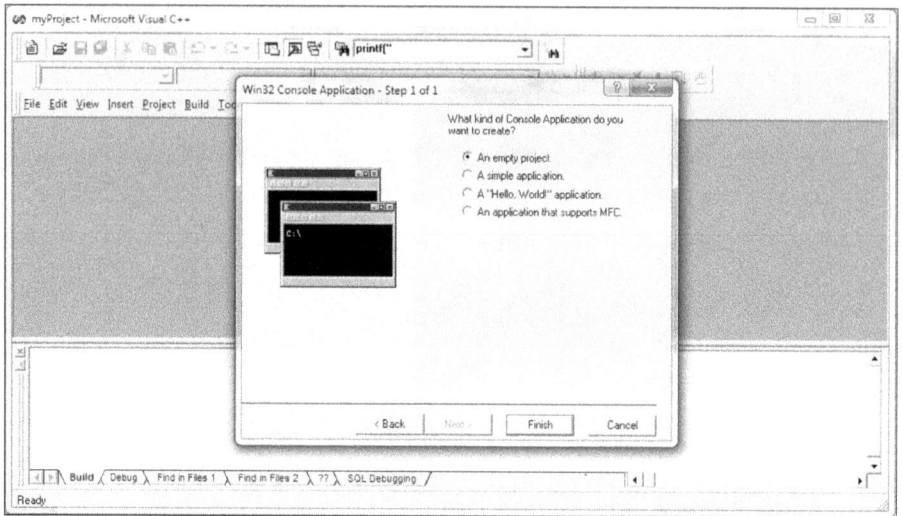

Step 3: The following window appears, in the top left, click on **File** and then **New**.

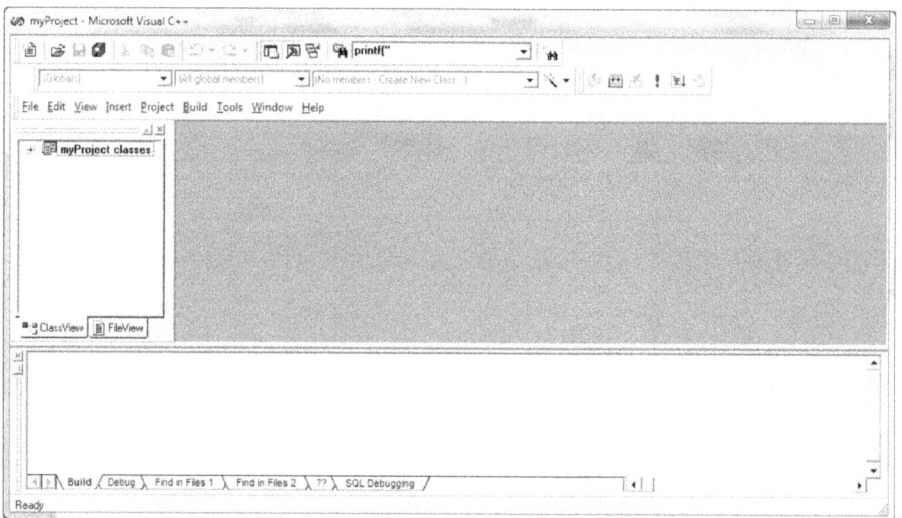

Step 4: Under the Files option, highlight the C++ Source File and provide a C++ file name with **.cpp** extension. In this case, Example.cpp is provided.

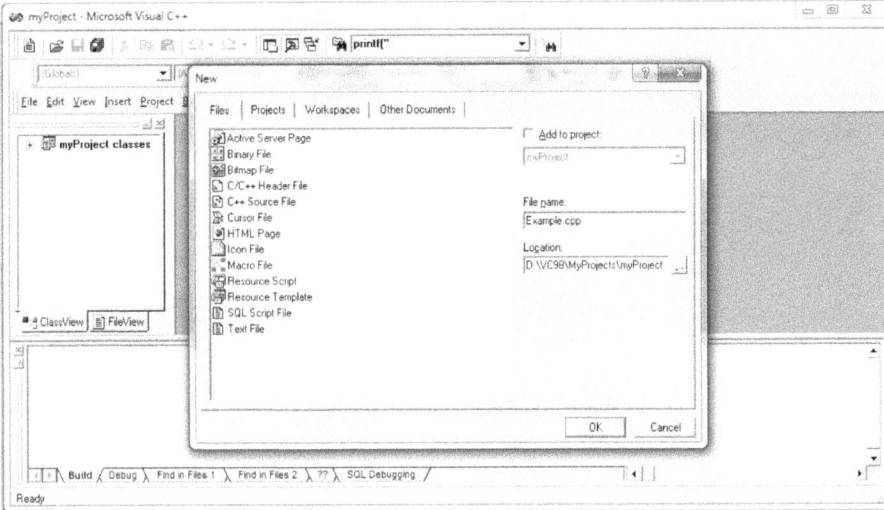

Step 5: Write the program in the space provided as shown in the following screenshot. To compile the program, select **Build** and then **Compile** option, or
press **Ctrl+F7**.

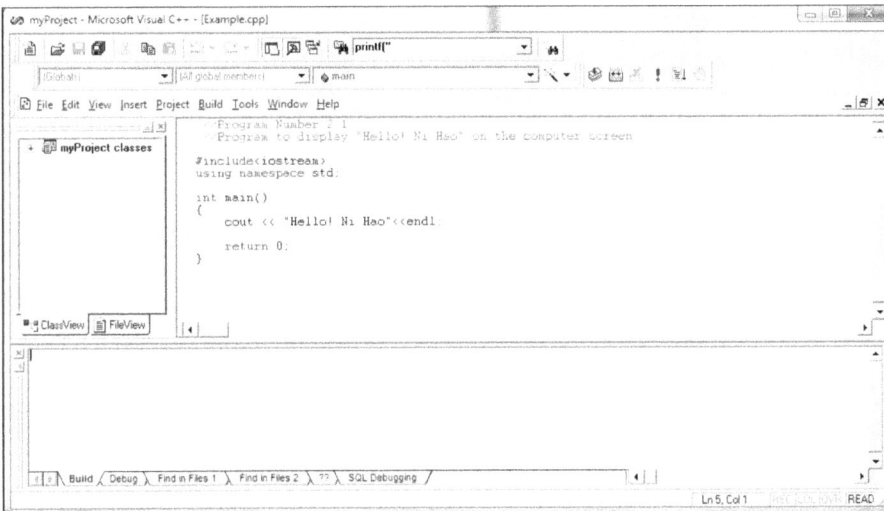

Step 6: To execute the program, select the **Build** and **Execute** or press **Ctrl+F5**. The
results are displayed in the given screenshot:

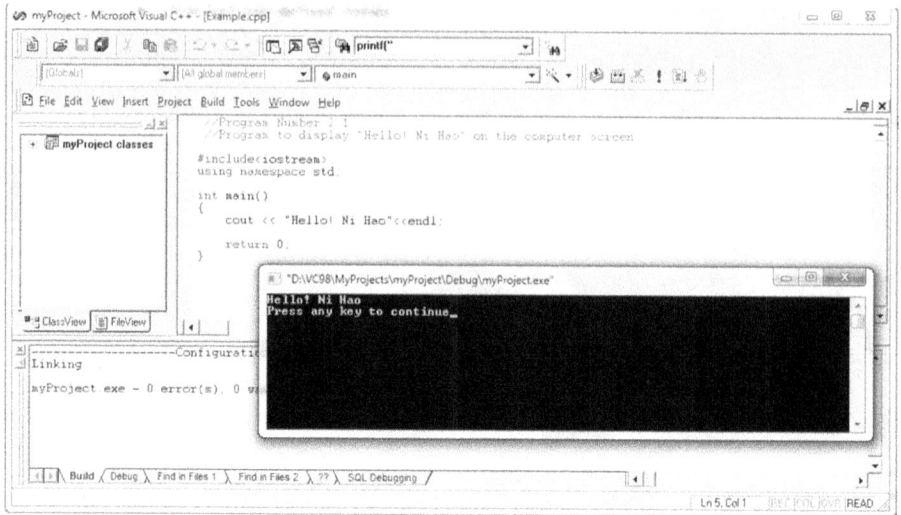

2.10 Running C++ programs in codeblocks IDE

Code::Blocks is a free, open-source, cross-platform C, C++, and Fortran IDE that supports multiple compilers including GCC, Clang, and Visual C++, which is being developed for Windows. This is a framework for working with source code and using compilers and linkers. Here, we will describe the ways of obtaining Code::Blocks and the procedure to compile C++ programs successfully. The details are described step by step.

Step 1: Visit the website of Code::Blocks, http://codeblocks.org/

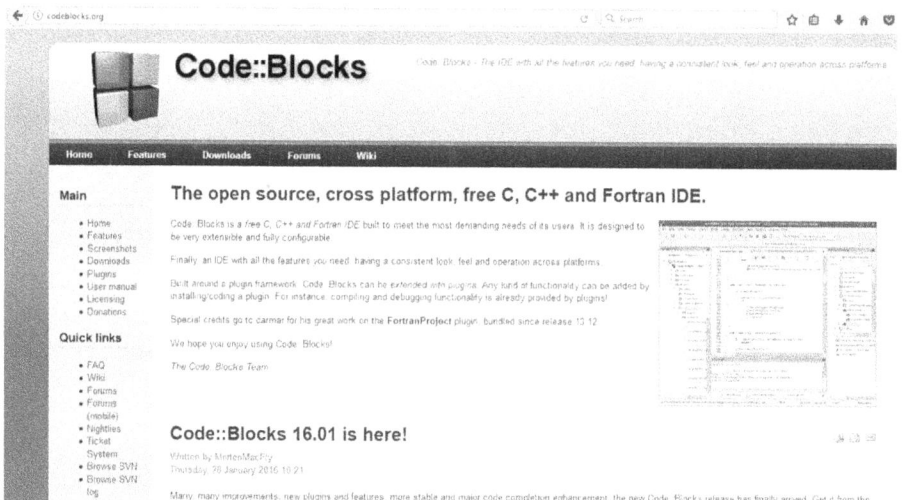

Step 2: Select the Downloads option from the left menu (http://www.codeblocks.
org/downloads), the details of downloading are shown in the following
screenshot. In the Downloads, select – Download the binary release.

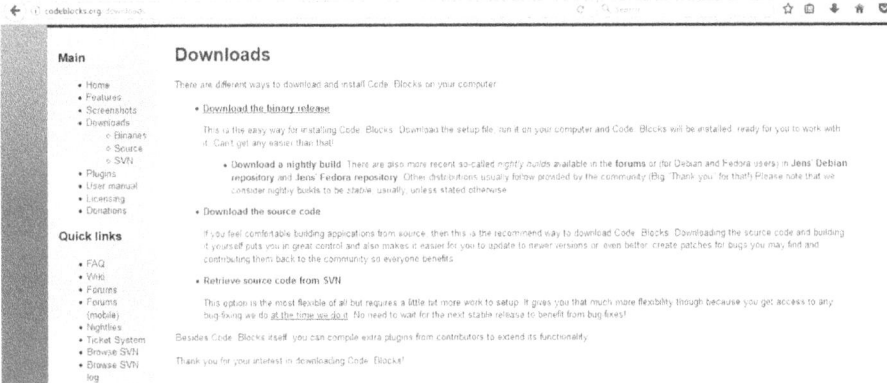

Step 3: Select the operating system of the system platform; in this case, we have
selected Windows XP/Vista/7/8.x/10

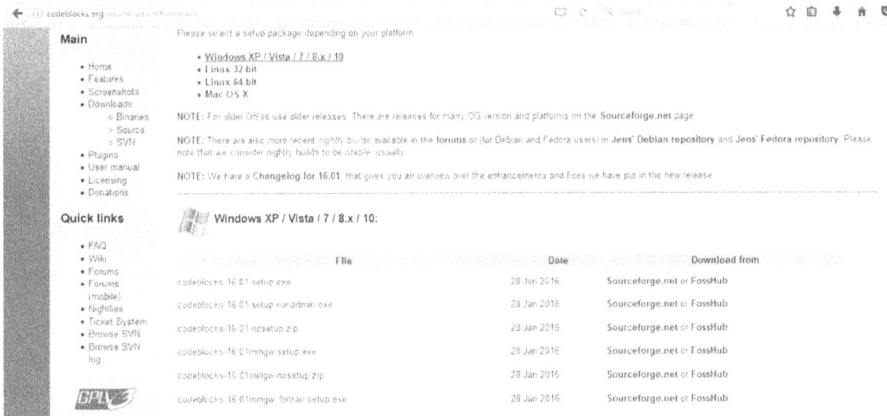

Step 4: As shown in the screen, we can see a variety of download options for Code::
Blocks. For beginners, we recommend to download codeblocks-16.01mingw-
setup.exe because this is included with GNN/GCC compiler. As per the Code::
Blocks website, the codeblocks-16.01mingw-setup.exe file includes additional GCC/G++ compiler and GDB debugger.

Step 5: After selecting the right file to download, we can choose downloading it either from Sourceforge.net or FossHub. In the current case, we have selected Sourceforge.net. The downloading may take around 4–8 min depending on the Internet speed. The downloaded file will be stored in a default location in your computer.

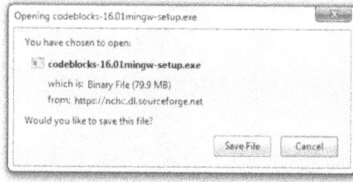

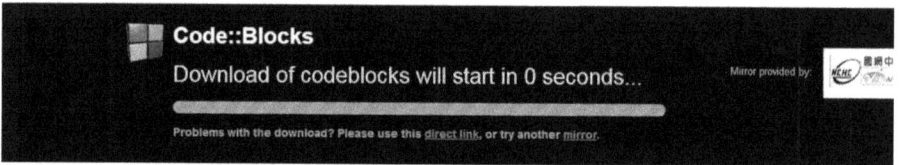

Step 6: Double click on the downloaded file and install with administrative rights, and then click **Next** button.

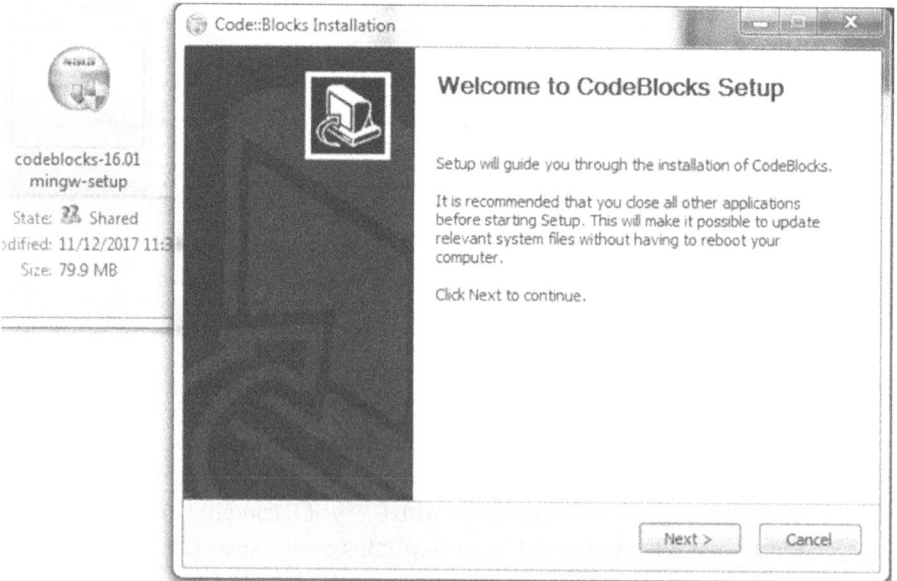

Step 7: After clicking **Next** button, we will get the window for the License Agreement. After agreeing to the license agreement, we can follow the default instructions, and press **Next**. The next step is to choose the components and then we can continue with default options and choose the install location afterwards. If we have followed the instructions properly, then we will be prompted with Installation Complete and Completing CodeBlocks Setup windows as shown in the following screenshots. Click **Finish** to complete the installation.

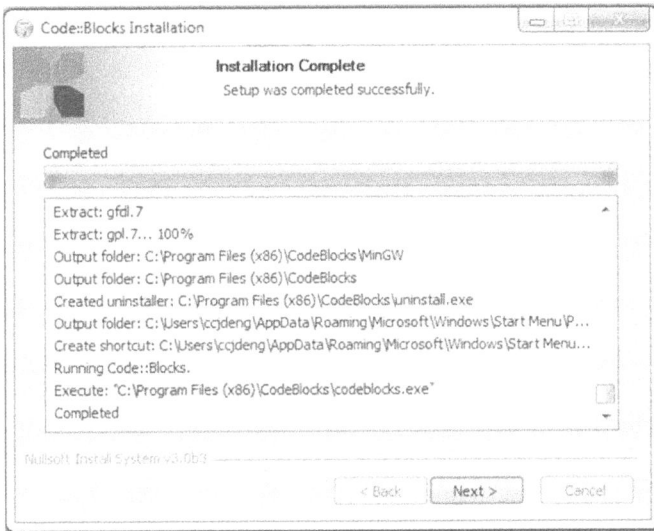

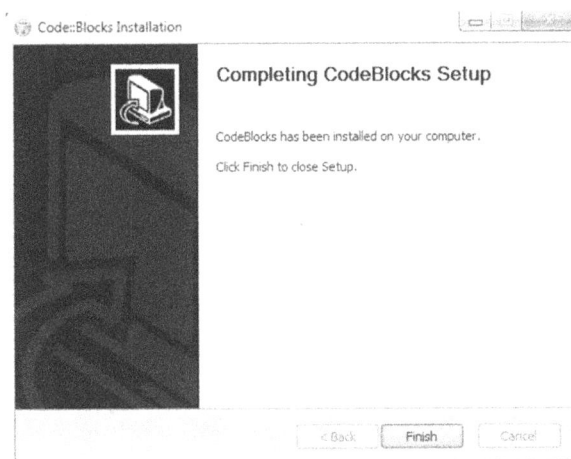

Step 8: If the CodeBlocks is installed properly in your computer, the next step is to launch the CodeBlocks from the Windows start button by choosing the option CodeBlocks as shown in the screenshot or CodeBlocks for desktop (in some cases).

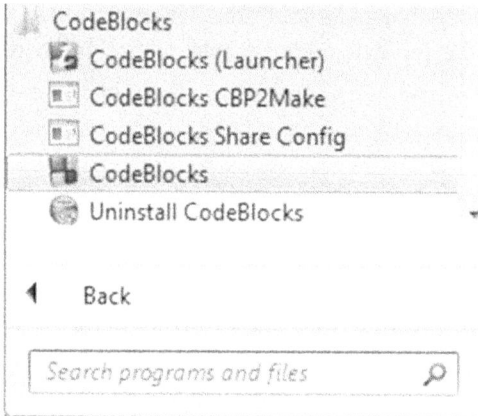

CodeBlocks
  CodeBlocks (Launcher)
  CodeBlocks CBP2Make
  CodeBlocks Share Config
  CodeBlocks
  Uninstall CodeBlocks   ▼

◀   Back

Search programs and files   🔎

Step 9: While launching the CodeBlocks IDE, it may prompt you a window as shown in the screenshot. Select the option, "Yes, associate Code::Blocks with C/C++ file types," and then select **OK**.

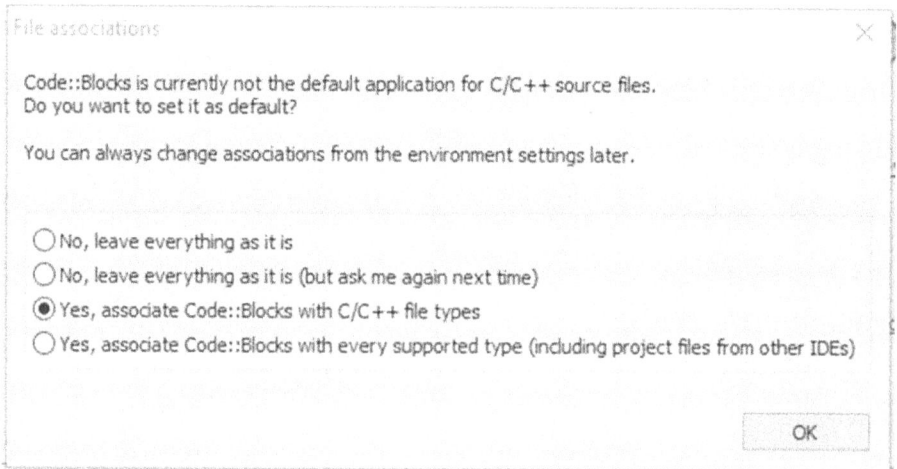

File associations   ✕

Code::Blocks is currently not the default application for C/C++ source files.
Do you want to set it as default?

You can always change associations from the environment settings later.

○ No, leave everything as it is
○ No, leave everything as it is (but ask me again next time)
◉ Yes, associate Code::Blocks with C/C++ file types
○ Yes, associate Code::Blocks with every supported type (including project files from other IDEs)

                                                        OK

Step 10: After we finish the step 9, we will arrive at CodeBlocks main interface window as shown in the screenshot:

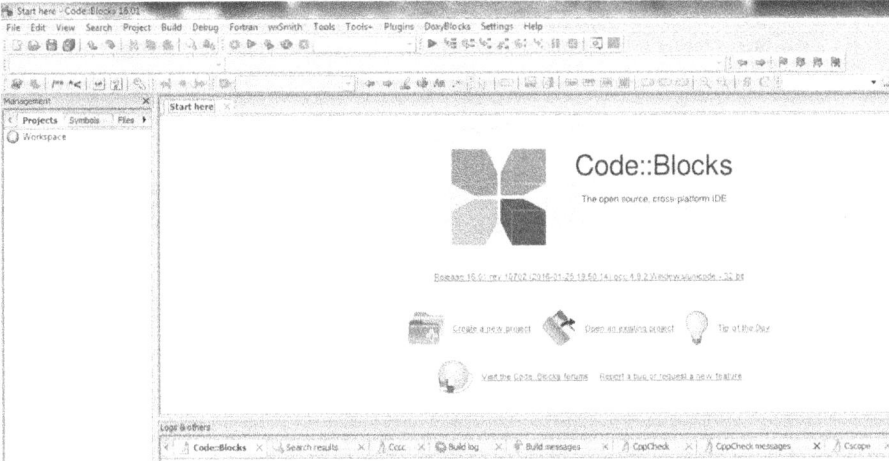

Step 11: To finalize the installation, we still have to check for the path of the compiler so that the CodeBlocks automatically detects the path of the compiler. For this, choose the **Settings** from the CodeBlocks Main menu, and select the compiler; the window will appear as shown in the screenshot. In this window, select Global Compiler Settings and then click on Reset Defaults.

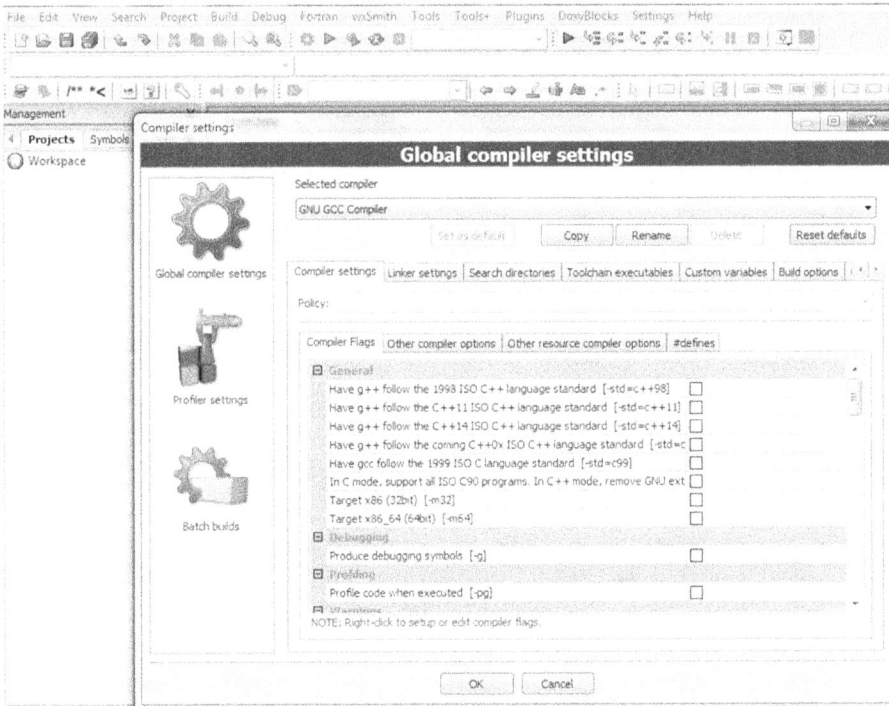

Step 12: Once we finish the step 11, we are prompted with pop-up windows asking questions such as "Reset this Compiler's settings to the defaults?" and "Are you REALLY sure?". Press **OK** for both the questions. If everything is installed properly, the following window pops up:

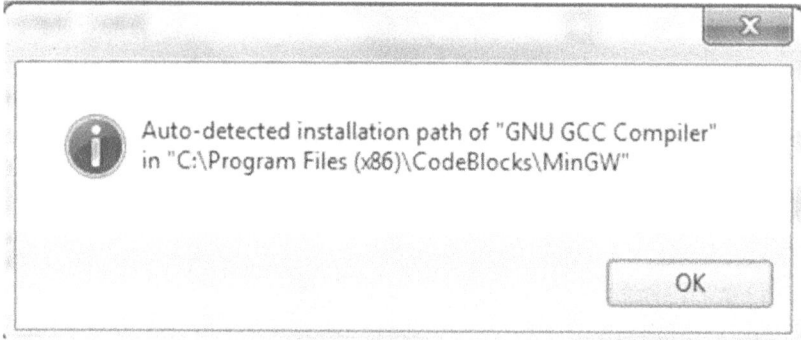

2.11 Writing the first C++ program in CodeBlocks IDE

Here, we will describe the steps involved in writing a simple C++ program in CodeBlocks and running it successfully.

Step 1: In the first step, we click on **File** from menu toolbar and take the cursor on **New** as shown in the following window:

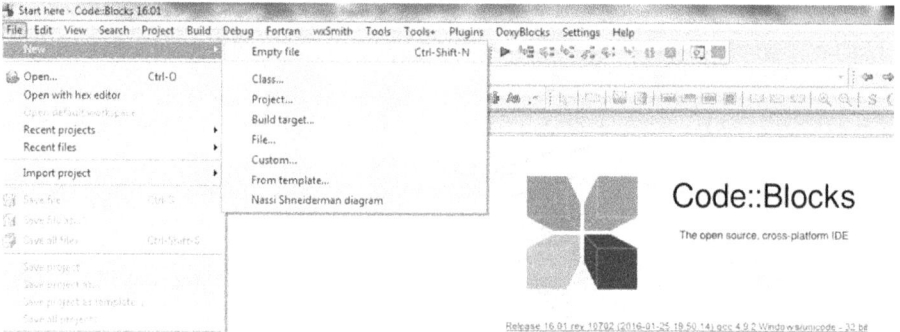

Step 2: Then, we have to name the file. By default, the file is named as ***Untiltled1** as shown in the screenshot, so we have to name this as a C++ file. If there is an asterisk (*) before a file name in editor, it means the content in editor is not saved. If an asterisk (*) is not preceding the file name, it means the content of the file is saved. Now, we have to select a directory to save this program and

give it an appropriate name. It is recommended to use underscores for long names than separating them using space. The file name should have an extension.**cpp**. After selecting proper directory and name for the program, click on the save button from the dialog box. It is important that the file name must end with an extension .**cpp**.

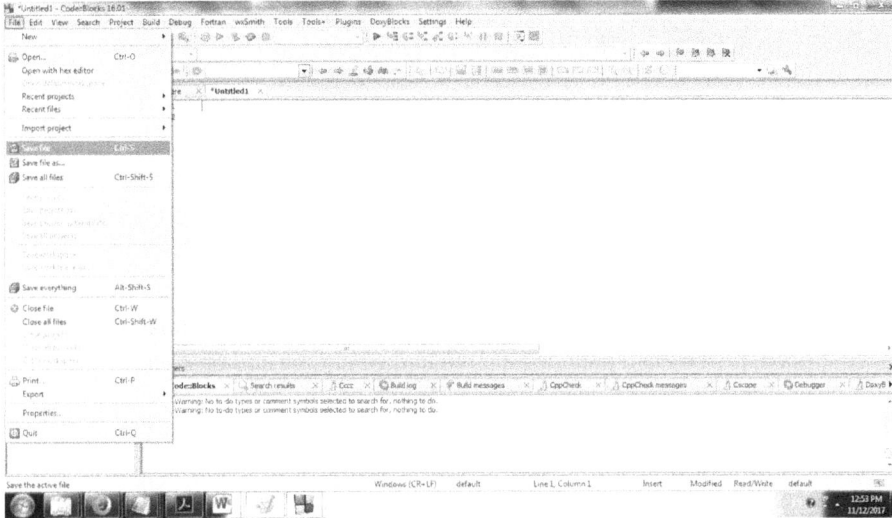

Step 3: For example, in the following window, a simple C++program is written in the CodeBlocks editor's space in a file called **hello.cpp**. We can start writing the program after naming the file. The file can be saved using the **Save** icon or by pressing **Ctrl+S**.

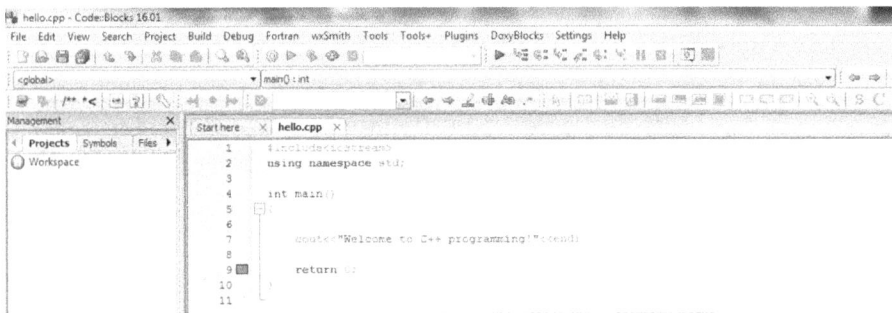

Step 4: Now, we can build the program using **Build** icon in the IDE. If there are no errors in the program as shown in the following screenshot, then at the bottom of IDE in **Build Log** it will show, "Process terminated with status

0," that is, program is error free. This statement will be followed by a number of errors and warning in the program, "0 error(s), 0 warning(s)." It is important to read the error message carefully to understand the error(s).

Step 5: If your program is error free then we can run it by clicking on **Run** icon as shown in the screenshot. After clicking on **Run**, a new terminal window will open, now we can provide an input to the program and then an output or the results will be displayed on the same screen.

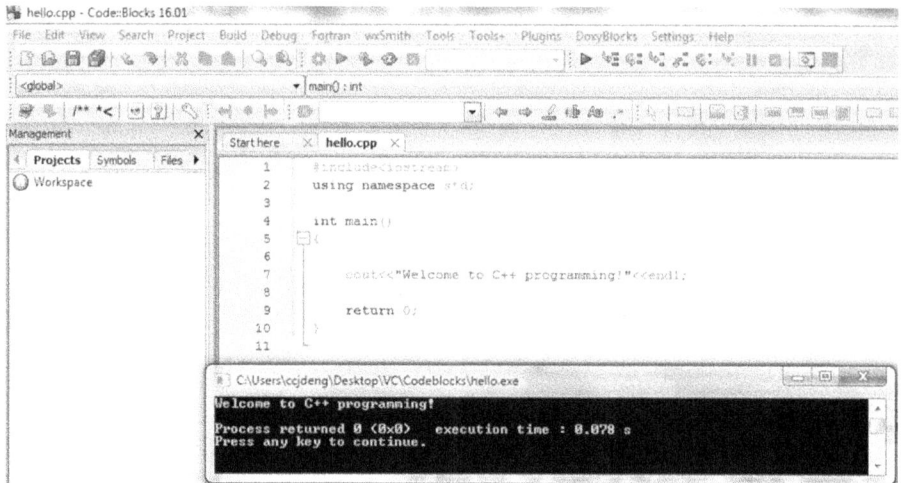

If there is an error (or errors) in the program, then it will be shown in **Build log** with the line number. One such example is shown in the following screenshots, where a semicolon is missing in the program, which is an error.

To open an existing file in CodeBlocks, we can go to **File** from menu toolbar, and click **Open**. This will provide the options to locate the existing files. We can also use the shortcut option by pressing **Ctrl+O**.

2.12 Comprehensive understanding of object-oriented concepts in C++

Here, we will describe a program that features most of the OOP concepts. In the subsequent chapters, we will understand most of the object-oriented concepts in depth. Program 2.2 includes most of the prominent features of OOP, such as classes, objects, access modifiers, constructors, information hiding, inheritance, and polymorphism. Usually, an **object** is called an instance of a **class**. An object has data and methods or behavior. A class is used to define data and methods. For example, Liu, Fang, and Yan all are students and they share many characteristics; these characteristics are expressed as data and methods and are defined in the class. So, a class is used to define data and methods, which are common to all of its objects. In Program 2.2, there are three classes: (1) Student, (2) Freshmen, and (3) Sophomore. Based on these classes, several objects can be created. For example, Fang, Yan, and Liu are objects created from the classes Student, Freshmen, and Sophomore, respectively. As described, each class may have many methods and variables. For example, collegename, student_number, name, and marks are variables in this program. The get_college_name(), get_name_number(), get_marks(), and class_grade() are methods within classes.

The constructors are one of the most powerful features of the object-oriented languages. Constructors are used for initializing objects during its creation.

Initialization of data members is necessary when we deal with multiple objects of the same class. A constructor is a special method that is executed when the object of that class is created. The name of the constructor must be the same as that of the class. For example, in the Program 2.2, the public: Student(){} is a constructor and it has the same name as its class Student. Constructors are useful to initialize the values automatically when the object of that class is created.

In an object-oriented programming, **inheritance** plays a major role in writing large programs. Inheritance property is highly required when we deal with many similar classes with minor changes. Inheritance enables us to define a new class based on an existing class definition. For example, in Program 2.2, Student is a **base class** while Freshmen and Sophomore are **derived classes**. This implies that many characteristics of Freshmen and Sophomore are derived from the class Student. In this case, we call the class of Student as **parent class** (or **super class** or **base class**) and the class of Freshmen and Sophomore as **child class** (or **subclass** or **derived class**).

In inheritance, we create or derive a new class similar to the existing class but will have some new characteristics. This is very useful when we are making modifications to the existing program. For example, a program A needs some modifications to make a new program B. In such cases, instead of developing program B from the scratch, we derive the existing features from program A. This makes the programming task easier. Thus, the main advantage of inheritance is code reuse.

Polymorphism is another most essential feature of an object-oriented programming. The polymorphism increases the ability of writing the programs simpler and with reusability. The **polymorphism** means many forms (such as many faces). For example, a person may be a father at home, an officer at office, or a customer in a restaurant. Here, a father, an officer, and a customer all refer to the same person. For example, in the Program 2.2, Freshmen is a **subclass** derived from Student class. It is also clear that, in general, freshmen or sophomore students are also students. So in C++, it is possible to make an instance of **subclass** object as a type of **base class**. Here, Sophomore object is a type of Student; it is possible since Sophomore class is derived from Student. An object can be used either as its own type or as an object of its base type. This is possible because of a property of C++ called **dynamic binding**. As in the program, a method call to get_college_name() will automatically invoke the method of Sophomore rather than the method of Student (Fig. 2.10).

```
// Program 2.2
// Comprehensive Program to understand most of the object-oriented
// concepts in C++

#include <iostream>
#include <cstring>
using namespace std;
```

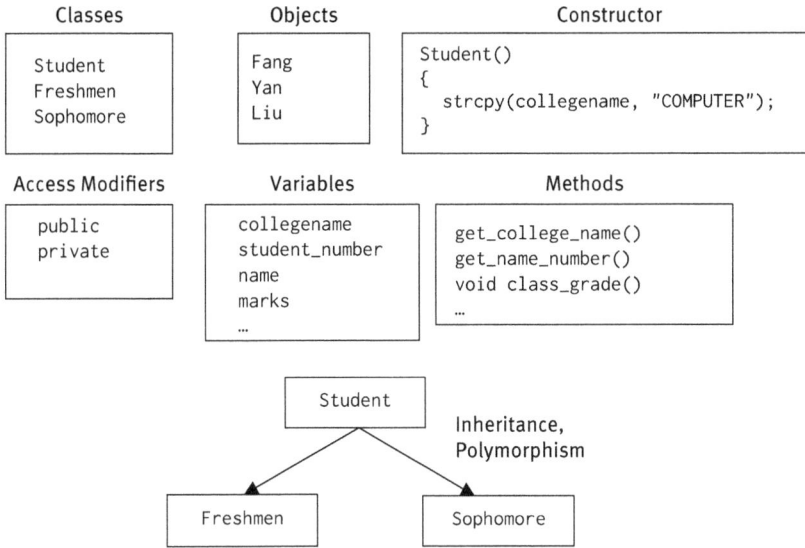

Fig. 2.10: Major components of an object-oriented programming as described in Program 2.2.

```cpp
class Student
{
    public:
        char collegename[30];

    public:
        Student()
        {
            strcpy(collegename, "COMPUTER");
        }

        int student_number;
        char name[20];

    private:
        int marks;

    public:
        virtual void get_college_name()
        {
        cout << "College Name: "<< collegename << endl;
        }

        void get_name_number()
        {
```

```cpp
            cout << "Student Number: " << student_number << endl;
            cout << "Student Name: " << name << endl;
        }
        void get_marks()
        {
            cout << "Student Marks: " << marks << endl;
        }
};

class Freshmen: public Student
{
    public:

        void class_grade()
        {
            cout << "Student Status: Freshmen Student" << endl;
        }
};

class Sophomore: public Student
{
    public:
        void get_college_name()
        {
            strcpy (collegename, "MECHANICAL");
            cout << "College Name: " << collegename << endl;
        }
};

int main()
{
    //Fang is an instance of object Student
    Student Fang;

    //Assigning values to member variables
    Fang.student_number = 2018189001;
    strcpy (Fang.name,"Zhang Yunxia");

    //Can't assign values to marks, as it is private variable

    //Values accessed through constructor
    cout << "College Name: " << Fang.collegename << endl;

    //Calling the method
    Fang.get_name_number();

    //Inheritance: subclass declaration
    Freshmen Yan;
```

```
    Yan.get_college_name();
    Yan.class_grade();

    //Polymorphism
    Student *Liu;
    Sophomore Zhang;
    Liu = &Zhang;
    Liu -> get_college_name();

    return 0;
}
```

The results of Program 2.2 are as follows:

```
    College Name: COMPUTER
    Student Number: 2018189001
    Student Name: Zhang Yunxia
    College Name: COMPUTER
    Student Status: Freshmen Student
    College Name: MECHANICAL
```

2.13 Review questions

1. List the various features of the object-oriented languages.
2. Briefly explain these terms: Objects, Classes, Modularity, Information hiding, Inheritance, Constructors, and Polymorphism.
3. Write a brief note on C++ programming language.
4. Define the following terms related to a C++ program: comments, header file, namespace, compound statement, extraction operator, and insertion operator.
5. Write a C++program to display your name, university name, and address on the computer screen.
6. Write a note on different versions of C++. How the later versions are different from the old versions?
7. Briefly describe the terms: high-level language, source file, object file, compiler, and linker.
8. Write the steps involved in running C++ program in the latest version of Visual Studio.
9. List the different freely available online C++ compilers. Describe your favorite online compiler and list the reasons for your choice.

3 Programming Basics

> The scholar who cherishes the love of comfort is not fit to be deemed a scholar.
> — Confucius

3.1 Introduction

It is important to understand simple C++ programs to study the basics of programming. Almost all C++ programs are wrapped around identifiers, variables, keywords, literals, data types, and methods. In this chapter, we will explain all of these fundamental concepts that are significant to understand the nuts and bolts of a programming language such as C++.

3.2 Variables and identifiers

Suppose, if we want to perform an operation, that is, calculate the sum of two numbers a and b and store the result in c, then it is represented as:

```
c = a + b
```

To perform this operation in a program, we must decide the kind of data types the numbers are. Let us say that all of them are *integers*, then we first declare a, b, and c as integers. Integers are natural and whole numbers that do not include decimals or fractions. Then, the statements in a program must include the following:

```
int a,b,c;
c = a + b;
```

The previous two statements are responsible for allocating memory locations to store data values a, b, and c, where a, b, and c are the names associated with respective memory allocations. These names are called **variables.**

The general syntax for variable declaration is as follows:

```
<data type><variables>;
Example: int a,b,c;
```

Here a, b, and c are variables and int is the data type. The above declaration can also be written as follows:

```
int a;
int b;
int c;
```

https://doi.org/10.1515/9783110593846-003

The names given to the variables are called **identifiers** that are also the names given to methods or functions and classes. To declare a variable as an identifier, it must satisfy the following conditions:

1. It must be composed of letters, numbers, and underscore (_).
2. It cannot contain blank spaces.
3. It can only begin with a letter or an underscore.
4. It cannot begin with a number.
5. All variable names are case-sensitive, for example, SMALL variable is not the same as small variable.
6. There should be no limit to the length of a C++ variable name.
7. C++ does not allow punctuation characters such as @, $, and % within identifiers.

Following are a few examples of valid variable names:

```
OneVariable
onevariable
ONEVARIABLE
One_Variable
o
n
_one
One_18
One18
_18One
```

Following are a few examples of invalid variable names:

```
One Variable  // Contains a blank space
9One          // Begins with a digit
One+Two       // Plus sign is not an alphanumeric character
One-Variable  // Hyphen (-) is not an alphanumeric character
```

3.3 C++ Keywords

The keywords are special words that can neither be used as identifiers nor as the names of program variables. All the C++ keywords are in **lower-case** instead of upper-case (or capitals). The following list shows some of the commonly used keywords in C++. Many of these keywords are also common to both C and C++. Please note that keywords are either added or deleted from time to time.

asm	else	new	this
auto	enum	operator	throw
bool	explicit	private	true

break	export	protected	try
case	extern	public	typedef
catch	false	register	typeid
char	float	reinterpret_cast	typename
class	for	return	union
const	friend	short	unsigned
const_cast	goto	signed	using
continue	if	sizeof	virtual
default	inline	static	void
delete	int	static_cast	volatile
do	long	struct	wchar_t
double	mutable	switch	while
dynamic_cast	namespace	template	

3.4 Data types

The variables in programming languages are used to store information such as integer, character, floating point numbers, etc. The variables are reserved memory locations that store values. The data types help to store information of different types such as integer, character, etc. The representation of data type is machine specific. On the basis of the data type of a variable, the operating system allocates memory and decides what can be stored in the reserved memory. The basic data types in C++ are int, long, char, float, and double. Some of the basic data types can be modified by using one or more of these type modifiers such as signed, unsigned, short, and long. Table 3.1 shows the variable type, number of bytes required to store the value in memory, and the maximum and minimum value that can be stored in such type of variables.

Table 3.1: Size and range of C++ basic data types.

Data Type	Byte(s)	Range
char	1	−128 to 127
unsigned char	1	0 to 255
signed char	1	−128 to 127
int	4	−2,147,483,648 to 2,147,483,647
unsigned int	4	0 to 4,294,967,295
signed int	4	−2,147,483,648 to 2,147,483,647
short int	2	−32,768 to 32,767
unsigned short int	2	0 to 65,535
signed short int	2	−32,768 to 32,767
long int	4	−2,147,483,648 to 2,147,483,647
signed long int	4	−2,147,483,648 to 2,147,483,647
unsigned long int	4	0 to 4,294,967,295
float	4	$\pm 3.4 \times 10^{\pm 38}$ with approximately 7-digit accuracy
double	8	$\pm 1.7 \times 10^{\pm 308}$ with approximately 15-digit accuracy
long double	8	$\pm 1.7 \times 10^{\pm 308}$ with approximately 15-digit accuracy

Here is an example of declaring data types:

```
int One_Variavle;
long bigNumber;
```

It is also possible to initialize a value to a variable at the time of declaration. For example:

```
int myAge = 26;
```

Program 3.1 explains data types in C++:

```
//Program 3.1
//Program to understand Data Types in C++
#include <iostream>
using namespace std;

int main(void)
{
    short b = 45;
    int c = 100;
    long d = 100000L;
    char e = 'C';
    float f = 100.99F;
    double g = 100E+4;

    cout << "Short Value: "<< b << endl;
    cout << "Integer Value: "<< c << endl;
    cout << "Long Value: "<< d << endl;
    cout << "Character Value: "<< e << endl;
    cout << "Float Value: "<<f << endl;
    cout << "Double Value: "<< g << endl;
    return 0;
}
```

The result of Program 3.1 is shown below:

```
Short Value: 45
Integer Value: 100
Long Value: 100000
Character Value: C
Float Value: 100.99
Double Value: 1e+006
```

As shown in Table 3.1, the sizes of variables are shown as **bytes**. However it is important to note that they might be different from those shown in the table, depending on the compiler and the computer we are using. The sizeof() operator helps us to display the correct size of various data types. Program 3.2 shows an example to obtain the size of various data types in a particular computer.

```
// Program 3.2
// Program to check the size of data Types in C++
#include <iostream>
using namespace std;

int main()
{
    cout << "Size of char : " << sizeof(char) << endl;
    cout << "Size of unsigned char : " << sizeof(unsigned char) << endl;
    cout << "Size of signed char : " << sizeof(signed char) << endl;
    cout << "Size of wchar_t : " << sizeof(wchar_t) << endl;
    cout << "Size of int : " << sizeof(int) << endl;
    cout << "Size of unsigned int : " << sizeof(unsigned int) << endl;
    cout << "Size of signed int : " << sizeof(signed int) << endl;
    cout << "Size of short int : " << sizeof(short int) << endl;
    cout << "Size of unsigned short int : "
         << sizeof(unsigned short int) << endl;
    cout << "Size of signed short int : "
         << sizeof(signed short int) << endl;
    cout << "Size of long int : " << sizeof(long int) << endl;
    cout << "Size of unsigned long int : "
         << sizeof(unsigned long int) << endl;
    cout << "Size of signed long int : "
         << sizeof(signed long int) << endl;
    cout << "Size of float : " << sizeof(float) << endl;
    cout << "Size of double : " << sizeof(double) << endl;
    cout << "Size of long double : " << sizeof(long double) << endl;
    return 0;
}
```

The result of Program 3.2 is shown below:

```
Size of char : 1
Size of unsigned char : 1
Size of signed char : 1
Size of wchar_t : 2
Size of int : 4
Size of unsigned int : 4
Size of signed int : 4
Size of short int : 2
Size of unsigned short int : 2
Size of signed short int : 2
Size of long int : 4
Size of unsigned long int : 4
Size of signed long int : 4
Size of float : 4
Size of double : 8
Size of long double : 8
```

3.5 C++ Literals and constants

The literals are used to denote constants. In programs, the literals directly represent a value. Constants that refer to fixed values that the program may not alter are called literals. For example, "Hello" is a literal constant. The commonly used literals are characters, strings, and numbers. So, constants can be of any data type, and they are divided into integer numerals, floating-point numerals, characters, strings, and Boolean values.

Integer literals

In general, we use the decimal numbers, however, an integer literal in C++ can also be octal or hexadecimal. For representing a hexadecimal number, the prefix 0x or 0X is used. For representing an octal number, 0 is used as prefix. However, nothing is used as prefix for representing a decimal number. An integer literal can also have a suffix that is a combination of U and L, for unsigned and long, respectively. The suffix can be uppercase or lowercase and can be in any order. Here are some examples of integer literals.

```
42      // decimal literal
015     // octal literal
0xFF    // hexadecimal literal
0X2ef   // hexadecimal literal
18u     // unsigned integer literal
78l     // long literal
56ul    // unsigned long literal
6555LU  // unsigned long literal
```

Program 3.3 demonstrates the use of integer literals in C++. Also note that the results are displayed in decimals equivalents of octal and hexadecimal numbers, however, C++ also provides ways of displaying them in original form.

```
// Program 3.3
// Integer Literals
#include <iostream>
using namespace std;

int main()
{
    int num1 = 42;          // decimal literal
    int num2 = 015;         // octal literal
    int num3 = 0xFF;        // hexadecimal literal
    int num4 = 0X2ef;       // hexadecimal literal
    int num5 = 18u;         // unsigned integer literal
```

```
int num6 = 781;          // long literal
int num7 = 56ul;         // unsigned long literal
int num8 = 6555LU;       // unsigned long literal

cout << "Decimal literal :"<< num1<< endl;
cout << "Octal literal :"<< num2 << endl;
cout << "Hexadecimal literal 1 :"<< num3 << endl;
cout << "Hexadecimal literal 2 :"<< num4 << endl;
cout << "Unsigned integer literal :"<< num5 << endl;
cout << "Long literal :"<< num6 << endl;
cout << "Unsigned long literal 1 :"<< num7 << endl;
cout << "Unsigned long literal 2 :"<< num8 << endl;
return 0;
}
```

The result of Program 3.3 is shown below:

```
Decimal literal :42
Octal literal    :13
Hexadecimal literal 1 :255
Hexadecimal literal 2 :751
Unsigned integer literal :18
Long literal     :78
Unsigned long literal 1 :56
Unsigned long literal 2 :6555
```

Floating-point literal

Any number with a decimal point such as 8.18 is treated as floating-type literal. A floating-point literal has an integer part, a decimal point, a fractional part, and an exponent part. We can represent floating-point literals either in decimal form or exponential form. To specify a number as float we have to add a suffix 'f' or "F," for example, 8.18F or 3.12f. The signed exponent is introduced by e or E.

In the decimal notation, nonempty sequence of decimal digits containing a decimal point is used. The nonempty sequence of decimal digits signifies the significant. The type specifier l, f, L or F also can be used as optional suffix. If there is no suffix, by default it is considered as double. The f or F suffix indicates the literal is of type float, and l or L indicates the literal is of type long double.

In the second type of exponential form notation, a nonempty sequence of decimal digits is used, which defines the significant along with e or E followed with optional minus or plus sign and nonempty sequence of decimal digits that defines exponent. The type specifier l, f, L, or F also can be used as optional suffix. Note that when we consider exponent, it is the power of 10 by which the significant is multiplied. For example, the mathematical meaning of 187e2 is 187×10^2. Program 3.4 demonstrates the use of floating point literals.

```cpp
//Program 3.4
//Floating-point literals
#include <iostream>
using namespace std;

int main()
{
    float num1 = 3.14f;
    float num2 = 18.89f;
    float num3 = 897.12F;
    long double num4 = 99877.8921;
    long double num5 = 17877.67L;
    double num6 = 893.46e-18;
    float num7 = 893.12E2;
    float num8 = 8e4f;
    cout << "num1 = : " << num1 << endl;
    cout << "num2 = : " << num2 << endl;
    cout << "num3 = : " << num3 << endl;
    cout << "num4 = : " << num4 << endl;
    cout << "num5 = : " << num5 << endl;
    cout << "num6 = : " << num6 << endl;
    cout << "num7 = : " << num7 << endl;
    cout << "num8 = : " << num8 << endl;
    return 0;
}
```

The result of Program 3.4 is shown below:

```
num1 = : 3.14
num2 = : 18.89
num3 = : 897.12
num4 = : 99877.9
num5 = : 17877.7
num6 = : 8.9346e-016
num7 = : 89312
num8 = : 80000
```

Boolean literal

There are two Boolean literals and they are `true` and `false`. They are also a part of standard C++ keywords. A value of `true` represents true, and a value of `false` represents false. Program 3.5 shows the demonstration of using Boolean literals in C++.

```
//Program 3.5
//Boolean literals
#include <iostream>
using namespace std;

int main()
{
    bool a = true;      // Boolean literal
    bool b = false;     //Boolean literal
    cout << a << endl;
    cout << b << endl;
    return 0;
}
```

The result of Program 3.5 is shown below:

```
1
0
```

Character literal

A character literal is enclosed within single quotes, for example, 'c'. A character literal is composed of a constant character. It is represented by the character surrounded by single quotation marks. A character literal can be a plain character (e.g., 'x'), an escape sequence (e.g., '\t'), or a universal character (e.g., '\u02C0'). There are certain characters in C++ that will have special meaning when they are preceded by a back-slash. They are used to represent characters such as newline ('\n') or tab ('\t'). These characters are called escape sequence characters. A backslash ('\') character is used to denote nonprinting character. These characters are very useful in programming, for example, to insert a blank space, jump to next line, etc. Table 3.2 summarizes some of the commonly used escape sequence characters.

Table 3.2: Commonly used escape sequence characters.

Escape Sequence	Meaning	Escape Sequence	Meaning
\n	New line	\t	Horizontal tab
\a	Sounds a beep	\v	Vertical tab
\'	Single quote	\r	Carriage return
\\	Backslash	\"	Double quotes
\b	Backspace	\?	Question mark
\f	Form feed	\0	Null character

Program 3.6 demonstrates the use and application of some of the escape sequence characters.

```
//Program 3.6
//Demonstration of escape sequence characters
#include <iostream>
using namespace std;

int main()
{
    char newline = '\n';        // Newline character:
    char tab = '\t';            // Tab character
    char backspace = '\b';      // Backspace character
    char backslash = '\\';      // Backslash character
    char nullChar = '\0';       // Null character
    char alarmbeep = '\a';      // Beep sound character

    cout << "Newline character: "
         << newline << "End of newline character" << endl;
    cout << "Tab character: " << tab <<"End of tab character"<< endl;
    cout << "Backspace character: "
         << backspace << "End of backspace character" << endl;
    cout << "Backslash character: "
         << backslash <<"End of backslash character" << endl;
    cout << "Null character: "
         << nullChar << "End of null character" << endl;
    cout << "Making a beep sound: " << alarmbeep << "End of beep"
         << endl;
    return 0;
}
```

The result of Program 3.6 is shown below:

```
Newline character:
End of newline character
Tab character:  End of tab character
Backspace character:End of backspace character
Backslash character: \End of backslash character
Null character:  End of null character
Making a beep sound: End of beep
```

String literal

The string literal is always enclosed in double quotes, and it represents a sequence of characters that together form a null-terminated string. A string contains characters that are similar to character literals such as plain characters, escape sequences, and universal characters, for example, "Hello! Ni Hao!" Remember that a single character enclosed within double quotes is also a string lateral rather than character literal itself. We can also break a long line into multiple lines using string literals and separate them using whitespaces.

Defining constants

In C++, we can define constants in two ways:(a) by using #define preprocessor, and (b) by using the const keyword. The standard form of using #define preprocess or for constants is as follows:

```
#define identifier value
```

For example, we can define an identifier PI with value 3.14 as follows:

```
#define PI 3.14
```

However, while using const keyword, the general form for defining constants is as follows:

```
const type variable = value;
```

For example, we can define an identifier PHI with value 1.618 as follows:

```
const floatPHI = 1.618;
```

Program 3.7 demonstrates the ways of using constants in C++. It is a common practice in programming to define constants in capital letters.

```
//Program 3.7
//Demonstration of constants
#include <iostream>
using namespace std;

#define PI 3.14
#define RAMANUJAN_NUM 1729

int main()
{
    const float PHI=1.618;

    cout << "The value of PI = :" << PI << endl;
    cout << "The value of PHI = :" << PHI << endl;
    cout << "The value of Ramanujan Number = :" << RAMANUJAN_NUM << endl;
    return 0;
}
```

The result of Program 3.7 is shown below:

```
The value of PI = :3.14
The value of PHI = :1.618
The value of Ramanujan Number = :1729
```

Defining synonyms for data types

We can create a new name for an existing type by using keyword `typedef`. The syntax to define a new type using `typedef` is as follows:

```
typedef type newname;
```

The `typedef` keyword enables us to define our own type name for an existing type. For example, we can define a type name `int_wholenum` as the standard `int` type with the declaration:

```
typedef int int_wholenum; // Defining int_wholenum as a type name
```

Now, the following declaration is perfectly legal and creates an integer variable called `width` with initial value as 23.

```
int_wholenum width=23; // Defining a int variable
```

The previous declaration is the same as follows:

```
int width=23; // Defining a int variable
```

Defining our own type name such as `int_wholenum` enables us to use both type specifiers within the same program for declaring different variables that will end up having the same type.

Variables with specific set of values

Sometimes, there is need for variables that have a limited set of possible values that can be usefully referred to by labels, such as the days of the week, colors in a rainbow, months of the year, or the suits in a card deck. There is a specific facility in C++ to handle this situation, it is called **enumeration**. Using enumerated data type is also another way of using constants. The enumerated data type is initiated by the keyword `enum`. An enumerated type declares an optional type name and a set of zero or more identifiers that can be used as values of the type. Each enumerator is a constant whose type is the enumeration. The general form of an enumeration type declaration is shown below.

```
enum enum-name { list of names } variable-list;
```

Here, the enum-name is the enumeration's type name. The list of names is separated by commas, and enclosed within flower brackets. For example, the following code defines an enumeration of week days called `Weekdays` and the variable `today` of type `Weekdays`.

```
enum Weekdays {Mon, Tues, Wed, Thurs, Fri, Sat, Sun} today;
```

The previous statement automatically defines a fixed integer value that will be type `int` by default. The first name in the list, `Mon`, will have the value 0, `Tues` will be 1, and so on. We can assign one of the enumeration constants as the value of the variable `today` shown below:

```
today = Thurs;
```

The value of `today` will be 3 because the symbolic constants that an enumeration defines are assigned values in sequence, starting with 0 by default. Each successive enumerator is one larger than the value of the previous one, but if we would prefer the implicit numbering to start at a different value, we can just write the following:

```
enum Weekdays {Mon = 1, Tues, Wed, Thurs, Fri, Sat, Sun} today;
```

Now, the enumeration constants will be equivalent to 1 through 7. The enumerators do not even need to have unique values. Let us consider another example shown below. In this case, `north` gets the value of 0, `south` gets the value of 1, `east` is equal to 40, and the `west` is equal to 41.

```
enum direction {north, south, east = 40, west};
```

Program 3.8 shows an example to demonstrate the enumerated data type in C++.

```cpp
//Program 3.8
//Demonstration of enumerated data types
#include <iostream>
using namespace std;

enum answer {FALSE, TRUE};
enum COLOR {RED, BLUE, GREEN, YELLOW};
enum direction {north, south, east = 40, west};

int main()
{
    cout << "This is TRUE as an integer: " << TRUE << endl;
    cout << "This is FALSE as an integer: " << FALSE << endl;
    cout << "This is RED as an integer: " << RED << endl;
    cout << "This is YELLOW as an integer: " << YELLOW << endl;
    cout << "This is south : " << south << endl;
    cout << "This is south : " << west << endl;
    return 0;
}
```

The result of Program 3.8 is shown below:

```
This is TRUE as an integer: 1
This is FALSE as an integer: 0
This is RED as an integer: 0
This is YELLOW as an integer: 3
This is south : 1
This is south : 41
```

3.6 Type casting

In Section 3.4, we studied about different data types in C++. Now, let us try to understand with the help of Program 3.9 what happens if we mix two different data types together.

```cpp
// Program 3.9
// Program to understand Type Casting in C++
#include  <iostream>
using namespace std;

int main()
{
    int a = 100;
    double b = 200;
    a = b;
    cout << "Value of a = :" << a << endl;
    cout << "Value of b = :" << b << endl;
    return 0;
}
```

In the previous statements, we are trying to assign value of b to a. This means that we are trying to **cast** data type of b to a. When we run the above program, we will get the following results.

```
Value of a = :200
Value of b = :200
```

This is an example for **implicit** conversions, which are automatically performed when a value is copied to a compatible type. We can consider another example shown below:

```cpp
short a = 1800;
int b;
b = a;
```

Here, the value of a is promoted from short to int without the need of any explicit operator. This is known as a **standard conversion**. Standard conversions affect fundamental data types and allow the conversions between numerical types such as short to int, int to float, double to int, etc. These types of conversions also happen in bool and some pointer conversions. However, converting to int from some smaller integer type, or to double from float is known as **promotion**, and it is guaranteed to produce the exact same value in the destination type. Other conversions between arithmetic types may not always be able to represent the same value exactly.

In some special cases, there is need for explicit conversion, which is widely known as **typecasting**. Type casting involves casting one type of data to another either implicitly or explicitly. There are two types of type casting, **explicit casting** and **implicit casting**. Explicit casting that occurs when we deliberately change the data type of value. Implicit conversions occur when two unequal types are represented in an equation, and they are adjusted to be of the same type. This happens internally without our knowledge. In Program 3.10, it is evident that by assigning a double to integer, the decimal portion is lost, however, this is the not the case if we use b = a; instead of a = b;

```
// Program 3.10
// Program to understand Type Casting in C++
#include <iostream>
using namespace std;

int main()
{
    int a = 100;
    double b = 3.145;
    a = b;
    cout << "Value of a = :" << a << endl;
    cout << "Value of b = :" << b << endl;
    return 0;
}
```

The result of Program 3.10 is shown below:

```
Value of a = :3
Value of b = :3.145
```

If we change the statement a = b; to statement b = a; then we will obtain the following results. This will be so because float, being the higher data type, can easily accommodate the value stored in an int.

```
Value of a = :100
Value of b = :100
```

3.7 Input and output manipulators

A **manipulator** modifies the way in which data output to (or input from) a stream is handled. In other words, they are helper functions that make it possible to control input/output streams using operator << or operator >>. Manipulators are defined in the standard library header file iomanip, so we need #include directive for it. Let us consider a statement that is shown below:

```
cout << "Hello, world!" << endl;
```

This statement contains a manipulator endl. This is an object, which when supplied to operator <<, causes a newline character to be put into the output stream, followed by a call of cout's flush function that causes the internal buffer to be immediately emptied. This makes sure that all of the output is displayed before the program goes on to the next statement. So manipulators are objects that cause the output stream object to do something, either to its output, or to its member variables. The manipulators with no arguments, such as endl, are included in <iostream>. The commonly used manipulators are listed in Table 3.3.

Table 3.3: Commonly used manipulators in C++.

Manipulator	Description
dec, hex, oct	Changes the base used for integer I/O
endl	Outputs '\n' and flushes the output stream
fixed, scientific	Changes formatting used for floating-point I/O
setfill	Changes the fill character
setiosflags	Sets the specified ios_base flags
setprecision	Changes floating-point precision
setw	Changes the width of the next input/output field

Program 3.11 shows an example that summarizes the application of manipulators. The setw(n) causes the output value that follows to be right-justified in a field that is n spaces wide, so setw(6) causes the next output value to be presented in a field with a width of six spaces. The setw() manipulator works only for the single-output value, and follows its insertion into the stream immediately. So, we have to insert the manipulator into the stream immediately preceding each value that we want to output within a given field width.

```
// Program 3.11
// Input and output manipulators
#include <iostream>
#include <iomanip>
```

```
using namespace std;

int main()
{
    float num1 = 0.1;
    float num2 = 1.0;
    float num3 = 1234567890.0;
    int num4 = 1234, num5 = 5678,num6 = 428;

    cout << "1. " << num1 << ", "
         << num2 << ", " << num3 << endl;
    cout << "2. " << fixed << num1 << ", "
         << num2 << ", " << num3 << endl;
    cout << "3. " << scientific << num1 << ", "
         << num2 << ", " << num3 << endl;
    cout << "4. " << fixed << setprecision(3) << num1 << ", "
         << num1 << ", " << num3 << endl;
    cout << "5. " << setprecision(20) << num1 << endl;
    cout << "6. " << setw(6) << num4 << setw(6) << num5 <<endl;
    cout << "7. " << setw(8) << setfill('*') << 34 << 45 << endl;
    cout << "8. " << setw(8) << 34 << setw(8) << 45 << endl;
    cout << "9. " << dec << num6 << endl;    // decimal
    cout << "10. " << hex << num6 << endl;   // hexidecimal
    cout << "11. " << oct << num6 << endl;   // octal
    return 0;
}
```

The result of Program 3.11 is shown below:

```
1. 0.1, 1, 1.23457e+009
2. 0.100000, 1.000000, 1234567936.000000
3. 1.000000e-001, 1.000000e+000, 1.234568e+009
4. 0.100, 0.100, 1234567936.000
5. 0.10000000149011612000
6.    1234   5678
7. ******3445
8. ******34******45
9. 428
10. 1ac
11. 654
```

3.8 Storage duration and scope

The variables in a program has finite lifetime. They have two properties: storage duration and scope. The first property, storage duration, is about how long a particular variable lasts. There are basically three different kinds of **storage durations** that a variable can have: **automatic, static**, and **dynamic**. The other property is called **scope**. The lifetime and scope of a variable are two different things. The **lifetime** is the period during execution from the time the variable was first created to the time when it was destroyed and the memory it occupies was freed for other uses. The scope of a variable is the region of a program code over which the variable can be declared and may be accessed. The scope of a variable defines the validity of a variable within a part of a program, that is, if the variable is outside the scope, it is not possible to use it. The variables we have defined so far are called automatic variables, and they have automatic storage duration.

The scope can be broadly classified into three categories: (a) inside a function or a block, as **local variables**, (b) in the definition of function parameters, as **formal parameters**, and (c) outside of all functions, as **global variables**. We will learn about function and its parameters in Chapter 10.

Automatic storage duration and local variables

Variables that are declared inside a function or block are called local variables or **automatic variables**. They can be used only by statements that are inside that function or block of code. Local variables are not known to functions outside of their own function. These variables are usually declared within a block and within a pair of braces. They have local scope or **block scope**. The automatic variables are created when they are defined. They are automatically destroyed at the end of the block. In automatic storage duration, objects exist only at certain points during execution. The objects are created and initialized (in case they are initialized) every time the block in which they are declared is entered. They exist only while the block is active, that is, its statements are being executed, and are destroyed when the block is exited. Their value is lost when they are destroyed. Let us consider a simple example of Program 3.12 to demonstrate the scope of automatic variables.

```
// Program 3.12
// Automatic variables
#include <iostream>
using namespace std;

int main()
{
    //Function scope starts here
    int var1 = 11;
    int var2 = 22;
    cout << "Value of outer var1 = " << var1 << endl;
    cout << "Value of outer var2 = " << var2 << endl;
    {
        // Beginning of new scope
        int var1 = 33; // Now, outer var1 has no scope here
```

```
    int var3 = 44;
    cout <<"Value of inner var1 = " << var1 << endl;
    var1 = var1+7;
    var2 = var2+var3;
    cout << "Value of inner var1 = " << var1 << endl;
    cout << "Value of inner var2 = " << var2 << endl;
  }
  cout << "Value of outer var1 = " << var1 << endl;
  cout << "Value of outer var2 = " << var2 << endl;
  //cout <<  var3 << endl; // trying to print var3 will give error
  return 0;
}
```

The result of Program 3.12 is shown below:

```
    Value of outer var1 = 11
    Value of outer var2 = 22
    Value of inner var1 = 33
    Value of inner var1 = 40
    Value of inner var2 = 66
    Value of outer var1 = 11
    Value of outer var2 = 66
```

The first two statements declare and define two integer variables, var1 and var2, with initial values of 11 and 22, respectively. Both these variables exist from this point to the closing brace at the end of the program. The scope of these variables also extends to the closing brace at the end of main(). Following the variable definitions, the value of var1 is written to cout to produce the first of the lines shown in the output. There is then a second brace, which starts a new block. Two variables, var1 and var3, are defined within this block, with values 33 and 44, respectively. The var1 declared here is different from the first var1. The first var1 still exists, but its name is masked by the second var1. Any use of the name var1 following the declaration within the inner block refers to the var1 declared within that block.

Static storage duration and global variables

In static storage duration, the objects have the life duration of entire program, that is, their value is maintained for the program duration. For static storage duration, objects storage is allocated and initialized only once, that is, prior to the execution of the first statement for these objects. This does not mean that these objects may be used anywhere and at any time; scope is a separate issue.

Global variables are defined and declared outside of all the functions, blocks, and classes, usually on top of the program, and are called **globals**. The global variables will hold their value throughout the lifetime of the program. A global variable can be accessed by any function. That is, a global variable is available for use throughout the entire program after its declaration. These variables have **global scope**, which is also called **global namespace scope** or **file scope**. Global-scope objects have static storage duration. This means that they are accessible throughout all the functions in the file, following the point at which they are declared. If we declare them at the very beginning of program, they will be accessible from anywhere in the file. Global variables have **static storage duration** by default. Global variables with static storage duration will exist from the start of execution of the program until execution of the program ends. If we do not specify an initial value for a global variable, it will be initialized with 0 by default. Initialization of global variables takes place before the execution of `main()` begins, so they are always ready to be used within any code that is within the variable's scope.

Program 3.13 is an example to understand both global and local variables. The variable var3, which appears at the beginning of the file, is declared at global scope, which appears before the function `main()`. The scope of each global variable extends from the point at which it is defined to the end of the file. A program can have same name for local and global variables but the value of local variable inside a function will take preference. For example, in Program 3.13, there is a local variable with name var3 inside the block within `main()`. In this case, local variable inside the block takes the preference.

```cpp
// Program 3.13
// Global Variables
#include <iostream>
using namespace std;

int var3 = 55;        //global variable var1

int main()
{
    //Function scope starts here
    int var1 = 11;
    int var2 = 22;

    cout << "Value of outer var1 = " << var1 << endl;
    cout << "Value of outer var2 = " << var2 << endl;
    cout << "Value of outer var3 = " << var3 << endl;
    {
        // Beginning of new scope
        int var1 = 33; // Now, outer var1 has no scope here
        int var3 = 44; //Now global variable var3, has no scope here
        cout << "Value of inner var1 = " << var1 << endl;
        var1 = var1 + 7;
        var2 = var2 + var3;
        cout << "Value of inner var1 = " << var1 << endl;
        cout << "Value of inner var2 = " << var2 << endl;
        cout << "Value of outer var3 = " << var3 << endl;
```

```
    }
    cout << "Value of outer var1 = " << var1 << endl;
    cout << "Value of outer var2 = " << var2 << endl;
    cout << "Value of outer var3 = " << var3 << endl;
    return 0;
}
```

The result of Program 3.13 is shown below:

```
        Value of outer var1 = 11
        Value of outer var2 = 22
        Value of outer var3 = 55
        Value of inner var1 = 33
        Value of inner var1 = 40
        Value of inner var2 = 66
        Value of outer var3 = 44
        Value of outer var1 = 11
        Value of outer var2 = 66
        Value of outer var3 = 55
```

Scope resolution operator (::)

As we have seen in Program 3.13, it is possible to hide a global variable by using local variable with the same name. But one may ask: What if the programmer also wants to use the global variable in the same block, where local variable also share the same name? This is possible using scope resolution operator (::). The scope resolution operator is used when we want to use a global variable that also has a local variable with same name. If the resolution operator is placed in front of the variable name then the global variable is referenced. When no resolution operator is placed, then the local variable is referenced. Now, we can modify Program 3.13, as shown in Program 3.14, where we can access both local and global var1 variable inside the block.

```
// Program 3.14
// Global Variables and scope resolution operator
#include <iostream>
using namespace std;
int var3 = 55;    //global variable var1

int main()
{
    //Function scope starts here
    int var1 = 11;
    int var2 = 22;

    cout << "Value of outer var1 = " << var1 << endl;
    cout << "Value of outer var2 = " << var2 << endl;
    cout << "Value of outer var3 = " << var3 << endl;
```

```
{
        // Beginning of new scope
        int var1 = 33; // Now, outer var1 has no scope here
        int var3 = 44; //Now global variable var3, has no scope here
        cout <<"Value of inner var1 = " << var1 << endl;
        var1 = var1 + 7;
        var2 = var2 + var3;
        cout << "Value of inner var1 = " << var1<< endl;
        cout << "Value of inner var2 = " << var2<< endl;
        cout << "Value of inner var3 = " << var3 << endl;
        cout << "Value of global var3 = " << ::var3 << endl;
    }
    cout << "Value of outer var1 = " << var1<< endl;
    cout << "Value of outer var2 = " << var2<< endl;
    cout << "Value of outer var3 = " << var3 << endl;
    return 0;
}
```

The result of Program 3.14 is shown below:

```
Value of outer var1 = 11
Value of outer var2 = 22
Value of outer var3 = 55
Value of inner var1 = 33
Value of inner var1 = 40
Value of inner var2 = 66
Value of inner var3 = 44
Value of global var3 = 55
Value of outer var1 = 11
Value of outer var2 = 66
Value of outer var3 = 55
```

The following statements describe the application of scope resolution operator. The first statement prints the value of local variable var3, whereas the second statement prints the value of global var3 by using scope resolution operator.

```
cout << "Value of inner var3 = " << var3 << endl;
cout << "Value of global var3 = " << ::var3 << endl;
```

Dynamic storage duration

Dynamic storage duration objects have a lifetime determined by the programmer. In the dynamic storage duration objects are created by the programmer with the new keyword, and they exist until they are destroyed by the programmer with the delete keyword. It is the programmer's responsibility to delete a dynamic storage duration object when it is no longer needed. Failure to do so results in memory leaks whereby memory consumed is not released and the supply eventually runs out.

3.9 Review questions

1. What is a variable? Explain.
2. How are identifiers different from variables? List the rules to declare a variable as an identifier.
3. What is a C++ keyword? List all the C++ keywords.
4. Briefly explain the following: (a) literal, (b) character literal, (c) string literal, (d) floating-point literal, and (e) integer literal.
5. Explain different data types in C++.
6. What is an escape sequence character? Describe at least eight escape sequence characters.
7. What are the common ways of declaring constants in C++? Explain with examples.
8. List the use of these keywords: (a) `enum`, (b) `const`, (c) `define`, and (d) `typedef`.
9. What is an enumerated data type? List its applications.
10. How should the synonyms be defined for data types in C++? Describe with an example program.
11. What is the meaning of variables with specific set of values? How are they useful in real-life applications.
12. What is type-casting? What are the different types of type-casting? Discuss.
13. What is the meaning of a manipulator? List the commonly used manipulators in C++.
14. Define storage duration and scope. What are the different kinds of storage durations?
15. How is the lifetime of a variable different from the scope of a variable? Discuss.
16. Discuss local variables with an example program.
17. Discuss global variables with an example program.
18. What is scope resolution operator? What is the benefit of using it in a program?

4 Operators and Expressions

> Integrity, wisdom, skill, intelligence – such things are forged in adversity.
> — Mencius

4.1 Introduction

In Chapter 3, we have studied about data types and variables. In this chapter, we will focus on various operators and expressions used in C++ programming. An operator is used along with one, two, or more operands. For example, let us look at a simple statement:

```
c = a + b;
```

Here a and b are two operands and + (plus) is an operator and c = a + b is an **arithmetic expression**. Operators are broadly classified in three categories:
1. Unary operators
2. Binary operators
3. Ternary operators

Unary operator is an operator used along with only one operand. For example,

```
c = -b;
```

In this statement – (minus) is used with only one operand b.
Binary operator is an operator used along with two operands.

```
For example: c = a + b;
```

Ternary operator, also called **conditional operator**, is a special operator that will be explained in later part of the chapter. In particular, the operators are broadly categorized as follows:
1. Relational and equality operators
2. Assignment operators
3. Arithmetic operators
4. Bitwise operators
5. Increment and decrement operators
6. Logical operators
7. Conditional operator

https://doi.org/10.1515/9783110593846-004

4.2 Relational and equality operators

These operators are used to compare or relate operands. Table 4.1 shows a list of relational and equality operators.

Table 4.1: List of relational and equality operators.

Operator	Meaning	Example Statement
>	Greater than	if(a > b) b = small;
>=	Greater than or equal to	if(a >= b) b = small;
<	Less than	if(a < b) b = big;
<=	Less than or equal to	if(a <= b) b = big;
==	Boolean equals	if(a == b) a = same;
!=	Not equal to	if(a != b) a = notSame;

Program 4.1 illustrates relational equality operators. In Table 4.1, we have used if statement. We will study about such decision-making statements in Chapter 5.

```
// Program 4.1
// Program to understand relational operators
#include <iostream>
using namespace std;

int main(void)
{
    int a = 18, b = 6;
    if (a > b)
        cout << "a is greater than b" << endl;
    if (a == b)
        cout << "a is equal to b" << endl;

    return 0;
}
```

The result of Program 4.1 is shown below:

```
a is greater than b
```

4.3 Arithmetic operators

The arithmetic operators are + (plus), – (minus), * (multiply), / (divide), and % (modulo). Table 4.2 shows a list of arithmetic operators.

The modulo (%) operator is used to find the remainder after division, for example, 3 % 2 = 1. Program 4.2 shows a simple example of applying arithmetic operators in C++.

Table 4.2: List of arithmetic operators.

Operator	Meaning	Example statement
+	Addition	c = a + b;
−	Subtraction	c = a - b;
*	Multiplication	c = a * b;
/	Division	c = a / b;
%	Modulo	c = a % b;

```
// Program 4.2
// Program to understand arithmetic operators
#include <iostream>
using namespace std;

int main()
{
    int a = 88;
    int b = 12;
    cout << "Addition example: a + b = "  << a + b << endl;
    cout << "Subtraction example: a - b = " << a - b << endl;
    cout << "Multiplication example: a * b = " << a * b << endl;
    cout << "Division example: a / b = " << a / b << endl;
    cout << "Modulo example: a % b = " << a % b << endl;
    return 0;
}
```

The result of Program 4.2 is shown below:

```
Addition example: a + b = 100
Subtraction example: a - b = 76
Multiplication example: a * b = 1056
Division example: a / b = 7
Modulo example: a % b = 4
```

As the result of Program 4.2 shows, after dividing 88 by 12, we get 7, because all the variables are integers, and module (%) provides the remainder after this division, that is, 4.

4.4 Bitwise operators

The computer can understand the binary number system. Binary numbers are base-two numbers; and consist of 0 and 1. A byte represents 8 bits; each bit can be a 0 or 1. So a

byte is a string of zeros and ones. The rightmost bit of a byte is known as least significant bit (LSB) and the leftmost bit is known as the most significant bit (MSB). A negative number is represented in a slightly different manner. (remember that integer can be signed or unsigned). If the leftmost bit is the sign bit and if it is 1, then the number is negative; if it is 0, then the number is positive. Bitwise operators provide the memory access needed without any hassle to write in machine language code. However, in day-to-day business usage, these operators are rarely used. These operators are used to perform operations on bits of a variable value. Bit operators, as the name suggests, are used to perform operations on binary digits. Table 4.3 lists various bitwise operators.

Table 4.3: List of bitwise operators.

Operator	Meaning	Example Statement
|	Bitwise OR	c = a | b;
^	Bitwise XOR	c = a ^ b;
&	Bitwise AND	c = a & b;
>>	Right shift	c = a << 1;
>>	Left shift	c = a << 2
~	Bitwise NOT	c = ~b;

Bitwise AND

The logical AND, represented by &(ampersand) symbol, evaluates as true (1) only if both operands are 1 as shown in the following truth table.

0 & 0	0
0 & 1	0
1 & 0	0
1 & 1	1

If number a is equal to 25 and b is equal to 77, then the bitwise AND between these two numbers, c = a & b, is evaluated, as shown below, resulting in number 9.

a	00011001	25
b	01001101	77
c = a & b	00001001	9

The bitwise AND operator is used for masking operations. This operator can be used to set specific bits of a number to 0. We can also use bitwise AND to test whether an integer is odd or even. In case of an odd integer, if we perform a bitwise AND operation on an integer with 1, the result will be true if the rightmost bit of the integer is 1. On the other hand, in case of an even integer, the rightmost bit of the integer will be 0.

Bitwise Inclusive OR (or Bitwise OR)

Bitwise OR is represented by a | (pipe) symbol. The binary representation of the two operands involved in bitwise OR is compared bit by bit. The bitwise inclusive OR operation is used when we want to set some specified bits of a number to 1. Each bit that is a 1 in the first operand or a 1 in the second operand will produce a 1 in the corresponding bit of the result as shown below.

0 | 0	0
0 | 1	1
1 | 0	1
1 | 1	1

For example:

```
int a = 2, b = 4;
```

Here, 010 represents variable a (in bitwise or binary) and 100 represents 4.
So, a | b is equal to 6
010 (bitwise OR) 100 =110 (all in binary)

Bitwise Exclusive OR (or Bitwise XOR)

The bitwise exclusive OR or XOR, which is represented by ^ (caret) symbol gives 1 if either bit is 1, but not for both. One important point to remember is that any value that is XORed with itself results in 0, as shown below. This is used by assembly language programmers to test the two values for equality.

0 ^ 0	0
0 ^ 1	1
1 ^ 0	1
1 ^ 1	0

It is possible to exchange two numbers without using a temporary location using bitwise XOR operator. This seems an interesting use of bitwise XOR operator. Program 4.3 shows one such example.

```
// Program 4.3
// Exchanging two numbers without using intermediate memory location
// Bitwise XOR
#include <iostream>
using namespace std;
```

```
int main()
{
    int a = 8;
    int b = 2;
    cout << "Value of numbers before exchange :"
        << " a = " << a << ", b= " << b <<endl;
    a = a ^ b;
    b = a ^ b;
    a = a ^ b;
    cout<<"Value of numbers after exchange :"
        << " a = " << a << ", b= " << b <<endl;
    return 0;
}
```

The result of Program 4.3 is shown below:

```
Value of numbers before exchange: a = 8, b = 2
Value of numbers after exchange: a = 2, b = 8
```

One's complement operator

The one's complement operator is represented as a tilde ~. This converts a value into its one's complement, in other words, all the zeros become ones and the ones become zeros. This is a unary operator that operates on an integer constant or expression, for example, ~12.

Shift operators

Left shift and **right shift** operations are analogous to multiplication and division by 10. When we divide a number by 10, we shift the digits once to the right by retaining the decimal point. When we multiply by ten we shift the number left and add 0 on the right. When a left shift operation (<<) is performed on an operand, the bits of the operand are shifted left. Bits that are shifted out of the high-order bit of the data item are lost and 0s are added through the low-order bit of the operand. If a is a variable with the value of 2, then a left shifting twice results in value 8 as shown in Table 4.4. Here, the number 2 represented using 8 bits. It is worth noting that bits that "fall off" from either end of the variable are lost.

Table 4.4: Example of left shift (<<) operation.

Operation	Bitwise Representation	Result
Initial bit position of number 2	00000010	a = 2
Shifting to left once, bit 1 is moved to left	00000100	a = 4
Shifting to left twice, bit 1 is moved to left	00001000	a = 8

In a right shift operation (>>), the bit on the right, that is, the low-order bit is lost and depending on the type of machine, either a 1 or 0 will be shifted into the leftmost bit. The shift operation is also sometimes referred to as rotating left and right. As shown in Table 4.5, the number b = 9 is shifted to right three times, resulting in value of 1.

Table 4.5: Example of right shift (>>) operation.

Operation	Bitwise Representation	Result
Initial bit position of number 9	00001001	b = 9
Shifting to right once, LSB bit 1 is lost	00000100	b = 4
Shifting to right twice, LSB bit 0 is lost	00000010	b = 2
Shifting to right thrice, LSB bit 0 is lost	00000001	b = 1

Program 4.4 illustrates summary of all bitwise operators in C++.

```cpp
// Program 4.4
// Program to understand bitwise operators
#include <iostream>
using namespace std;

int main(void)
{
    int a = 2, b = 9;
    cout << "Bitwise OR: "  << (a | b) << endl;
    cout << "Bitwise XOR: " << (a ^ b) << endl;
    cout << "Bitwise AND: " << (a & b) << endl;
    cout << "Right Shift: " << (b >> 3) << endl;
    cout << "Left Shift: "  << (a << 2) << endl;
    cout << "Bitwise NOT: " << (~a) << endl;
    return 0;
}
```

The result of Program 4.4 is shown below:

```
Bitwise OR: 11
Bitwise XOR: 11
Bitwise AND: 0
Right Shift: 1
Left Shift: 8
Bitwise NOT: -3
```

4.5 Assignment operators

The assignment operators are used to assign the values to variables or to values. Let us look at the following statement:

```
int a = 1,b = 2;
a = b;
```

After the second statement, both a and b values will be equal to 2. The " = " operator is called as **assignment operator.** We can combine many other operators with assignment operator. For example,

```
a = a + 2;
```

This can be written as follows:

```
a += 2;
```

A list of assignment operators is shown in Table 4.6:

Table 4.6: List of assignment operators.

Operators	Meaning	Example Statement
=	Assignment	a = b;
^=	Bitwise XOR and assign	a ^= b;
&=	Bitwise AND and assign	a &= b;
%=	Take remainder and assign	a %= 1;
+=	Add and assign	a += 2;
-=	Subtract and assign	a -= 7;
*=	Multiply and assign	a *= 10;
/=	Divide and assign	a /= 4;
|=	Bitwise OR and assign	a |= 3;
>>=	Shift bits right with sign extension and assign	a >>= 3;
<<=	Shift bits left and assign	a <<= 2;

4.6 Increment and decrement operators

These kinds of operators are used very commonly in many programs. There are two operators: ++ and −− . For example,

```
a = a + 1; can be written as a++ or ++a
a = a - 1; can be written as a-- or --a
```

Remember that a++ and ++a are different. Similarly a -- or --a are also different. The a++; statement first assigns and then increments. However, ++a; statement first increments and then assigns as shown in Table 4.7.

Table 4.7: Increment and decrement operators.

Operators	Meaning	Example Statement
++	Increment by one	a++; or ++a;
--	Decrement by one	a--;; or --a;

Program 4.5 illustrates increment and decrement operators:

```
// Program 4.5
// Program to understand increment and increment operators
#include <iostream>
using namespace std;

int main(void)
{
    int  b, a = 2 ;
    b = a++;
    cout << "a = " << a << ",  b = " << b <<endl;
    b = ++a;
    cout << "a = " << a << ",  b = " << b << endl;
    b = --a;
    cout << "a = " << a << ",  b = " << b << endl;
    b = a--;
    cout<< "a = " << a << ",  b = " << b << endl;
    b = a +++ -- a + b ;
    cout<< "a = " << a << ",  b = " << b << endl;
    return 0;
}
```

The result of Program 4.5 is shown below:

```
a = 3,   b = 2
a = 4,   b = 4
a = 3,   b = 3
a = 2,   b = 3
a = 2,   b = 5
```

Another interesting example of increment and decrement operators is shown in Program 4.6.

```
// Program 4.6
// Example to understand increment and increment operators
#include <iostream>
using namespace std;
```

```
int main()
{
    int x = 10;
    cout << "Value of x after pre-fixing ++ is " << ++x << endl;
    cout << "Value of x after post-fixing ++ is " << x++ << endl;
    cout << "Value of x after post-fixing ++ is " << x << endl;
    cout << "Value of x after pre-fixing -- is " << --x << endl;
    cout << "Value of x after post-fixing -- is " << x-- << endl;
    cout << "Value of x after post-fixing -- is " << x << endl;
    return 0;
}
```

The result of Program 4.6 is shown below:

```
Value of x after pre-fixing ++ is 11
Value of x after post-fixing ++ is 11
Value of x after post-fixing ++ is 12
Value of x after pre-fixing -- is 11
Value of x after post-fixing -- is 11
Value of x after post-fixing -- is 10
```

4.7 Logical operators

The logical operators are used along with Boolean expressions. The commonly used logical operators are Boolean AND, Boolean OR, and Boolean NOT. Table 4.8 illustrates the use of logical operators.

Table 4.8: List of logical operators.

Operators	Meaning	Example Statement
&&	Boolean AND	if((a == 5) && (a <= 10)) b = 5;
||	Boolean OR	if((a == 5) || (a <= 10)) b = 5
!	Boolean NOT	if(!(a == 5)) b = 5;

4.8 Conditional operator

The conditional operator (?:) is a special type of operator. It uses three operands and is also called **ternary** operator, for example, (a>b)?a:b;. In this example, if a is greater than b, then it returns the value of a else b. To understand more about conditional operators, let us look at Program 4.7.

```
// Program 4.7
// Program to understand Conditional operators
#include <iostream>
using namespace std;

int main(void)
{
    int   a=1,b=8;
    cout<<"Bigger Number:   "<<((a>b)?a:b)<<endl;
    return 0;
}
```

The result of Program 4.7 is shown below:

```
Bigger Number: 8
```

4.9 Operator precedence

Many operand and operators together make an expression. During evaluation of such expressions, which operator is evaluated first? This is decided by operator precedence in C++. Operator precedence decides how an expression is evaluated. Table 4.9 lists the precedence and associativity of C++ operators. Operators are listed from top to bottom in descending precedence.

Table 4.9: Precedence and associativity of C++ operators.

Precedence	Operator	Description	Associativity
1	::	Scope resolution	Left to right
2	++	Suffix/postfix increment and decrement,	
	--	e.g., a++,a--	
	type()	Functional cast	
	type{}		
	()	Function call, e.g., a()	
	[]	Subscript, e.g., a[]	
	.->	Member access	
3	++a	Prefix increment and decrement, e.g., ++a,--a	Right to left
	--a		
	+	Unary plus and minus, e.g., +a,-a	
	-		
	!	Logical NOT and bitwise NOT	
	~		
	(type)	C-style cast	

(continued)

Table 4.9 (Continued)

Precedence	Operator	Description	Associativity
	*	Indirection (dereference), e.g., *a	
	&	Address-of, e.g., &a	
	sizeof	Size-of	
	new	Dynamic memory allocation	
	new[]		
	delete	Dynamic memory deallocation	
	delete[]		
4	.*	Pointer-to-member	Left to right
	->*		
5	*	Multiplication, division, and remainder,	
	/	e.g., a*b, a/b, a%b	
	%		
6	+	Addition and subtraction, e.g., a+b, a-b	
	-		
7	<<	Bitwise left shift and right shift	
	>>		
8	<	For relational operators < and ≤, respectively	
	<=		
9	==	For relational operators = and ≠, respectively	
	!=		
10	&	Bitwise AND, e.g., a&b	
11	^	Bitwise XOR (exclusive OR)	
12	|	Bitwise OR (inclusive OR)	
13	&&	Logical AND	
14	||	Logical OR	
15	?:	Ternary conditional, e.g., a?b:c	Right to left
	throw	Throw operator	
	=	Direct assignment, provided by default for C++ classes	
	+=	Compound assignment by sum and difference	
	-=		
	*=	Compound assignment by product, quotient, and	
	/=	remainder	
	%=		
	&=	Compound assignment by bitwise AND, XOR, and OR	
	^=		
	|=		
16	,	Comma	Left to right

Let us look at this following expression.

```
c = a + b * d;
```

In this expression, b*d is evaluated first and then a is added to the multiplied result. Table 4.9 decides and explains the complete operator precedence in C++. Program 4.8 summarizes the importance of operator and precedence with example statements.

```
// Program 4.8
// Program to understand operator precedence and associativity
#include <iostream>
using namespace std;

int main()
{
    float a = 18, b = 28, c =12 ;
    int d = 18;
    float  result1, result2;
    result1 = a + b / c ;
    result2 = a * b / c * a;
    d = d +++ 6;
    cout << "result1 = " << result1 << endl;
    cout << "result2 = " << result2 << endl;
    cout << "d= " << d << endl;
    return 0;
}
```

The result of Program 4.8 is shown below:

```
result1 = 20.3333
result2 = 756
d = 25
```

4.10 Review questions

1. What is an operator? What are the different types of operators in C++?
2. What are the commonly used arithmetic operators in C++? Describe with an example program.
3. What is the difference between division (/) and modulo (%) operators?
4. What are the different types of bitwise operator? Describe them.
5. How to exchange two numbers using bitwise XOR operators? Describe with an example.

6. What is a ternary operator? Explain with a program.
7. Explain the difference between post-increment (i++) and pre-increment (++i) statements.
8. What are the different logical operators available in C++. Describe each of them.
9. What is operator precedence and associativity? Explain its role in evaluating expressions.

5 Selection Statements

> The person attempting to travel two roads at once will get nowhere
> —Xun Zi

5.1 Introduction

As we have seen in previous chapters, almost all programs executed sequentially. This means that all statements executed one after another. This is called **sequential flow of execution**. Actually, in real situations, we may not wish to execute all the statements every time. We may choose to execute some statements instead of all statements or we may execute different statements depending on the context. This is called **decision-making**. Decision-making is important in our everyday life. For example, if you have more money in your bank account, you may either buy a car or go for a motorbike. These kinds of situations are quite common in all programming problems. In such cases, we will make use of **selection statements**. In this chapter, we will discuss about various selection statements supported in C++. The various selection statements are: `if`, `if-else`, and `switch` statements.

5.2 The `if` statement

The `if` statement is used to alter the sequential flow of execution of statements. This is very useful when we want to execute some statements only after a particular condition is met or satisfied. The general form of `if` statement is as follows:

```
if(Boolean-expression)
    statement;
```

Here, `Boolean-expression` is an expression that returns the result as `true` or `false`. If the expression evaluates to `true`, then the statements inside the `if` block are executed otherwise statements following `if` block are executed. The `Boolean-expression` may use relational operators, such as <,<=, ==,>, and >=, to make a conditional expression that evaluates to `true` or `false`.

A `if` block may contain a single statement or multiple statements. The general form of an `if` statement with multiple statements is as follows:

```
if(Boolean-expression)
{
    statement-1;
```

https://doi.org/10.1515/9783110593846-005

```
        statement-2;
        statement-3;
        ....

        ....
        statement-n;
}
```

Program 5.1 illustrates a simple if statement. Here, a statement inside the if block is executed only if the yourMarks is equal to or above 60, else it would be skipped and the statement following the if statement will be executed.

```
// Program 5.1
// Program to understand simple if statement
#include <iostream>
using namespace std;

int main ()
{
    int yourMarks = 65;
    if (yourMarks >= 60)
        cout << " You Pass the Exam " << endl;
    cout << " You Know your Result " << endl;
    return 0;
}
```

The result of Program 5.1 is as follows:

```
        You Pass the Exam
        You Know your Result
```

Program 5.1 can be well understood by the diagram shown in Fig. 5.1.

Program 5.2 illustrates the use of multiple statements in an if block. Here, we have to use the opening and closing braces ({}) to execute these multiple statements as apart of if block.

```
// Program 5.2
// Program with multiple statements in a if block
#include <iostream>
using namespace std;

int main ()
{
    int yourMarks = 65;
    if (yourMarks >= 60)
    {
        cout << " You Pass the Exam " << endl;
```

```
        cout << " Well Done! " << endl;
    }
    cout << " You Know your Result " << endl;
    return 0;
}
```

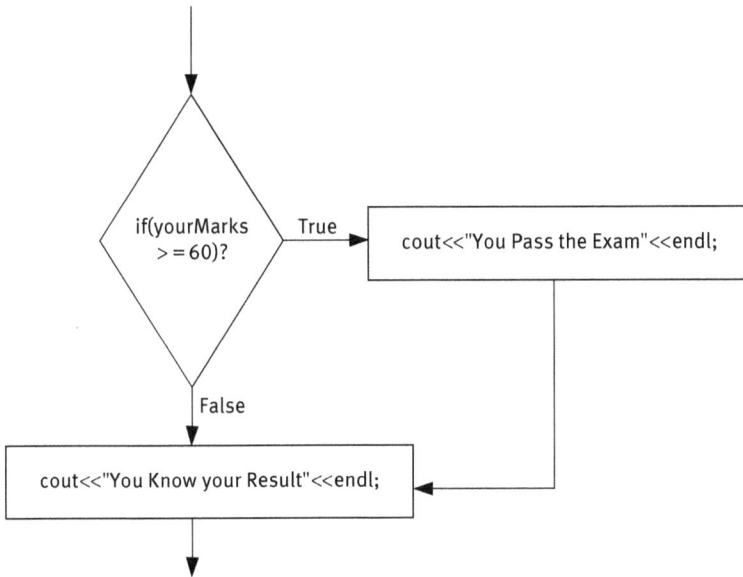

Fig. 5.1: Control flow of if statement.

The result of Program 5.2 is as follows:

```
You Pass the Exam
Well Done!
You Know your Result
```

5.3 The if-else statement

In Section 5.2, we studied about if statement, where we have noticed that statements inside the if block are executed only if the yourMarks value is equal to or greater than 60. What if the yourMarks is less than 60? In such cases, we make use of if-else statement. Here, the if branches into two blocks – (1) if block and (2) else block. If the condition evaluates to true, the execution control branches to if block; if it is false, it branches to else block. Program 5.3 shows implementation of if-else statement:

```
// Program 5.3
// Program with if-else statements
#include <iostream>
using namespace std;

int main()
{
    int yourMarks = 45;
    if (yourMarks >= 60)
        cout << " You Pass the Exam " << endl;
    else
        cout << " You are Failed " << endl;
    cout << " You Know your Result " << endl;
    return 0;
}
```

The result of Program 5.3 is as follows:

```
You are Failed
You know your result
```

Program 5.3 can be well understood by the diagram shown in Fig. 5.2.

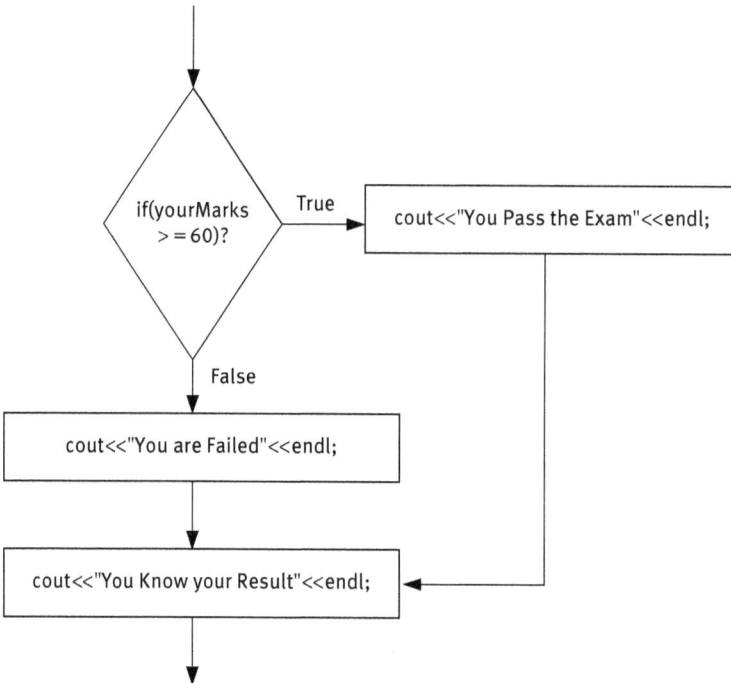

Fig. 5.2: Control flow of if-else statement.

5.4 The `if-else-if` statement

In Program 5.3, we have seen that the execution control branches into two. In C++, we can again branch a block further by including `else-if` statements. The general form of this statement is as follows:

```
if(Boolean-expression-1)
{
    statement-1;
}
else if(Boolean-expression-2)
{
    statement-2;
}
else if(Boolean-expression-3)
{
    statement-3;
}
....
....
....
else
    statement-n;
....
next statement;
....
```

Here, there are many Boolean expressions. If one of the Boolean expressions evaluates to `true`, the statement associated with it is executed and the control is moved to the `next statement` leaving rest of the statements in the if-else-if blocks. Let us consider an example of grading marks scored in a subject by students in a university. The grading of students is done on the basis of following rules (Table 5.1):

Table 5.1: The grading of students on the basis of marks.

Marks	Result	Grade
<60	Fail	No grade
≥ 60 and <70	Pass	Grade C
≥ 70 and <80	Pass	Grade B
>80 and ≤ 100	Pass	Grade A

To write a program to simulate aforementioned conditions, we will make use of `if-else-if` statements. Program 5.4 demonstrates `if-else-if` statements.

```
// Program 5.4
// Program with if-else-if statements
#include <iostream>
using namespace std;

int main ()
{
    int yourMarks = 85;
    if (yourMarks < 60)
    {
        cout << " You are Failed " << endl;
        cout << " Sorry! You have No Grade " << endl;
    }
    else if (yourMarks >= 60 && yourMarks < 70)
    {
        cout << " You Pass the Exam " << endl;
        cout << " Your grade is C " << endl;
    }
    else if (yourMarks >= 70 && yourMarks < 80)
    {
        cout << " You Pass the Exam " << endl;
        cout << " Your grade is B " << endl;
    }
    else if (yourMarks >= 80 && yourMarks <= 100)
    {
        cout << " You Pass the Exam " << endl;
        cout << " Your grade is A " << endl;
    }
    else
        cout << " No Results for you " << endl;

    cout << " You know your result "<< endl;
    return 0;
}
```

The result of Program 5.4 is as follows:

```
You Pass the Exam
Your grade is A
You know your result
```

5.5 Nested if-else statement

A if statement may have another if statement as its statement. This is called **nesting** of if statements. This is also true for else statement. The general form of nesting of if-else statements is as follows:

```
if(Boolean-expression-1)
{
        if(Boolean-expression-2)
        {
                Statement-1;
        }
        else
        {
                Statement-2;
        }
}
else
{
        Statement-3;
}
Next-statement;
```

Nested if-else statement

Here, if the first Boolean-expression-1 evaluates to true, then the second Boolean-expression-2 is evaluated and continues as another if statement, otherwise statement-3 is executed. If the Boolean Expression-2 evaluates to true, then Statement-1 is executed otherwise Statement-2 is executed. Here, the if statement containing Boolean-expression-2 is called a **nested** if statement as it is inside another if statement.

Let us consider the following example, where we can develop a scenario of application of nested if statement. In a university, there are two kinds of grading systems, one for juniors and another for seniors (Tables 5.2 and 5.3).

Table 5.2: The grading system for juniors.

Marks	Result	Grade
<60	Fail	No grade
>= 60 and <70	Pass	Grade C
>= 70 and <80	Pass	Grade B
>80 and <= 100	Pass	Grade A

Table 5.3: The grading system for seniors.

Marks	Result	Grade
<60	Fail	No grade
>= 60 and <80	Pass	Grade B
>= 80 and <= 100	Pass	Grade A

Here, we notice that the grading methods applied for the senior students are different from that of juniors. This problem is solved by using nested if statements as shown in Program 5.5.

```cpp
// Program 5.5
// Program with nested if-else statements
#include <iostream>
using namespace std;

int main ()
{
    int yourMarks = 85;
    char yourStudentType = 'S'; // Code 'S' for senior
    if (yourStudentType == 'J')
    {
        cout << "You are a Junior student" << endl;
        if (yourMarks < 60)
        {
            cout << " You Fail the Exam " << endl;
            cout << " Sorry! You have No Grade " << endl;
        }
        else if (yourMarks >= 60 && yourMarks < 70)
        {
            cout << " You Pass the Exam " << endl;
            cout << " Your grade is C " << endl;
        }
        else if (yourMarks >= 70 && yourMarks < 80)
        {
            cout << " You Pass the Exam " << endl;
            cout << " Your grade is B " << endl;
        }
        else if (yourMarks >= 80 && yourMarks <= 100)
        {
            cout << " You Pass the Exam " << endl;
            cout << "Your grade is A " << endl;
        }
    }
    else
    {
        cout << " You are a Senior student " <<endl;
        if (yourMarks < 60)
        {
            cout << " You Fail the Exam " << endl;
            cout << " Sorry! You have No Grade " <<endl;
        }
        else if (yourMarks >= 60 && yourMarks < 80)
        {
            cout << " You Pass the Exam " << endl;
```

```
            cout << " Your grade is B " << endl;
        }
        else if (yourMarks >= 80 && yourMarks <= 100)
        {
            cout << " You Pass the Exam " << endl;
            cout << " Your grade is A " << endl;
        }
    }
    cout << " You know your result " << endl;
    return 0;
}
```

The result of Program 5.5 is as follows:

```
You are a Senior student
You Pass the Exam
Your grade is A
You know your result
```

5.6 The switch statement

The switch statement is used to select a statement based on a condition among many choices. Here, the expression of the switch statement generates an integer value; based on this value a particular statement is selected. The switch statement is very much useful when we deal with many if-else statements. Instead of writing long and time-consuming if-else statements, we may use switch statement. The general form of the switch statement is as follows:

```
switch(Expression)
{
    case : Expression-Value-1: Statement-1; break;
    case : Expression-Value-2: Statement-2; break;
    case : Expression-Value-2: Statement-2; break;

    ....
    ....
    ....
    default: Statement-n;
}
```

Remember that a statement in switch may be a simple statement with one statement or a compound statement with many statements together as a block. In switch statement, the Expression refers to any expression that produces an integer result. Depending on the value of expression, the statement following each expression value is executed. It means, if the expression produces Expression-Value-1 as a result, the Statement-1 is executed and the break following the Statement-1 takes the control to jump to the end of the switch body. It is important to remember that the break statement is not compulsory in switch statement. The default statement is executed only if Expression result is not matching with any of the expression values. Note that default statement is not having break since it is the last statement of the switch statement.

To understand switch statement, let us consider the students' result table in a university.

Table 5.4: The students' result in a university.

Student Number	Student Name	Result	Grade
23	Sally	Pass	A
45	Fang	Pass	B
67	Anil	Fail	No grade
88	Hong	Pass	C

To retrieve a student's result from Table 5.4, we will make use of switch statement as shown in Program 5.6.

```
// Program 5.6
// Program with switch statement
#include <iostream>
using namespace std;

int main ()
{
    int yourNumber = 23;
    switch(yourNumber)
    {
        case 23:
            cout << " Name    :Sally " << endl;
            cout << " Result :Pass " << endl;
            cout << " Grade   :A " << endl;
            break;
        case 45:
            cout << " Name    :Fang " << endl;
            cout << " Result :Pass " << endl;
            cout << " Grade   :B " << endl;
            break;
        case 67:
            cout << " Name    :Anil " << endl;
            cout << " Result :Fail " << endl;
```

```
            cout << " Grade   :No Grade " << endl;
            break;
        case 88:
            cout << " Name     :Hong " << endl;
            cout << " Result   :pass " << endl;
            cout << " Grade    :C " << endl;
            break;
        default:
            cout << " Sorry! No Results for you " << endl;
    }
    return 0;
}
```

The result of Program 5.6 is as follows:

```
    Name:Sally
    Result:Pass
    Grade:A
```

In the switch statement, the Expression must be an integer or a character expression. Program 5.7 illustrates an example with character expression. In this example, each game name is represented by a character code. If the code is "H," it is Hockey game. If it is "F, " it is Football, etc. The program will display the name of the game according to the character code (Table 5.5).

Table 5.5: Representation of the name of the game by a character code.

Name of the Game	Character Code
Basketball	B
Football	F
Hockey	H
Cricket	C
Ping-pong	P

In Table 5.5, each character code identifies a game. This can be written as a program using switch statement as shown here:

```
// Program 5.7
// Program with switch statement
#include <iostream>
using namespace std;

int main ()
{
```

```
        char getChar = 'C';
        switch (getChar)
        {
            case 'B':
                cout << " Basketball " << endl;
                break;
            case 'C':
                cout << " Cricket " << endl;
                break;
            case 'F':
                cout << " Football " << endl;
                break;
            case 'H':
                cout << " Hockey " << endl;
                break;
            case 'P':
                cout << " Ping-Pong " << endl;
                break;
            default:
                cout << " No game for this code " << endl;
        }
        return 0;
}
```

The result of Program 5.7 is as follows:

```
        Cricket
```

The Expression in switch statement can be any expression that produces an integral result. Program 5.8 shows the use of the arithmetic expression to select among many options.

```
// Program 5.8
// Program with switch statement
#include <iostream>
using namespace std;

int main ()
{
    int a = 10,  b = 20;
    switch(a + b)
    {
        case 10:
            cout << " Result is 10 " << endl;
            break;
        case 20:
            cout << " Result is 20 " << endl;
            break;
```

```
        case 30:
            cout << " Result is 30 " << endl;
            break;
        default:
            cout << " No Result " << endl;
    }
    return 0;
}
```

The result of Program 5.8 is as follows:

```
    Result is 30
```

5.7 The ternary operator

In the previous chapters, we have studied about **unary** and **binary** operators. In this section, we will study about a special operator called **ternary** operator. This is also called a conditional operator, which is briefly covered in Section 4.8. This is also called ternary because it uses three operands. It is discussed here because its operation has a lot of similarities to if-else statement. The ternary operator has the following general form:

```
    Operand-1 = Boolean Expression ? Operand-2 : Operand-3
```

For example:

```
    big = a > b ? a : b;
```

In the aforementioned statement, if the number a is bigger than b, then big is assigned to a else to b. Let us consider the example as given in Program 5.9 with · if-else statement.

```
// Program 5.9
// Program to find maximum of two numbers using if-else statement
#include <iostream>
using namespace std;

int main ()
{
    int a = 67,  b = 99,  big;
    if(a > b)
        big = a;
```

```
    else
        big = b;
    cout << " The Biggest Number is : " << big << endl;
    return 0;
}
```

The result of Program 5.9 is as follows:

```
    The Biggest Number is :99
```

The same program can be written using a ternary operator as shown in Program 5.10.

```
// Program 5.10
// Program to find maximum of two numbers using ternary operator
#include <iostream>
using namespace std;

int main()
{
    int a = 67,  b = 99,  big;
    big = a > b ? a : b;
    cout << " The Biggest Number is : " << big << endl;
    return 0;
}
```

The result of Program 5.10 is as follows:

```
    The Biggest Number is :99
```

Also, remember that the ternary operator returns a value based on the expression and does not execute a statement or a set of statements as in if-else statement. A ternary operator may have an expression as an operand. Program 5.11 is written to find maximum of three numbers using ternary operators.

```
// Program 5.11
// Program to find maximum of three numbers using ternary operator
#include <iostream>
using namespace std;

int main ()
{
    int a = 167,  b = 991,  c = 185,  big;
    big = c > ((a > b) ? a : b) ? c :((a > b) ? a : b);
    cout << " The Biggest Number is : " << big << endl;
    return 0;
}
```

The result of Program 5.11 is as follows:

```
The Biggest Number is :991
```

5.8 Review questions

1. Describe these terms related to programming: sequential flow, decision-making, selection statements, and Boolean expression.
2. Explain the following statements in C++: if, if-else, and if-else-if.
3. What is a nested if statement? What is the difference between nested if and a compound (if block with many statements) if?
4. Write a program to find maximum of four integer numbers using if-else statements.
5. What is the use of switch statement? Compare switch statement with if-else statement.
6. What is a ternary operator? Write a program to find maximum of four numbers using the ternary operator.
7. Write a program to find the roots of a quadratic equation $Ax^2+Bx+C=0$ for non-zero values of A, B, and C.

6 Looping Statements

> To accomplish anything whatsoever one must have standards.
> None have yet accomplished anything without them.
> —Mo Zi

6.1 Introduction

The looping is necessary to execute many statements of similar behavior. There are many different types of the looping statements. In this chapter, we will study about the looping statements such as while, do-while, and for. In addition, we will also describe the use of break and continue statements. These statements are used in almost every program and are called as **repetitive** or **iterative** statements.

6.2 The while loop

The general form of while loop is as follows:

```
while(Boolean-expression)
{
    Statements;
}

Next-statements;
```

Here, the Boolean-expression is evaluated first; if it is true, the statement inside the while is executed else the next statements are executed. The statements inside the loop are executed until the Boolean-expression evaluates to false. This means, the statements inside the while loop are executed repeatedly as long as the Boolean-expression is true. Program 6.1 illustrates the use of the while loop.

```
// Program 6.1
// Program to understand while loop
#include <iostream>
using namespace std;

int main ()
{
    int i = 1;
    while(i <= 5)
    {
```

https://doi.org/10.1515/9783110593846-006

```
        cout << " Statement :   inside while loop " << endl;
        i = i + 1;
    }
    cout << " Statement :   outside while loop " << endl;
    return 0;
}
```

The result of Program 6.1 is as follows:

```
Statement :  inside while loop
Statement :  inside while loop
Statement :  inside while loop
Statement :  inside while loop
Statement :  inside while loop
Statement :  outside while loop
```

The aforementioned program is represented pictorially in Fig. 6.1:

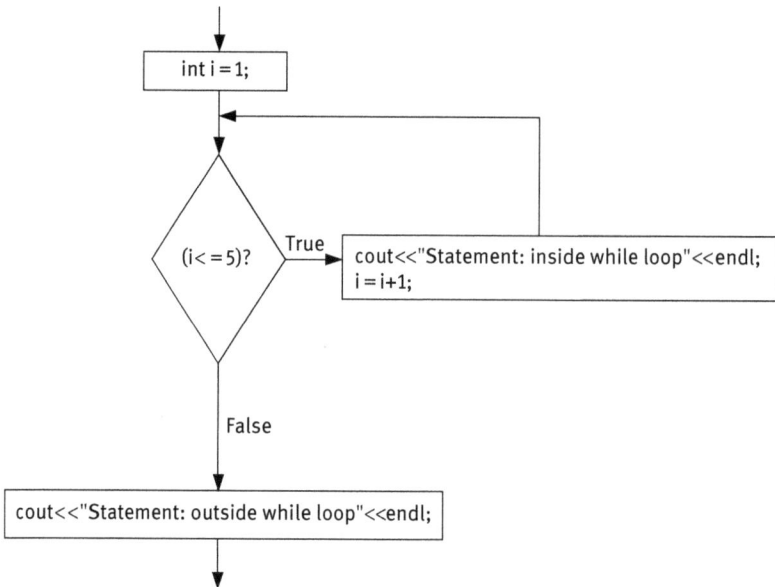

Fig. 6.1: Control flow of while statement.

In Program 6.1, we have noticed that the increment (or sometimes the decrement) statement i++ is separated from the Boolean-expression. It is possible to combine the increment or the decrement operators together along with the Boolean-expression. Program 6.1 can be rewritten as shown in Program 6.2.

```
// Program 6.2
// Program to understand while loop
#include <iostream>
using namespace std;

int main ()
{
    int i = 1;
    while(i++ <= 5)
    {
        cout << " Statement : inside while loop " << endl;
    }
    cout << " Statement : outside while loop " << endl;
    return 0;
}
```

The result of Program 6.2 is as follows:

```
Statement : inside while loop
Statement : inside while loop
Statement : inside while loop
Statement : inside while loop
Statement : inside while loop
Statement : outside while loop
```

Infinite while Loop

In few cases, it may be necessary to execute some statements all the time. In such cases, we use infinite looping statements. In this situation, the Boolean-expression always evaluates to true.

```
// Program 6.3
// This program to execute the statements for infinite number of times
#include <iostream>
using namespace std;

int main ()
{
    int i = 1;
    while(i == 1)
    {
        cout << " Infinite while loop " << endl;
    }
    return 0;
}
```

Program 6.4 also runs infinite times by using the while loop.

```
// Program 6.4
// Program which runs infinitely
#include <iostream>
using namespace std;

int main ()
{
    while(true);
    return 0;
}
```

6.3 The do-while loop

In Section 6.2, we have studied about the while loop and noticed that the statements inside the loop are executed only if the Boolean-expression evaluates to true. It means that the statements are not executed even a single time if the Boolean-expression is false. The difference between the do-while and the while statement is that the statements inside the do-while are executed at least once, even if the Boolean-expression evaluates to false. The general form of the do-while is as follows:

```
do
{
    Statements
}
while (Boolean-expression);

Next-statements;
```

As we mentioned earlier, the Boolean-expression is evaluated after the execution of statements inside the loop. The execution of statements continues until the Boolean-expression evaluates to false. The following program illustrates the use of the do-while loop:

```
// Program 6.5
// A program with do-while statement
#include <iostream>
using namespace std;

int main ()
{
    int i = 1;
    do
    {
```

```
        cout << " Statement :  inside do-while loop " << endl;
        i = i + 1;
    }
    while(i <= 5);
    cout << " Statement :  outside do-while loop " << endl;
    return 0;
}
```

The result of Program 6.5 is as follows:

```
Statement :  inside do-while loop
Statement :  inside do-while loop
Statement :  inside do-while loop
Statement :  inside do-while loop
Statement :  inside do-while loop
Statement :  outside do-while loop
```

Program 6.5 is shown in Fig. 6.2:

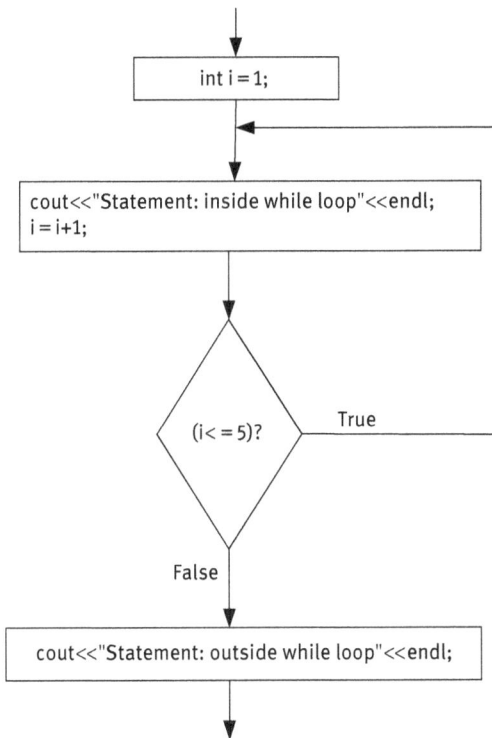

Fig. 6.2: Control flow of do-while statement.

Program 6.5 can be rewritten by combining the increment statement along with the Boolean-expression as shown in Program 6.6:

```cpp
// Program 6.6
// A program with do-while statement
#include <iostream>
using namespace std;

int main ()
{
    int i = 1;
    do
    {
        cout << " Statement : inside do-while loop " << endl;
    }
    while(i++ <= 5);
    cout << " Statement : outside do-while loop " << endl;
    return 0;
}
```

Program 6.7 illustrates the difference between the do-while and the while. Here, the statements inside the do-while are executed even if the Boolean-expression is false (i != 1).

```cpp
// Program 6.7
// Program to understand do-while statement
#include <iostream>
using namespace std;

int main ()
{
    int i = 1;
    do
    {
        cout << " Statement : inside do-while loop " << endl;
    }
    while(i != 1);
    cout << " Statement : outside do-while loop " << endl;
    return 0;
}
```

The result of Program 6.7 is as follows:

```
Statement : inside do-while loop
Statement : outside do-while loop
```

Infinite do-while Loop

In few cases, it may be necessary to execute some statements all the time. In such cases, we use infinite looping statements. In this situation, the Boolean-expression always evaluates to true (Program 6.8):

```
// Program 6.8
// This program to execute the statements for infinite number of times
#include <iostream>
using namespace std;

int main ()
{
    int i = 1;
    do
    {
        cout << " Infinite do-while loop " << endl;
    }
    while(i == 1);
    return 0;
}
```

The code shown in Program 6.9 also runs infinite times using the do-while loop.

```
// Program 6.9
// Program which runs infinitely
#include <iostream>
using namespace std;

int main ()
{
    do{ }while(true);

    return 0;
}
```

6.4 The for loop

In the previous sections, we have seen the while loop and the do-while loop and it is possible only to evaluate the Boolean-expressions in the while and do-while statements. The initialization of values is done before the loop. The for loop solves this problem as it is a modified version of while loop and do-while loop where we can include initialization statements, the Boolean-expression, and the increment and decrement statements together as a part of the for loop.

The general form of the for loop is as follows:

```
for(initialization operation; Boolean-expression; increment or decrement)
{
    Statements;
}
    Next-statements;
```

Program 6.10 illustrates the use of the for loop:

```
// Program 6.10
// Program with for loop
#include <iostream>
using namespace std;

int main ()
{
    for(int i = 1; i <= 5; i++)
    {
        cout << " Statement :  inside for loop " << endl;
    }
    cout << " Statement :  outside for loop " << endl;
    return 0;
}
```

The result of Program 6.10 is as follows:

```
Statement :  inside for loop
Statement :  inside for loop
Statement :  inside for loop
Statement :  inside for loop
Statement :  inside for loop
Statement :  outside for loop
```

Here, i = 1 is the initialization operation, i < =5 is the Boolean-expression, and i++ is an increment operation. Program 6.10 is pictorially represented in Fig. 6.3.

A for loop may include multiple initialization operations and increment or decrement operations together in a single for statement. In Program 6.11, there are two initialization operations, i = 1 and j = 1, separated by a comma and an increment operation i++ and a decrement operation j--.

```
// Program 6.11
// A program to understand a for loop with
// multiple initialization and increment and decrement operations
```

```cpp
#include <iostream>
using namespace std;

int main ()
{
    int i, j;
    for(i = 1, j = 15; i <= 5; i++,  j--)
        cout << " Hello " << i << " " << j << endl;
    return 0;
}
```

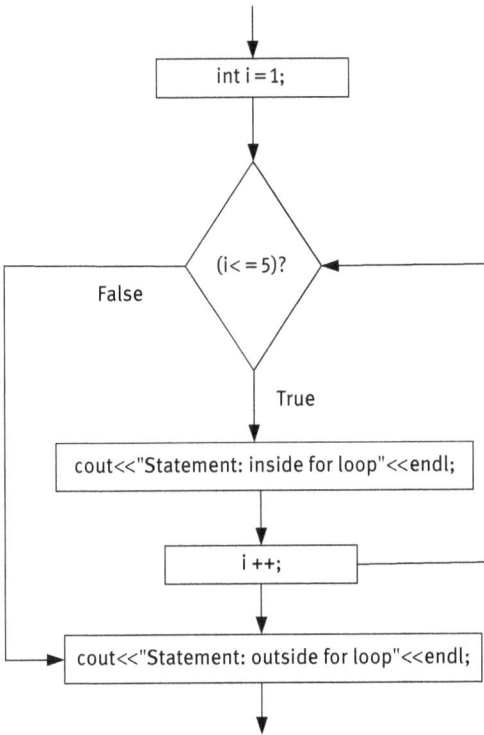

Fig. 6.3: Control flow of the for statement.

The result of Program 6.11 is as follows:

```
Hello    1 15
Hello    2 14
Hello    3 13
Hello    4 12
Hello    5 11
```

A for statement can be written without increment or decrement operation. In Program 6.12, the increment operation (i++) is separated from the for loop.

```
// Program 6.12
// The for statement without increment or decrement operator
#include <iostream>
using namespace std;

int main ()
{
    int i = 1;
    for(; i <= 5;)
    {
        cout << " Hello "<< i << endl;
        i++;
    }
    return 0;
}
```

The result of Program 6.12 is as follows:

```
Hello   1
Hello   2
Hello   3
Hello   4
Hello   5
```

A for statement can also be written with the Boolean-expression only. The initialization and the increment or decrement operations are written in separate statements. This is shown in Program 6.13:

```
// Program 6.13
// The for statement with only Boolean Expression
#include <iostream>
using namespace std;

int main ()
{
    int i = 1;
    for(;i <= 5;)
    {
        cout << " Hello " << i << endl;
        i++;
    }
    return 0;
}
```

The result of Program 6.13 is same as that of Program 6.12.

Infinite for Loop

In few cases, it may be necessary to execute some statements all the time. In such cases, we use infinite looping statements. In this situation, the Boolean-expression always evaluates to true. Programs 6.14 and 6.15 are examples for infinite execution.

```
// Program 6.14
// This program to execute the statements for infinite number of times
#include <iostream>
using namespace std;

int main ()
{
    for(; ;)
    {
        cout << " Infinite Loop " << endl;
    }
    return 0;
}

// Program 6.15
// A Program runs infinitely
#include <iostream>
using namespace std;

int main ()
{
    for(; ;);
    return 0;
}
```

6.5 Nesting of loops

Till now we have studied different types of looping statements in C++. It is also possible to have looping statement inside another loop. This is called **nesting of looping statements**. This is very useful in many cases. For example, a for loop may contain another for loop as a statement or while statement. This is true for while and do-while statements as well. Program 6.16 illustrates a simple nesting of for loops. The program generates a right-angled triangle of numbers.

```
// Program 6.16
// A program to generate number triangle using nested for loops
// Value of n = 6
#include <iostream>
using namespace std;
```

```
int main ()
{
    int sum = 0,  n = 6;
    for(int i = 1; i <= n; i++)
    {
        for(int j = 1; j <= i; j++)
        {
            cout << j << " ";
        }
        cout << endl;
    }
    return 0;
}
```

The result of Program 6.16 is as follows:

```
1
1 2
1 2 3
1 2 3 4
1 2 3 4 5
1 2 3 4 5 6
```

6.6 The break statement

The break statement is used simply to exit a loop or switch statement. It is useful when we need to exit a loop on some condition. It is frequently used with the switch statement. It is generally used together with the while, for, do-while, and switch statements. Program 6.17 illustrates the use of break statement. Here, the break statement simply exits for loop after single iteration. Many times break statements are used to terminate the loop unconditionally. The statements written after break statement are meaningless and such a program generates an error during compilation. Many programmers try to avoid break statement due its debugging problems.

```
// Program 6.17
// This is a program to understand break statement.
#include <iostream>
using namespace std;

int main ()
{
    for(int i = 1 ;i <10; i++)
    {
        cout << " Value of i = " << i << endl;
        break;
```

```
    }
    return 0;
}
```

The result of Program 6.17 is as follows:

```
    Value of i = 1
```

Program 6.18 illustrates the break statement upon a condition. Here, if the value of i is greater than 3, then the for loop exits from execution.

```
// Program 6.18
// The break statement used with a condition
#include <iostream>
using namespace std;

int main ()
{
    for(int i = 1; i < 10; i++)
    {
        if(i > 3)
        {
            cout << " Break The Program " << endl;
            break;
        }
        else
        {
            cout << " Value of i = " << i << endl;
        }
    }
    return 0;
}
```

The result of Program 6.18 is as follows:

```
    Value of i = 1
    Value of i = 2
    Value of i = 3
    Break The Program
```

The break statement can be used with while, do-while, and switch statements too. The following sections of this chapter illustrate such examples.

```
// Program 6.19
// The break statement used with a while statement

#include <iostream>
```

```
using namespace std;

int main ()
{
    int i = 1;

    while( i <= 10)
    {
        cout << " Value of i = " << i << endl;
        if(i >= 5)
            break;
        i++;
    }
    return 0;
}
```

The result of Program 6.19 is as follows:

```
Value of i = 1
Value of i = 2
Value of i = 3
Value of i = 4
Value of i = 5
```

An example of a break statement used in do-while statement is presented in Program 6.20.

```
// Program 6.20
// The break statement used with a do-while statement
#include <iostream>
using namespace std;

int main ()
{
    int i = 1;
    do
    {
        cout << " Value of i = " << i << endl;
        if(i >= 5)
            break;
        i++;
    }
    while(i <= 10);
    return 0;
}
```

The result of Program 6.20 is as follows:

```
        Value of i = 1
        Value of i = 2
        Value of i = 3
        Value of i = 4
        Value of i = 5
```

Program 6.21 illustrates the use of break statement in switch. The program will skip rest of the case statements.

```
// Program 6.21
// The break statement used with a switch statement
#include <iostream>
using namespace std;

int main ()
{
    int i = 1;
    switch(i)
    {
        case 1:
            cout << " Value of i = " << i << endl;
            break;
        default:
            cout << " Hello " << endl;
    }
    return 0;
}
```

The result of Program 6.21 is as follows:

```
        Value of i = 1
```

Remember that the break statement exits from the enclosing loop and not from the outer loop. In Program 6.22, only innermost loop exits but outer loop continues its execution until condition fails.

```
// Program 6.22
// The break statement used in nested for loops
#include <iostream>
using namespace std;

int main ()
{
    for(int i = 1; i < 3; i++)
    {
        for(int j = 1; j < 3; j++)
        {
```

```
            cout << " Value of j = " << j << " break " << endl;
            break;
        }
        cout << " Value of i = " << i << << endl;
    }
    return 0;
}
```

The result of Program 6.22 is as follows:

```
Value of j = 1 break
Value of i = 1
Value of j = 1 break
Value of i = 2
```

6.7 The continue statement

The continue statement return to the beginning of the enclosing loop. The rest of the statements after the continue statement remain unexecuted. The continue statement is quite opposite to break statement operation. The continue statement can be used together with while, do-while, and for loops. Program 6.23 illustrates the basic operation of continue statement.

```
// Program 6.23
// This program illustrates the use of continue statement.
#include <iostream>
using namespace std;

int main ()
{
    for(int i = 1; i <= 10; i++)
    {
        if(i <= 5)
            continue;
        cout << " Value of i = " << i << endl;
    }
    return 0;
}
```

The result of Program 6.23 is as follows:

```
Value of i = 6
Value of i = 7
```

```
Value of i = 8
Value of i = 9
Value of i = 10
```

Program 6.24 illustrates a `continue` statement in a nested `for` loops. The `continue` statement returns the control to the beginning of the innermost loop.

```cpp
// Program 6.24
// The continue statement used in nested for loops
#include <iostream>
using namespace std;

int main ()
{
    for(int i = 1; i < 3; i++)
    {
        for(int j = 1; j < 3; j++)
        {
            if(j == 1)
                continue;
            cout << " Value of j = " << j << endl;
        }
        cout << " Value of i = " << i << endl;
    }
    return 0;
}
```

The result of Program 6.24 is as follows:

```
Value of j = 2
Value of i = 1
Value of j = 2
Value of i = 2
```

6.8 Review questions

1. Explain the following looping statements with an example program for each: `while`, `for`, and `do-while`.
2. What is the difference between `while` and `do-while`? Explain with an example program.
3. Explain `break` and `continue` statements with programs.
4. Compare `while`, `do-while`, and `for` loops. Which is better and why?

5. Write a program to generate *N* Fibonacci numbers. The Fibonacci numbers are the numbers where each number in the series is the sum of the two preceding numbers.

   0 1 1 2 3 5 8 13 21 34 ...

   if *N* = 4 then the output should be

   0 1 1 2

6. Write a program to generate *N* prime numbers. For example, if *N* = 4, the result will be

   2 3 5 7

7. Write a program to calculate the sum of the digits of a given integer number, for example, if the number is 1234 the result is 10.

8. Write different programs to generate the following number triangles using for loops, for the input *N*. For example, for *N*=6, the results are as follows:

1	1	1
1 2	1 2	1 1
1 2 3	1 2 3	1 2 1
1 2 3 4	1 2 3 4	1 2 3 2 1
1 2 3 4 5	1 2 3 4 5	1 2 3 4 3 2 1
1 2 3 4 5 6	1 2 3 4 5 6	1 2 3 4 5 4 3 2 1

9. Repeat the Exercise 8 using while loop.

10. Write a program to generate the following series of output (where value of *N* = 4):

    a) 1 + 2*2 + 3*3*3 + 4*4* 4 +....
    b) 1 + 1*2 + 1*2*3 + 1*2*3*4 +....
    c) 1*1 + 2*2 + 3*3 + 4* 4...

11. Find the difference between Programs 6.25 and 6.26:

```
// Program 6.25
#include <iostream>
using namespace std;
int main ()
{
    while(true);
    cout << " Hello " << endl;
    return 0;
}


// Program 6.26
#include <iostream>
```

```
using namespace std;
int main ()
{
    cout << " Hello " << endl;
    while(true);
    return 0;
}
```

12. Find the difference between Programs 6.27 and 6.28:

```
// Program 6.27
#include <iostream>
using namespace std;
int main ()
{
    cout << " Infinite Loop " << endl;
    for(; ;);
    return 0;
}
```

```
// Program 6.28
#include <iostream>
using namespace std;
int main ()
{
    for(; ;);
        cout << " Infinite Loop " << endl;
    return 0;
}
```

13. Guess the result of Program 6.29 without executing it.

```
// Program 6.29
#include <iostream>
using namespace std;
int main ()
{
    break;
        return 0;
}
```

14. Check for the result of Program 6.30.

```
// Program 6.30
#include <iostream>
using namespace std;
```

```
int main ()
{
    for(; ;){break;}
    return 0;
}
```

15. Check for the result of Program 6.31

```
// Program 6.31
#include <iostream>
using namespace std;
int main ()
{
    for(int i = 1; i < 3; i ++)
    {
        for(int j = 1; i < 3; j ++)
        {
            cout << i * j << endl;
        }
    }
    return 0;
}
```

7 Arrays

> Flow with whatever may happen and let your mind be free. Stay centered by accepting
> whatever you are doing. This is the ultimate.
> — Zhuangzi

7.1 Introduction

In this chapter we explore the concept of arrays. Before proceeding to understand this
concept, let us first look at an example – list of marks scored by 10 students in a class.
What should we do to find the average marks of students in a class? How do we write
a program to find average score of all the 10 students? One way to solve this problem
is by assigning all the 10 scores to distinct variables. Let the example marks scored by
10 students are as shown below.

67,89,90,68,78,91,87,56,77,66

So, average marks = (67+89+90+68+78+91+87+56+77+66)/10.0

This can be converted to a C++ code as shown below:

```
int m1=67,m2=89,m3=90,m4=68,m5=78,m6=91,m7=87,m8=56,m9=77,m10=66;
float Average = (m1+m2+m3+m4+m5+m6+m7+m8+m9+m10)/10.0;
```

As we can see from the above code, we have used 10 different variables to denote
different marks of students. This is the case where there are only 10 students. What if
there are 200 students in a college? How can we declare distinct variables for all 200
students? This is really a problem and a waste of time. By using arrays we can solve
these problems. An **array** is a set of values of same data type. It is used to store
collection of data, where series of elements of the same type placed in contiguous
memory locations can be individually referenced by adding an index to a unique
identifier. In the discussed example, all 10 variables m1–m10 are integers. Here, all 10
variables share same data type. The arrays in C++ can be declared as:

```
data type <variable name>[arraySize];
```

For example: int marks[10];

This statement allocates memory for 10 values of data type integer. We can initialize
the array with predefined values as shown below:

```
int marks[10] = {67,89,90,68,78,91,87,56,77,66};
```

https://doi.org/10.1515/9783110593846-007

The arrays are used in many applications. For example, to read and store the names of students in a college, to store marks of students in a college, to sort the values in ascending order, to solve matrix problems, and so on.

7.2 One-dimensional arrays

In Section 7.1, we studied the fundamentals of arrays. Let us look at the above example again. To solve this problem using arrays, we will use **one-dimensional array.** The one-dimensional array is simply a list of values stored in a **row** or **column**, such as a row of trees and a row of students. As in a classroom, some students sit in row-wise and others in column-wise. Here, each row or column is a one-dimensional array. To understand the one-dimensional array, let us look at Fig. 7.1.

1	2	3
4	5	6
7	8	9

Fig. 7.1: Array of numbers.

Here, there are 9 numbers, out of which 1, 2, and 3 are in the first row; 4, 5, 6 in the second row; and 7, 8, and 9 are in third row. In the same way, we notice that 1, 4, 7 are in first column; 2, 5, and 6 in second column; and 3, 6, and 9 are in third column. Here, each column or row is a one-dimensional array. So, in this array, there are three one-dimensional rows of arrays or three one-dimensional columns of arrays. As we see in the Section 7.3, the entire grid of rows and columns together makes a **two-dimensional array.**

The scores of 10 students can be assigned to 10 elements in an array instead of different variables as shown below:

```
int marks[10] = {67,89,90,68,78,91,87,56,77,66};
```

The above statement is same as:

```
int marks[10];

marks[0] = 67;
marks[1] = 89;
marks[2] = 90;
```

```
marks[3] = 68;
marks[4] = 78;
marks[5] = 91;
marks[6] = 87;
marks[7] = 56;
marks[8] = 77;
marks[9] = 66;
```

All 10 different marks are stored at 10 different locations in the array starting from marks [0] to marks [9]. A point worth remembering is, if the array size is n, then the index of array ranges from 0 to n-1 and not 1 to n. All 10 marks are stored in a **consecutive** order. This means that marks 67 is stored in marks[0] and marks 89 is stored in marks[1], and so on. Fig. 7.2 shows the meaning of terms **array index, array element,** and **array value** with an example. The complete program to calculate average marks using arrays is shown in Program 7.1.

Array index	Array element	Value
0	marks [0]	67

Fig.7.2: Description of array terms.

```
// Program 7.1
// A program to find average marks of 10 students using arrays
#include <iostream>
using namespace std;

int main ()
{
    int marks [] =  {67,89,90,68,78,91,87,56,77,66};
    int i;
    float average  =  0, sum  =  0;
    for(i = 0; i < 10 ; i++)
        {
          sum = sum + marks [i];
        }
        average = sum / 10;
        cout << " The Average Marks of 10 Students = "  << average << endl;
        return 0;
}
```

The result of Program 7.1 is shown as follows:

```
The Average Marks of 10 Students = 76.9
```

Arrays can be used in variety of applications. It can be used to solve many real-time problems that we face in everyday life. Program 7.2 generates the following series of output using one-dimensional arrays

```
Input    Output
12       12 5
23       23 25
34       34 125
45       45 625
56       56 3125
```

To generate powers of 5, we will make use of pow() function. Moreover, as this is a **library function** defined in the include file <math.h>, we have to include this in the program. The following statement

m = pow(5,2); returns the value of m = 25 as the square of 5.

```
// Program 7.2
// A program to display powers of 5 using arrays
#include <iostream>
using namespace std;
#include <math.h>
#define Array_Length 5

int main ()
{
        int list[5] = {12,23,34,45,56};
        int i;
        for(i = 0; i < Array_Length; i++)
        {
                cout << list[i] << " "  << pow(5,(i + 1)) << endl;
        }
        return 0;
}
```

The result of Program 7.2 is shown as follows:

```
12    5
23    25
34    125
45    625
56    3125
```

In Program 7.2, the Array_Length is defined as 5, which is the size or length of the array. One-dimensional arrays can be used in variety of applications, such as sorting and searching, which will be discussed in Chapter 9.

7.3 Multidimensional arrays

In Section 7.2, we studied about one-dimensional arrays. As we have seen, one-dimensional arrays are just a collection or list of items. In this section, we will discuss about multidimensional arrays. The multidimensional arrays include two or more one-dimensional arrays. Consider the following Table 7.1.

Table 7.1: Three one-dimensional arrays forming a two-dimensional array.

1	2	3
4	5	6
7	8	9

In Table 7.1, there are three rows or three one-dimensional arrays that form a two-dimensional array. In this case, numbers are arranged in rows and columns. A two-dimensional array can be declared as

```
data type <variable name>[arraySize1][arraySize2];
```
For example:
```
int marks[][];
```
or
```
int marks[10][10];
```

The statement `int marks[10][10];` allocates memory for 100 (10×10) values of data type integer. We can also initialize two-dimensional array as shown:
```
int marks[2][3] =
{
     {68,78,91},
     {87,56,77}
};
```

The aforementioned statement is same as

```
    int marks[2][3];

    marks[0][0] = 68;
    marks[0][1] = 78;
    marks[0][2] = 91;
    marks[1][0] = 87;
```

```
marks[1][1] = 56;
marks[1][2] = 77;
```

We can notice that the numbers are arranged in two rows and three columns. Using two-dimensional array to find the average of six students is shown in Program 7.3 by modifying Program 7.1

```cpp
// Program 7.3
// A program to find average marks of 6 students using two-dimensional
// arrays
#include <iostream>
using namespace std;
int main ()
{
    int marks[2][3] =
    {
        {68,78,91},
        {87,56,77}
    };
    int i, j;
    float average = 0, sum = 0;
    for(i = 0; i < 2; i++)
    {
        for(j = 0; j < 3; j++)
        {
            sum = sum + marks [i][j];
        }
    }
    average = sum / 6;
    cout << " The Average Marks of 6 Students = "  << average << endl;
    return 0;
}
```

The result of Program 7.3 is as follows:

```
The Average Marks of 6 Students = 76.1667
```

Notice that we may use an array with more than two dimensions. For example, Program 7.4 stores eight values in a three-dimensional array and displays them:

```cpp
// Program 7.4
// A program to understand three-dimensional arrays
#include <iostream>
using namespace std;
```

```
int main ()
{
    int list [2][2][2] =
    {
        {
                {1,2},
                {3,4}
        },
        {
                {5,6},
                {7,8}
        }
    };
    int i,  j, k;

    for(i = 0; i < 2; i++)
    {
        for(j = 0; j < 2; j++)
        {
            for(k = 0; k < 2; k++)
            cout << " list[ " << i << " ][ " << j << " ][" << k << " ]
                = " <<list[i][j][k] << endl;
        }
    }
    return 0;
}
```

The result of Program 7.4 is as follows:

```
list[0][0][0] = 1
list[0][0][1] = 2
list[0][1][0] = 3
list[0][1][1] = 4
list[1][0][0] = 5
list[1][0][1] = 6
list[1][1][0] = 7
list[1][1][1] = 8
```

7.4 Applications of two-dimensional arrays

The two-dimensional arrays are used in many mathematical applications to solve problems. It is primarily used to solve matrix-related problems. In this section, we will describe some of the widely used applications of two-dimensional arrays, for example, the matrix problems such as matrix addition, subtraction, and multiplication can be solved using two-dimensional arrays.

Let A[3][3] be a matrix with the following values:

```
4 5 6
7 7 6
8 5 7
```

Let B[3][3] be a matrix with the following values:

```
1 2 1
2 2 1
1 3 2
```

The result after adding two matrices will be, that is, A + B:

```
5 7 7
9 9 7
9 8 9
```

The result after subtracting two matrices will be, that is, A - B:

```
3 3 5
5 5 5
7 2 5
```

The result after multiplying two matrices will be, that is, A × B:

```
20 36 21
27 46 26
25 47 27
```

Program 7.5 illustrates matrix addition program. Remember to add and subtract matrix A and matrix B, the number of rows and columns of first matrix should be equal to number of rows and columns of second matrix, respectively.

```cpp
// Program 7.5
// Matrix addition program
#include <iostream>
using namespace std;

int main ()
{
    int r_A = 3, c_A = 3;   //Rows in Matrix A = 3 and Columns = 3
    int r_B = 3, c_B = 3;   //Rows in Matrix B = 3 and Columns = 3
    int i,  j;

    int A[3][3] =
    {                       //Matrix A Values
        {4,5,6},
        {7,7,6},
        {8,5,7},
    };
    int B[3][3] =
```

```
{                           //Matrix B Values
    {1,2,1},
    {2,2,1},
    {1,3,2},
};
int C[3][3];                        //Declaration of Matric C

//check for row and columns of two matrices
if(r_A == r_B && c_A == c_B)
{
    //Initialize all elements of C matrix as zeroes
    for(i = 0; i < r_A; i++)
    {
        for(j = 0; j < c_A; j++)
        {
            C[i][j] = 0;
        }
    }

    //Matrix Addition
    for(i = 0; i < r_A; i++)
    {
        for(j = 0; j < c_A; j++)
        {
            C[i][j] = A[i][j] + B[i][j];
        }
    }

    //Print Matrix A
    cout << endl << " The Matrix A "  << endl;
    for(i = 0; i < r_A; i++)
    {
        for(j = 0; j < c_A; j++)
        {
            cout << A[i][j] << "  " ;
        }
        cout << endl;
    }

    //Print Matrix B
    cout << endl << " The Matrix B " << endl;
    for(i = 0; i < r_A; i++)
    {
        for(j = 0; j < c_A; j++)
        {
            cout << B[i][j] << "  " ;
        }
        cout << endl;
    }
```

```
        //Print Result Matrix C
        cout << endl << " The Matrix C = A+B " << endl;
        for(i = 0; i < r_A; i ++)
        {
                for(j = 0; j < c_A; j++)
                {
                        cout << C[i][j] << "   " ;
                }
                cout << endl;
        }
    }
    else
    {
        cout << " Matrix Addition is Not Possible" << endl;
        cout << " To add two matrices row and columns of two matrices must be same"
             <<    endl;
    }
    return 0;
}
```

The result of Program 7.5 is as follows:

```
    The Matrix A

    4 5 6
    7 7 6
    8 5 7

    The Matrix B

    1 2 1
    2 2 1
    1 3 2

    The Matrix C = A+B

    5 7 7
    9 9 7
    9 8 9
```

Program 7.5 can be modified for matrix subtraction by changing the following statements after initialization of matrix C.

```
    //Matrix Subtraction
    for(i = 0; i < r_A; i++)
    {
            for(j = 0; j < c_A; j++)
```

```
        {
                C[i][j] = A[i][j] - B[i][j];
        }
}
```

Matrix multiplication is little complex method as compared with matrix addition and subtraction. It is possible to multiply matrices, if and only if the columns of matrix A are equal to rows of matrix B. The following piece of code illustrates matrix multiplication.

```
//Matrix Multiplication
for(i = 0; i < r_A; i++)
{
        for(j = 0; j < c_B; j++)
        {
                C [i][j] = 0;
                for(k = 0; k < c_A; k++)
                {
                        C[i][j] = C[i][j] + A[i][k]  *  B[k][j];
                }
        }
}
```

Two-dimensional arrays can be used to solve **n** linear equations with **n** unknowns. Look at the following list of linear equations.

$$2x + 3y + 6z = 26$$
$$4x + 6y - 2z = 10$$
$$8x - 3y + 6z = 20$$

These equations can be represented as i.e. A×X = R

$$\begin{matrix} 2 & 3 & 6 \\ 4 & 6 & -2 \\ 8 & -3 & 6 \end{matrix} \quad \begin{matrix} x = 26 \\ y = 10 \\ z = 20 \end{matrix}$$

Here, matrix X comprises of unknown variables x, y, and z and can be obtained by

$$X = A^{-1} \text{ (inverse)} * R$$

Program 7.6 illustrates the above example of solving three linear equations.

```
//Program 7.6
//Program to solve three linear equations
#include <iostream>
using namespace std;
```

```
int main ()

{
    float A [3][3] =
    {
        {2, 3, 6},
        {4, 6, - 2},
        {8, - 3, 6}
    };

    //AX = R
    float X [3][1];
    float R [3][1] =
    {
        {26},
        {10},
        {20}
    };

    int n = 3;
    int i, j, k;

    //Find the determinant of matrix A
    float  det = A[0][0] * (A[1][1] * A[2][2]    - A[2][1] * A[1][2]) -
    A[0][1] * (A[1][0] * A[2][2] - A[2][0] * A[1][2])+
    A[0][2] * (A[1][0] * A[2][1] - A[2][0] * A[1][1]);

    //B is the inverse matrix of A
    float  B[3][3];
    B[0][0] = A[1][1] * A[2][2] - A[2][1] * A[1][2];
    B[0][1] = - (A[0][1] * A[2][2] - A[2][1] * A[0][2]);
    B[0][2] = A[0][1] * A[1][2] - A[1][1] * A[0][2];
    B[1][0] = - (A[1][0] * A[2][2] - A[2][0] * A[1][2]);
    B[1][1] = (A[0][0] * A[2][2] - A[2][0] * A[0][2]);
    B[1][2] = - (A[0][0] * A[1][2] - A[1][0] * A[0][2]);
    B[2][0] = A[1][0] * A[2][1] - A[2][0] * A[1][1];
    B[2][1] = - (A[0][0] * A[2][1] - A[2][0] * A[0][1]);
    B[2][2] = A[0][0] * A[1][1] - A[1][0] * A[0][1];

    //To find inverse of A
    for(i = 0;i < n; i++)
    {
        for(j = 0; j < n; j++)
        {
            B[i][j] = B[i][j] / det;
        }
    }

    // X  =  (inverse of A = B) * R
```

```
for(i = 0;i < n; i++)
{
    for(j = 0; j < 1; j++)
    {
        X[i][j] = 0;
        for(k = 0;k < n ; k++)
        {
            X[i][j] = X[i][j] + B[i][k] * R[k][j];
        }
    }
}
cout << " The Solutions to the equations are " << endl;
cout << " X = "   << X[0][0] << endl;
cout << " Y = "   << X[1][0] << endl;
cout << " Z = "   << X[2][0] << endl;
return 0;
}
```

The result of Program 7.6 is as follows:

```
The Solutions to the equations are
X = 1
Y = 2
Z = 3
```

Another interesting program of generating **magic square** is presented further. Consider Tables 7.2 and 7.3. They are magic squares. Magic square is a grid of n×n cells with positive integers starting from 1, 2, 3, and 4…up to n×n. The grid is filled in such a way that sum of numbers in each row, column, and diagonals are equal. However, Program 7.7 works only for all magic squares, where n is odd. The magic square, where $n = 3$ and sum of elements in a row or column is 15 is shown in Table 7.2.

Table 7.2: Magic square where $n = 3$ and the elements in a row or column add upto 15.

6	1	8
7	5	3
2	9	4

The magic square, where $n = 5$, with elements in a row or column adding to 65 is shown in Table 7.3.

Table 7.3: Magic square where $n = 5$ and the elements in a row or column add upto 65.

15	8	1	24	17
16	14	7	5	23
22	20	13	6	4
3	21	19	12	10
9	2	25	18	11

```cpp
// Program 7.7
// Magic Square Program
#include <iostream>
using namespace std;

int main ()
{
    int square [100][100];
    int n;
    cout << " Enter the value of n (odd number only) : " << endl;
    cin >> n;
    int i,  j, k = 0,l = 0,key = 2;

    for(i = 0;i < n; i ++)
        for(j = 0; j < n; j ++)
            square[i][j] = 0;

    i = 0;
    j = (n - 1) / 2;
    square[i][j] = 1;

    while(key <= n * n)
    {
        k = (i - 1) % n;
        if(k == - 1)
            k = n - 1;

        l = (j - 1) % n;
        if(l == - 1)
            l = n - 1;

        if(square[k][l] == 0)
        {
            i = k;
            j = l;
        }
        else
```

```
        {
            i = (i + 1) % n;
        }

        square[i][j] = key;
        key = key + 1;
    }
    cout << endl << " The Magic Square for n = " << n << endl;
    for(i = 0; i < n; i++)
    {
        for(j = 0; j < n; j ++)
            cout << square[i][j] << "   " ;
        cout << endl;
    }
    return 0;
}
```

The result of Program 7.7 is as follows:

```
Enter the value of n (odd number only):
3

The Magic Square for n = 3
6 1 8
7 5 3
2 9 4
```

7.5 Review questions

1. What is an array? How to declare an array?
2. What is a two-dimensional array? How it is different from one-dimensional arrays.
3. List the advantages of arrays in programming.
4. Modify Program 7.3 to find the average of marks of six students using three-dimensional arrays.
5. Write a program to multiply following two matrices.

```
2 3 4 5          2 3 4
7 8 9 2          7 6 4
3 5 6 7          8 6 7
7 8 9 7          1 2 3
(4×4)            (4×3)
```

6. Write a program to copy elements from a two-dimensional array to one-dimensional array.

7. Write a program to generate the following output from the given input using two-dimensional arrays.

```
1 2 3 4        1 2 3 4
1 2 0 4        1 2 4 0
1 0 3 4        1 3 4 0
1 0 0 4        1 4 0 0
(Input)        (Output)
```

8. Write a program to generate the following output from the given input. Remember that the first row in the output matrix indicates total number of rows and columns and non-zero elements in the input matrix

```
6 0 0 0 1 0              5 6 6
0 0 0 0 0 8              0 0 6
9 0 0 0 0 0              0 4 1
0 0 0 0 0 4              1 5 8
0 0 3 0 0 0              2 0 9
(Input Matrix 5×6)       3 5 4
                         4 2 3
                         (Output Matrix 7×3)
```

9. Write a program to find inverse of a matrix.

8 Strings and Pointers

> No benefit is more constant than simplicity; no happiness more constant than peace.
> – Han Feizi

8.1 Introduction

In this chapter, we will study about strings and pointers. Although the strings and pointers are not closely related they are discussed together because in many instances, we use pointers along with arrays, and strings are set of character arrays. The C++ provides two types of string representations. The first one is C-style character string, which originated from the C language and continues to be supported within C++. The other type is the string supported from string class in C++. We will cover these aspects in general in this chapter.

A string is a one-dimensional array of characters. The last element in a string is the NULL terminator ('\0'). So, a string is an array with one element more than the maximum number of actual characters. Thus, a null-terminated string contains the characters that comprise the string followed by a null. We do not have to place the null character at the end of a string constant. The C++ compiler automatically places the '\0' at the end of the string when it initializes the array. In C++, a character is always represented within single quotes. For example, char c = 'a', however, strings are represented using double quotes, as in "Hello". Even if a single character is enclosed within double quotes, it is still considered as string, instead of character. The following declaration and initialization creates a string consisting of the word "Hello".

```
char examplestr[6] = {'H','e','l','l','o','\0'};
```

Let us understand a simple example of character array, as shown already. In this statement, we declared the size of the string as 6. However, the actual size of the string is 5, because there are only 5 characters excluding the null character. One should remember that the array index starts from 0 and not 1. The size of the array or the string cannot be changed or redefined by a programmer. In the aforementioned statement, the characters of the string will be numbered from 0 to 5. Fig. 8.1 shows memory presentation of the already defined string in C/C++.

The Program 8.1 shows an example to use the above string. In this program, three different strings are initialized in three different ways. All these initializations are acceptable, and a programmer can use the best method depending on the requirement. In the first initialization statement: char example1[6] = {'H','e','l','l','o','\0'};, the string is initialized character by character,; however, in the second (char example2[5] = "Good";) initialization, the entire string is initialized directly. In this case, the string is

https://doi.org/10.1515/9783110593846-008

Index	0	1	2	3	4	5
Value	H	e	l	l	o	\n

Fig. 8.1: Memory representation of a string.

enclosed within double quotes. The difference between the second and third initialization statement (char example3[] = "Morning";) is about the array index. In the third initialization, the array index is unspecified. However, if we use an array of size less than the number of character the compiler generates an error.

```
// Program 8.1
// String initialization program
#include <iostream>
using namespace std;

int main ()
{
    char example1[6]  =  {'H',  'e', 'l', 'l', 'o', '\0'};
    char example2[5]  =  "Good";
    char example3[ ]  =  "Morning";
    cout << " Example string 1  =  " << example1 << endl;
    cout << " Example string 2  =  " << example2 << endl;
    cout << " Example string 3  =  " << example3 << endl;
    return 0;
}
```

The result of Program 8.1 is as follows:

```
Example string 1  =  Hello
Example string 2  =  Good
Example string 3  =  Morning
```

An example where a string can be read from the keyboard and displayed back to screen using cin and cout statements is presented in Program 8.2.

```
// Program 8.2
// String input and output
#include <iostream>
using namespace std;

int main ()
{
    char str [10];
    cout <<     " Enter a string : ";
    cin >> str;
```

```
    cout << " The entered string is  = " << str << endl;
    return 0;
}
```

The sample result of Program 8.2 is as follows:

```
    Enter a string : Qingdao
    The entered string is = Qingdao
```

We can also write a program to copy one string to another.

```
// Program 8.3
// Program to copy one string to another
#include <iostream>
using namespace std;

int main ()
{
    char str1 [10] ,   str2 [10];
    int i = 0;
    cout << " Enter a string ,   str1 : ";
    cin >> str1;
    cout << " The entered string is  : " << str1 << endl;
    while((str2 [i]  = str1 [i] )!='\0')
        i++;
    cout << " String,   str2 contains  :" << str2 << endl;
    return 0;
}
```

A sample result of Program 8.3 is as follows

```
    Enter a string,   str1 : qingdao
    The entered string is  :qingdao
    String,   str2 contains :qingdao
```

In Program 8.3,two arrays are declared, str1 and str2, both with maximum capacity of 10 characters, including a null character. This means, the maximum length of strings (both str1 and str2) must be less than or equal to 9. The while statement directly assigns the str1 characters one by one to str2 array in the respective locations, starting from 0, and this operation is performed including the null character. But once the null character is also copied from str1 to str2, the operation stops because of the condition within the while statement. So, it is important to remember that when character arrays or a string in a program is used a '\0' or NULL terminator is added at the end of the string. Programs 8.4 and 8.5 show examples to understand the importance of null character while managing strings.

```
// Program 8.4
// Program to understand the role of null character
#include <iostream>
using namespace std;

int main ()
{
    char str [10];
    int i = 0;
    cout << " Enter a string  : ";
    while( (str [i++]  = getchar( )) != '\n');
    cout << " Entered string is  : " << str << endl;
    return 0;
}
```

A sample result of Program 8.4 is as follows:

```
Enter a string  : Beijing
Entered string is  : Beijing
¡¡¡¡ê ?
```

In Program 8.4, the while loop is used to read the character one by one using the getchar() library function until the user presses the enter key (so '\n' is supplied to perform this). We will describe more about the string library or built-in functions in Section 8.2 (to understand the meaning of functions, see Chapter 10). The getchar() function gets characters from standard input (stdin). This function reads in a character and returns the character as the ASCII value of that character. This function will wait for a key to be pressed before continuing with the program. Once the enter key is pressed, the reading of characters is stopped into string str. As shown in the sample result of Program 8.4, it is evident that the results display unexpected characters in its output. This is because the string str is unable to guess the end of the string as we have not added the null ('\0') character at the end of the str. So, the modified version of Program 8.4 is shown in Program 8.5. As shown in this program, a new statement str [i] = '\0'; is added after reading the characters to delimit the end of the string str.

```
// Program 8.5
// Program to understand the role of null character

#include <iostream>
using namespace std;

int main ()
{
    char str [10];
```

```
    int i = 0;
    cout << " Enter a string  : ";
    while( (str [i++]  = getchar( )) !='\n');
    str [i] ='\0';
    cout << " Entered string is  : "<< str<< endl;
    return 0;
}
```

A sample result of Program 8.5 is as follows:

```
    Enter a string  : Beijing
    Entered string is  : Beijing
```

8.2 String library functions

In this section, we will briefly describe some of the commonly used string library functions in C++. The 'cstring' library defines various string functions that can be used to perform various operations on strings. This section describes some of the string functions that are mostly used in the programs. However, #include <cstring> needs to be written in order to use any of the functions mentioned in Table 8.1.

Program 8.6 shows an example to demonstrate some of the string functions in C++.

```
// Program 8.6
// Functions manipulating strings
#include <iostream>
#include <cstring>
using namespace std;

int main ()
{
    char str1 [20] = "Great";
    char str2 [20] = "Wall";
    char str3 [20];

    //Finding the length of str1
    cout << "strlen(str1) : " << strlen(str1) << endl;

    // Copying str1 into str3
    strcpy( str3,   str1);
    cout << "strcpy( str3,   str1) : " << str3 << endl;

    // Concatenation of str1 and str2
    strcat( str1,   str2);
```

```
    cout << "strcat( str1,   str2) : " << str1 << endl;
    return 0;
}
```

Table 8.1: String functions and their descriptions

Function	Description
strlen (str);	This function returns the length of the string str. The length of the string is the number of characters in the string without the terminating character '\0'
strcpy (dest, src);	This is a string copy function. The first parameter is the destination string and the second parameter is the source string. The function strcpy will copy the contents of source string to the destination string, including the terminating null character '\0'
strcat (dest, src);	This is a string concatenation function. The first parameter is the destination string and the second parameter is the source string. The function strcat() will concatenate/append the contents of source array to the destination array. The terminating null character of the destination array is overwritten by the first character of the source array and a null character is introduced in the destination string at the end of the new string
strcmp (str1, str2);	This function compares two strings. The first parameter is str1 and the second parameter is str2 which will be compared by this function. It starts by comparing the first character of both the strings. It compares till it finds a non-matching character or the terminating null character. This function returns an integral value. The 0 is returned when both the strings are equal. A negative value is returned when the non-matching character encountered has a lower value in str1 than str2. A positive value is returned when the non-matching character encountered has a greater value in str1 than str2
strchr(str, ch);	This function returns a pointer to the first occurrence of character ch in string str. This function is used to locate the first occurrence of character in the string. This can also be located in order to retrieve a pointer to the end of a string.
strstr(str1, str2);	This function is used to locate a substring, and returns a pointer to the first occurrence of string str2 in string str1 or a null pointer if str2 is not part of str1.

The result of Program 8.6 is as follows:

```
    strlen(str1)  : 5
    strcpy(str3,  str1)  : Great
    strcat(str1,  str2) : GreatWall
```

8.3 Array of strings

As we have mentioned earlier, collection of characters is called string. For example, place names, names of persons, and names of plants are strings. However, in several applications, it is important to process several thousands of strings. For example, a classroom management program needs to read all the students' names, or in other words it is required to read array of strings. The arrays of strings can be created by declaring an array by using a method of a two-dimensional character array. String arrays are multidimensional arrays, that is, an array of strings or an array of characters. Consider the following expression:

```
char names [10][40];
```

The above variable is an array of strings with 10 names and up to 39 characters in each. C++ allows arrays of any dimension to be defined, the first index of the array refers to the row number, and the second index number refers the column number. Two-dimensional arrays are initialized in the same manner as a one-dimensional array. Program 8.7 shows an example of reading five names from keyboard and displaying them onto the screen.

```
// Program 8.7
// Array of strings
#include <iostream>
#include <cstring>
using namespace std;

int main ()
{
    char names [10][40];
    int i = 0;
    cout << " Enter five names one by one : " << endl;
    for(i = 0; i<5; i ++)
        cin >> names [i];
    cout << endl<<"Entered names are :" << endl;
    for(i = 0; i<5; i++)
        cout << names [i] << endl;
    return 0;
}
```

A sample result of Program 8.7 is as follows:

```
Enter five names one by one  :
Linda
Jessica
```

```
Ashan
Cicely
Amila

Entered names are  :
Linda
Jessica
Ashan
Cicely
Amila
```

8.4 Introduction to pointers

A pointer is a variable in C++ (or C) that points to a memory location. It does not directly contain a value such as int or float. One can access this value indirectly through the pointer variable. A pointer is declared as follows:

```
int *ptr1;
int i;
ptr1  =  &i;
```

Here, we have to understand the role played by characters '*' and '&' in front of variables. The character '*' in front of the variable is used to declare a pointer variable and it is also used in front of a pointer variable to access and retrieve the value contained by a pointer variable, not the address. However, the character '&' is used to access the address of an integer variable pointed by the pointer. In the above example, we declare an integer pointer "ptr1" and an integer variable i. Then we make the pointer ptr1 point to the address of the variable i. Consider Program 8.8 to understand the concept of pointers.

```
// Program 8.8
// Program to understand pointers
#include <iostream>
using namespace std;

int main ()
{
    int *ptr;
    int i = 18;
    ptr  =  &i;
    cout << " The value of i is " << i << endl;
    cout << " The pointer ptr (*ptr) contains the value "
```

```
        << *ptr << endl;
     return 0;
}
```

The result of Program 8.8 is as follows:

```
    The value of i is 18
    The pointer ptr (*ptr) contains the value 18
```

Different from other normal variables that can store values, pointers are special variables that can hold the address of a variable. Since they store memory address of a variable, the pointers are very commonly said to **"point to variables."** As shown in Program 8.8, a normal variable i might have an address, for example, 5060, and holds the value 18. However, the pointer variable ptr1 has its own address too, but stores 5060, which is address of variable i. Fig. 8.2 shows this illustration.

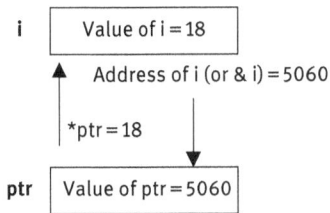

Fig. 8.2: Understanding pointers.

A pointer can be declared as:

```
    < pointer-type >  *< pointer-name >; or
```

```
    < pointer-type >* < pointer-name >;
```

The pointer-type specifies the type of pointer. It can be int,char,float, etc. This type specifies the type of variable whose address this pointer can store. The pointer-name can be any variable name specified by the user. It is a common practice that most of the pointer variables start with lowercase letter 'p', or end with 'ptr'. In Program 8.8, the int *ptr; is the pointer declaration. The int data type specifies the pointer type and the *ptr is the name of the pointer. In other words, the ptr is a variable that can store the address of an integer, and *ptr returns the value stored in that address. Now, let us modify Program 8.8 to display the address of the pointer and confirm our understanding.

```
// Program 8.9
// Program to understand pointers
#include <iostream>
using namespace std;

int main ()
{
    int *ptr;
    int i = 18;
    ptr = &i;
    cout << " The value of i is " << i << endl;
    cout << " The pointer ptr (*ptr) contains the value "
        << *ptr << endl;
    cout << " The address of i = " << &i << endl;
    cout << " The value of ptr  = " << ptr << endl;

    return 0;
}
```

A sample result of Program 8.9 is as follows:

```
The value of i is 18
The pointer ptr (*ptr) contains the value 18
The address of i =  0018FF40
The value of ptr  =  0018FF40
```

As shown in the results, the '&' operator is used to access the address of any variable type. In Program 8.9, the values stored in variable ptr as well as the address of i are same. However, the address of the variable may change from computer to computer. So, it is wrong to expect the same address when a user tests Program 8.9. We can also initialize a pointer in the following way:

```
<pointer declaration(except semicolon)> = <address of a variable>;
```

Or

```
<pointer declaration>;
<name-of-pointer> = <address of a variable>;
```

For example, the character pointers can be initialized as shown further. In the code mentioned, we declared a character variable ch that stores the value 'c'. Now, we declared a character pointer 'chptr' and initialized it with the address of variable 'ch'.

```
char ch = 'c';
char *chptr = &ch;
```

or

```
char ch  = 'c';
char *chptr;
chptr =  &ch
```

Program 8.10 shows an example of pointers, which include all types of common pointers in C++.

```
// Program 8.10
// Common pointers
#include <iostream>
using namespace std;

int main ()
{
    char ch ='c'  ;
    char *chptr = &ch;
    int i = 18;
    int *intptr = &i;
    float f = 3.14f;
    float *fptr = &f;
    char *sptr = "Hello World!";
    cout << " Value of (char) *chptr  =  " << *chptr << endl;
    cout << " Value of (int) *intptr  =  " << *intptr << endl;
    cout << " Value of (float) *fptr  =  " << *fptr << endl;
    cout << " Value of (char) *sptr =  " << *sptr << endl;
    cout << " Value of (string)  =  " << sptr << endl;
    return 0;
}
```

The result of Program 8.10 is as follows:

```
Value of (char) *chptr  =  c
Value of (int) *intptr  =  18
Value of (float) *fptr  =  3.14
Value of (char) *sptr =  H
Value of (string)  =  Hello World!
```

Program 8.10 shows an example that covers all the common pointers. The int, char, and float pointers are easy to understand, and they are straightforward. However, string pointers are quite different. As shown in the statement:char *sptr = "Hello World!";, the character pointer *sptr points to a string. As it can be seen, the statement includes a string instead of a single character. This shows that character and string pointers are used in the same way although their applications are different.

When we point a pointer to a string, by default it holds the address of the first character of the string. So, when we try to print *sptr, it only displays the first character 'H'. This means that any character pointer pointing to a string stores the address of the first character of the string. In the code above, 'sptr' holds the address of the character 'H'. So, when we apply the 'value of' operator '*' to 'sptr', the 'H' is displayed as output. However, if we try to display sptr, the compiler prints the entire string.

8.5 Pointer to pointer

So far, we have studied that the pointers are special variable that stores the address of another variable. Here, a question might arise: Is it possible to store the address of the pointer itself? The answer is Yes. In C and C++, it is perfectly legal for a pointer to point to another pointer. Let us consider an interesting assumption here.

> One day, while locating a street number in Beijing, you discover a person A, who agrees to guide you. Unfortunately, the person A is unable to locate the street you are looking for; instead he calls his friend B to guide him. Friend B also failed to locate the street, and calls his friend C to locate it. Let us assume that C is finally able to guide B, and then B is able to convey the message to A. In the end, you receive the required information to locate the street from A.

Now, in this scenario, lets us assume that information you are looking for is just an integer number (such as street number). Then, we can make you as the pointer to A (because you point him for information), and A as pointer to B, and B as pointer to C; finally C has the correct street number. Program 8.13 shows an example where we can demonstrate the above scenario with pointers that point to other pointers.

```
// Program 8.11
// Pointers to pointers

#include <iostream>
using namespace std;
int main ()
{
    int stNo = 1818;   //street number
    int *C;            //pointer C to store the address of stNo
    int **B;           //pointer to pointer,   to store the address of C
    int ***A;          //pointer to pointer,   to store the address of B
    int ****meptr;     //pointer to pointer,   to store the address of A

    C = &stNo;
    B = &C;
    A = &B;
```

```
    meptr = &A;

    cout << " Value of meptr = : " << meptr << endl;
    cout << " Value of *meptr = : " << *meptr << endl;
    cout << " Value of **meptr = : " << **meptr << endl;
    cout << " Value of **meptr = : " << **meptr << endl;
    cout << " Value of ***meptr = : " << ***meptr << endl;
    cout << " Value of ****meptr = : " << ****meptr << endl << endl;

    cout << " Value of A   = : " << A << endl;
    cout << " Value of *A   = : " << *A << endl;
    cout << " Value of **A   = :" << **A << endl;
    cout << " Value of ***A   = : " << ***A << endl << endl;

    cout << " Value of B   = : " << B << endl;
    cout << " Value of *B   = : " << *B << endl;
    cout << " Value of **B   = : " << **B << endl << endl;

    cout << " Value of C   = : " << C << endl;
    cout << " Value of *C   = : " << *C << endl;
    return 0;
}
```

The result of Program 8.11 is as follows:

```
        Value of meptr    =    :0018FF38
        Value of *meptr   =    :0018FF3C
        Value of **meptr  =    :0018FF40
        Value of **meptr  =    :0018FF40
        Value of ***meptr  =    :0018FF44
        Value of ****meptr  =    :1818

        Value of A    =    :0018FF3C
        Value of *A   =    :0018FF40
        Value of **A  =    :0018FF44
        Value of ***A  =    :1818

        Value of B    =    :0018FF40
        Value of *B   =    :0018FF44
        Value of **B  =    :1818

        Value of C    =    :0018FF44
        Value of *C   =    :1818
```

However, the address values may change from computer to computer. Fig. 8.3 shows such scenario and depicts how the addresses are stored in different pointer variables. It is worth noting from the results that the values of ****meptr, ***A, **B, and *C are all equal to 1818, which is equal to stNo.

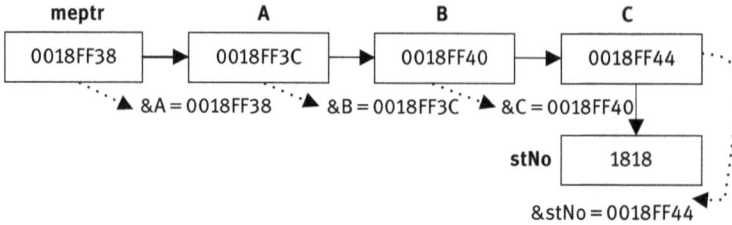

Fig. 8.3: Example for pointer to pointers.

8.6 Pointers and arrays

In C and C++, pointers and arrays are closely related. Pointers are very useful in array manipulation. Declaration of a pointer to an array is just like an integer pointer or a float pointer.

```
int *ptr;
int arr [5];
ptr  =  &arr [0];
```

Here, the pointer contains the address of the first element of the array. The other alternative for pointing to the first element of an array is `ptr = arr`. It is important to remember that the name of an array not followed by a subscript, is a pointer to the first element in the array.

Once a pointer has been set to point at an element of an array, it is possible to use the increment ++ and decrement -- operator to point to subsequent or previous elements of the array, respectively. But incrementing or decrementing the pointer to point beyond an array's boundary produces a runtime error, and program may crash or may overwrite other data or code sections of our program. So, it is the responsibility of the programmer to use the pointer to an array wisely. One more factor to consider is the size of the data type that the pointer points to. Suppose an integer pointer is pointing to an integer array, when we increment the pointer, the pointer points to the next element of the array. But in reality the pointer will contain an address that is typically 4 bytes greater than the address of the first element of the array.

Another aspect to consider is the array transformation rule. If `arr1` is an array, then the expression `arr1+1` is the address of the second element of the array, regardless of `arr1`'s data type. We can now use the indirection operator * in front of the variable to retrieve the value stored at this location. Thus, `*(arr1+1)`gives the value stored in the array's second element. Parentheses are required because the indirection operator * has a higher precedence over the addition operator. So, we can use this transformation rule to convert any array reference to its equivalent pointer expression.

    arr1[0]   is equivalent to *(arr1 + 0)
    arr1[1]   is equivalent to *(arr1 + 1)
    arr1[2]   is equivalent to *(arr1 + 2)

Without the parentheses the expression *arr1+1 evaluates to something totally different, as this retrieves the value stored in the array's first element and adds 1 to it. However, there are some key differences between arrays and pointers. A pointer's value can be changed to point to some other memory location. But the pointer represented by an array name cannot be changed. It is treated as a constant.

```
float TotAmt[10];
TotAmt  ++;      // illegal statement
TotAmt  - =  1;  // illegal statement
```

One more point to remember is that array names are initialized to point to the first element in the array whereas pointers are uninitialized when declared. They have to be explicitly initialized before usage otherwise a run time error will occur. Examples of using arrays and pointers together are presented in Programs 8.12 and 8.13.

```
// Program 8.12
// Arrays and pointers
#include <iostream>
using namespace std;

int main ()
{
    int arr[5]  = {11, 8, 45, 47, 9};
    int *ptr;
    ptr = &arr [0];
    cout << " Value of *ptr is  =  " << *ptr << endl;
    cout << " Value of *ptr+1 is  =  " << *ptr+1 << endl;
    cout << " Value of arr [1] is  =  " << arr [1] << endl;
    cout << " Value of *ptr+1 is  =  " << *(ptr+1) << endl;
    return 0;
}
```

The result of Program 8.12 is as follows:

```
Value of *ptr is  =  11
Value of *ptr+1 is  =  12
Value of arr [1]  is  =  8
Value of *ptr+1 is  =  8
```

Program 8.13 shows another challenging example of using arrays and pointers along with increment operator.

```
// Program 8.13
// Arrays and pointers
#include <iostream>
using namespace std;

int main ()
{
    int a[5] = {11, 8, 45, 47, 9};
    *a = *(a + 2) + (*a)++;
    cout << " The value of *a = " << a[0] << endl;
    return 0;
}
```

The result of Program 8.13 is as follows:

```
The value of *a  =  57
```

8.7 Array of pointers

In addition to the close relationship between arrays and pointers, we can also have array of pointers similar to array of integers or characters. An array of pointers can be declared as follows:

<type> *<name> [<number-of-elements];

For example: char *ptr[3];

The above line declares an array of three character pointers. Program 8.14 shows an example of using array of character pointers. We have selected the array of character pointers intentionally, as they have multiple benefits when using strings because as the array holds addresses of strings, we can easily display the strings using the pointer names. In this program, initially we created three character pointers and then assigned them to an array of pointers. So, now the array holds the address of strings.

```
// Program 8.14
// Array of pointers example
#include <iostream>
using namespace std;

int main(void)
{
    char *p1 =  "Liu";
    char *p2 =  "Shan";
    char *p3 =  "Jinan";

    char *arr[3];

    arr [0] =  p1;
    arr [1] =  p2;
    arr [2] =  p3;

    cout << " p1 = " << p1 << endl;
    cout << " p2 = " << p2 << endl;
    cout << " p3 = " << p3 << endl;

    cout << " arr[0] =  " << arr[0]  << endl;
    cout << " arr[1] =  " << arr[1]  << endl;
    cout << " arr[2] =  " << arr[2]  << endl;

    return 0;
}
```

In Program 8.14, we took three pointers pointing to three strings. Then we declared an array that can contain three pointers. We assigned the pointers 'p1', 'p2', and 'p3' to the 0, 1, and 2 index of array, respectively. The result of Program 8.14 is as follows:

```
p1  =  Liu
p2  =  Shan
p3  =  Jinan
arr [0]   =  Liu
arr [1]   =  Shan
arr [2]   =  Jinan
```

8.8 Review questions

1. Explain strings in C++ with an example.
2. Write a program to copy one string to another string using character arrays and without using standard string library functions such as strcpy.

3. What is the role of NULL terminator in strings? Explain with an example.
4. List at least five built-in string functions in C++.
5. Write a C++ program to understand the following string functions: `strcmps`, `strcpy`, `strcat`, `strtev`, and `strlen`
6. Write a C++ program to convert a lowercase string to uppercase string.
7. What is a pointer? How to declare an integer pointer in C++?
8. Write a C++ program to understand pointers.
9. Write a C++ program to demonstrate functions using pointers.
10. Describe the relationship between pointers and arrays using an example program.
11. List the difference between arrays and pointers in C++ using examples.
12. Write a program to demonstrate a pointer pointing to another pointer.

9 Searching and Sorting

> To know and not to act is not to know.
> – Wang Yangming

9.1 Introduction

In this chapter, we will study about different **sorting** and **searching** methods. The sorting and searching methods are very useful in today's computing environment and are used in almost all kinds of applications such as students' database, telephone-directory, employee database information, and travel database applications. Sorting is useful to arrange the different kinds of data, for example, numbers, names, and pictures, in a definite order, whereas searching is used to search an item in the given list.

9.2 Searching

There are different kinds of searching methods but we will be focusing on the most common methods. In searching, the objective is to search an item from the set of items in a given list. The list may be of numbers, values, or strings. Searching is very useful in retrieving information from a large database. The database may have huge amount of data and to retrieve the necessary data from such a database may take time. To solve such problems, we use most commonly used searching algorithms such as **linear search** and **binary search** methods.

9.3 Linear search

The linear searching is the simplest and easy searching method. It is also called **sequential search**. It has a precondition (i.e., condition necessary before searching) that there should not be any multiple or duplicate entries of the same data. To understand this, let us consider the following list of numbers:

23,45,67,89,45,34,99

In the above list there are total seven numbers, but the number 45 is repeated twice. So, linear search method will not apply to this list as there are multiple entries of same data item. Let us consider following list of numbers:

1,34,67,18,11,78

https://doi.org/10.1515/9783110593846-009

Here, there are together six numbers. Let us assume that we want to search the number 18 in the list. How do we search manually? As we know, we start from first element 1 and compare it with search value 18. If they are same, then we stop the search, otherwise we will compare the next element in the list; we will continue this operation until we reach end of the list. This is how the linear search method works. Here, we search from the beginning to end until we find a successful match of the search value. Program 9.1 illustrates the operation of linear search assuming that there are no duplicate entries in the list.

Here,

list[]	is an array of integer numbers
searchValue	is the data item to be searched in the list
location	returns the location of the data item

```cpp
//Program 9.1
// Linear Search program
#include<iostream>
using namespace std;
#define   Array_Length 6

int main()
{
    int list[6] = {1,34,67,18,11,78};
    int searchValue = 18;
    int i=0,location = -1;
    bool found = false;

    for (i = 0; i < Array_Length && !found ; i++ )
    {
        if (list[i] ==  searchValue)
        {
            found = true;
            location = i;
        }

    }
    if (found)
        cout << "The number is Found at Location "
            << location + 1 << endl;
    else
        cout << "The number is Not Found" << endl;

    return 0;
}
```

The result of Program 9.1 is as follows:

```
The number is Found at Location 4
```

The list of explanation to understand the complete execution flow of Program 9.1 is as follows. list[6] is the name of the array with 6 elements, 1, 34, 67, 18, 11, and 78. The Array_Length is total number of elements in the array list[6]. Table 9.1 shows the sequence of execution of Program 9.1. Notice that the actual location of the searchValue is location+1 as the array starts from 0.

Table 9.1: Execution steps in linear search program.

	searchValue	i	list[i]	found	location
Before	18	·		false	−1
Iteration1	18	0	1	false	−1
Iteration2	18	1	34	false	−1
Iteration3	18	2	67	false	−1
Iteration4	18	3	18	true	3

9.4 Binary search

In Section 9.3, we studied **linear search**. In this section, we will study about an improved method of linear search called **binary search**. This is also used to search an item from a given list. The binary search is little faster than the linear search, but the precondition for this method is that the list must be in sorted order. This means that the members of the list must be arranged in ascending order (from smaller data item to larger) or descending order (from larger data item to smaller).

In binary search method, we first compare the item to be searched with the item in the middle position of the list. In this case the result may be of the following type:

1. The item to be searched is same as the item in the middle location of the array. This means that the item is found and the location is one added to the middle location.
2. The item to be searched is smaller than the item in the middle location of the array. This means that the item must be in the first half of the array.
3. The item to be searched is greater than the item in the middle location of the array. This means that the item must be in the second half of the array.

We assume that there are no duplicate entries of the same items in the given list. Let us consider the following list of numbers:

```
1,11,18,34,67,78,118,121
```

This can be declared as array list[8]

```
int list[8]={1,11,18,34,67,78,118,121};
```

The item to be searched is 118

```
i.e., int searchValue=118;
```

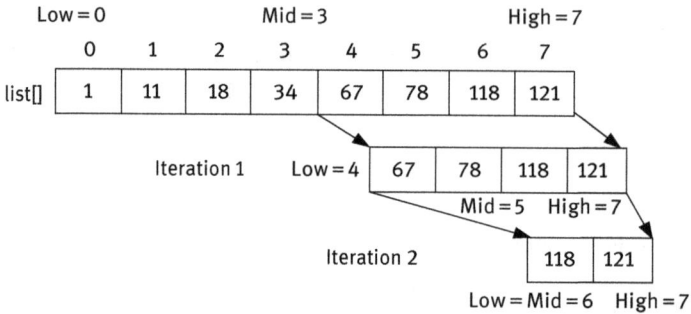

Fig. 9.1: Steps to illustrate binary search program.

Fig. 9.1: illustrates searching of item 118 in the above list.

Here,

list[8]	is an array of integer numbers
searchValue	is the data item to be searched in the list
location	returns the location of the data item

```
// Program 9.2
// Binary search program
#include<iostream>
using namespace std;
#define  Array_Length 8

int main()
{
    int list[8]={1,11,18,34,67,78,118,121};
    int searchValue = 118;
    int low = 0, high = Array_Length-1,mid = (low + high)/2;

    while(low <= high && list[mid] != searchValue)
    {
        if(list[mid] < searchValue)
        {
            low = mid + 1;
        }
        else
        {
            high = mid-1;
        }
        mid = (low + high)/2;
    }
    if(low > high)
        cout << "The number is Not Found" << endl;
    else
        cout<< "The number is Found at Location " << mid + 1 << endl;
```

```
    return 0;
}
```

The result of Program 9.2 is as follows:

```
    The number is Found in location 7
```

The analysis of the result is as follows. The list[8] is an array with values 1, 11, 18, 34, 67, 78, 118, and 121. All of them are in ascending order. The Array_Length is equal to 8. The execution steps and values of variables are summarized in Table 9.2.

Table 9.2: Execution steps to understand binary search program.

	searchValue	low	high	mid	list[mid]
Before	118	0	7	3	34
Iteration 1	118	4	7	5	78
Iteration 2	118	6	7	6	118

9.5 Sorting

In the previous sections, we have studied about the various searching methods. As we have seen in Binary search method, the precondition to search an item in a list is that the list must be in sorted order, that is, in ascending or descending. In this section, we will study about commonly used sorting techniques such as **insertion sort, selection sort,** and **bubble sort.** Sorting is arranging the numbers in an ordered way. It may be ascending order, descending order, or ascending and descending together. For example, if we want to know who is the tallest in a class of 20 students, then we enter the heights of all 20 students in an array of numbers and sort them in ascending order to find the tallest student in the class.

Let us look at the following unsorted list of heights of students (in centimeters)

```
156,190,163,145,178,167,155,176,154,191,169,175,187,173,165
```

The above list looks as following, if we sort it in **ascending** order

```
145 154 155 156 163 165 167 169 173 175 176 178 187 190 191
```

The above list looks as following, if we sort it in **descending** order

```
191 190 187 178 176 175 173 169 167 165 163 156 155 154 145
```

In the next sections, we will study about various commonly used **sorting** methods

9.6 Insertion sort

This section describes the **insertion** sort, where first an item or number in the list is picked and compared with next and the previous items and inserted into its position in the list. After the item is placed at its position, the algorithm tries to place the next item. At the end of the procedure, we will see that all items are sorted in ascending order. This is similar to arranging playing cards. We first pick a card and insert it in its correct location. Then we try to insert the next item in the list. Insertion sort works in the same way.

The following code illustrates the insertion sort algorithm to sort in ascending order.

```
for(i = 1; i < Array_Length; i++)
{
    temp = list[i];
        j = i;
        while (list[j-1] > temp )
        {
            list[j] = list[j-1];
            j = j-1;
            if(j <= 0)break;
        }
        list[j] = temp;
}
```

Program 9.3 illustrates the insertion program. This program sorts seven integer numbers in ascending order. Fig. 9.2 illustrates the execution steps to understand insertion sorting method.

```
//Program 9.3
//Insertion Sort Program

#include<iostream>
using namespace std;
#define  Array_Length 7

int main()
{
    int list[7] = {62, 45, 38, 11, 27, 77, 59};
    int i = 0,j = 0,temp = 0;
    for(i = 1; i < Array_Length; i++)
    {
        temp = list[i];
        j = i;
        while (list[j-1] > temp )
        {
            list[j] = list[j-1];
```

```
            j = j-1;
            if(j <= 0)break;
        }
        list[j] = temp;
    }
    cout << "The list of items in ascending order" << endl;
    for(i = 0; i < Array_Length; i++)
    {
        cout <<  list[i] << " ";
    }
    return 0;
}
```

The result of Program 9.3 is as follows:

```
    The list of items in ascending order
    11 27 38 45 59 62 77
```

Here, the list[] is an array of integer numbers 62, 45, 38, 11, 27, 77, and 59. The Array_Length is the length of the array, which is equal to 7. The analysis of the result is shown in Table 9.3 and Fig. 9.2. Table 9.3 shows the values of different variables in different iterations and Fig. 9.2 shows the values of the array in different iterations. As can be seen, all the elements of list array have been sorted in ascending order.

List before sorting:

62	45	38	11	27	77	59

Iteration 1

45	62	38	11	27	77	59

Iteration 2

38	45	62	11	27	77	59

Iteration 3

11	38	45	62	27	77	59

Iteration 4

11	27	38	45	62	77	59

Iteration 5

11	27	38	45	62	77	59

Iteration 6

11	27	38	45	59	62	77

Fig.9.2: Execution steps to illustrate insertion sort program.

Table 9.3: Execution steps to understand insertion sort program.

	i	list[i]	j	temp
Before	0	0	0	0
Iteration 1	1	45	0	45
Iteration 2	2	38	0	38
Iteration 3	3	11	0	11
Iteration 4	4	27	1	27
Iteration 5	5	77	5	77
Iteration 6	6	59	4	59

9.7 Selection sort

In selection sort, the objective is to find the largest or the smallest element and move it to the end of the array. In ascending order sorting, the method finds the smallest item and moves it to the first index of the list. After smallest element being moved to the first index of the array, the procedure is repeated to find the next smallest (bigger than the earlier one) in the array leaving the first element, since it is already sorted. As we move further, we will notice that the sorting continues with less number of elements in the array. At the end of the sorting method, all elements are sorted in ascending order.

In the case of descending order sorting, the method finds the largest item and moves it to the last index of the list. After the largest element is moved to the last index of the array, the procedure is repeated to find the next largest (smaller than the earlier one) in the array leaving the last element. Swapping the elements from one index to another to the last or first does the movement of elements. This method is called **selection sort** because it selects the smallest or largest elements and places at its correct position. This is same for rest of the elements in the array too. The following code illustrates the selection sort algorithm to sort in ascending order.

```
for(start = 0; start <= length-2; start++)
{
    min = start;
    for(i = start + 1; i <= length-1; i++)
    {
        if(list[i] < list[min])
        //Select the location of the smallest element in the list
        min = i;
    }
    //Swap the smallest element to its location
    temp = list[start];
    list[start] = list[min];
    list[min] = temp;
}
```

Program 9.4 illustrates the sorting of seven numbers into ascending order using selection sort procedure.

```
// Program 9.4
// Selection Sort Program

#include<iostream>
using namespace std;
#define  Array_Length 7

int main()
{
    int list[7] = {62, 45, 38, 11, 27, 77, 59};
    int start, min, length, temp,i;
    length = Array_Length;
    for(start = 0; start <= length-2; start++)
    {
        min = start;
        for(i = start+1; <= length-1; i++)
        {
            if(list[i] < list[min])
                min = i;
        }
        temp = list[start];
        list[start] = list[min];
        list[min] = temp;
    }
    cout << "The list of items in ascending order" << endl;
    for(i=0; i < Array_Length; i++)
    {
            cout << list[i] << " ";
    }

    return 0;
}
```

The result of Program 9.4 is as follows:

```
The list of items in ascending order
11 27 38 45 59 62 77
```

Here, the list[7] is an array of integer numbers 62, 45, 38, 11, 27, 77, and 59. The Array_Length is the length of the array, which is equal to 7. The analysis of the result is shown in Table 9.4 and Fig. 9.3. Table 9.4 shows the values of different variables in different iterations, and Fig. 9.3 shows the values of the array in different iterations. As can be seen, all the elements of list[] array have been sorted in ascending order.

Table 9.4: Execution steps to understand selection sort program.

	min	list[min]	start	temp
Before	–	–	–	–
Iteration 1	3	11	0	62
Iteration 2	4	27	1	45
Iteration 3	2	38	2	38
Iteration 4	4	45	3	62
Iteration 5	6	59	4	62
Iteration 6	6	62	5	77

List before sorting:

62	45	38	11	27	77	59

Iteration 1

11	45	38	62	27	77	59

Iteration 2

11	27	38	62	45	77	59

Iteration 3

11	27	38	62	45	77	59

Iteration 4

11	27	38	45	62	77	59

Iteration 5

11	27	38	45	59	77	62

Iteration 6

11	27	38	45	59	62	77

Fig.9.3: Execution steps to illustrate selection sort program.

9.8 Bubble sort

The bubble sorting is the commonly used sorting algorithm and is easy and simple to understand. This method can be explained in the following ways.

1. To start with the first and second elements in the array are compared; if they are in order (may be ascending or descending), then the comparison continues to second and third elements in the array until the last element is reached. If they are in wrong order, then the two neighboring elements are swapped and arranged in required order. This procedure is continued until the end of the array.

2. After the first iteration, algorithmically the largest element is bubbled (swapped) to the end of the array, in case of ascending order. In case of

descending order, smallest element will be swapped to the first index of the array.

3. The above methods are repeated until the end of the array, leaving the last element as it is already sorted, in the case of ascending order sorting. In case of descending order sorting, the steps 1 and 2 are repeated leaving the first element in the array, as it is already in sorted order.

4. At the end of the sorting procedure, all elements are sorted in the desired order.

Unfortunately, this method takes more number of iterations than many other methods and thus executes very slowly. The following code illustrates bubble sort algorithm to sort in ascending order.

```cpp
for (i = 0; i < Array_Length-1; i++)
{
    for (j = 0; j < Array_Length-1-i; j++)
    {   //Compare two adjacent elements for desired order
        if (list[j+1] < list[j])
        {
            //If they are not in order, swap the elements
            temp = list[j];
            list[j] = list[j+1];
            list[j+1] = temp;
        }
    }
}
```

Program 9.5 shows the implementation of Bubble sort algorithm.

```cpp
// Program 9.5
// Bubble sort program
#include<iostream>
using namespace std;
#define  Array_Length 7

int main()
{
    int list[7] = {62, 45, 38, 11, 27, 77, 59};
    int i,j,temp;
    for (i = 0; i < Array_Length-1; i++)
    {
        for (j = 0; j < Array_Length-1-i; j++)
        {
            if (list[j+1] < list[j])
            {
                temp = list[j];
```

```
                list[j] = list[j+1];
                list[j+1] = temp;
            }
        }
    }
    cout<<"The list of items in ascending order"<<endl;

    for(i = 0;i < Array_Length; i++)
    {
        cout << list[i] << " ";
    }
    return 0;
}
```

The result of Program 9.5 is as follows:

```
        The list of items in ascending order
        11 27 38 45 59 62 77
```

Here, the list[] is an array of integer numbers, 62, 45, 38, 11, 27, 77, and 59. The Array_Length is the length of the array, which is equal to 7. The analysis of the result is shown in Table 9.5 and Fig. 9.4. Table 9.4 shows the values of different variables in different iterations and Fig. 9.4 shows the values of the array in different iterations. As can be seen, all the elements of list[] array have been sorted in ascending order.

List before sorting:

62	45	38	11	27	77	59

Iteration 1

45	62	38	11	27	77	59

Iteration 2

45	38	62	11	27	77	59

Iteration 3

45	38	11	62	27	77	59

Iteration 4

45	38	11	27	62	77	59

Iteration 5 (same as iteration 4)

45	38	11	27	62	77	59

Iteration 6

45	38	11	27	62	59	77

Iteration 7

38	45	11	27	62	59	77

Iteration 8

38	11	45	27	62	59	77

Iteration 9

38	11	27	45	62	59	77

Iteration 10

38	11	27	45	62	59	77

Iteration 11

38	11	27	45	59	62	77

Iteration 12

11	38	27	45	59	62	77

Iteration 13

11	27	38	45	59	62	77

Iterations 14 to 21 (same as iteration 13)

11	27	38	45	59	62	77

Fig. 9.4: Execution steps to illustrate Bubble sort program.

Table 9.5: Execution steps to understand bubble sort program.

	i	j	list[j]	temp
Before	0	0	0	0
Iteration 1	0	0	45	62
Iteration 2	0	1	38	62
Iteration 3	0	2	11	62
Iteration 4	0	3	27	62
Iteration 5	0	4	62	62
Iteration 6	0	5	59	77
Iteration 7	1	0	38	45
Iteration 8	1	1	11	45
Iteration 9	1	2	27	45
Iteration 10	1	3	45	45
Iteration 11	1	4	59	62
Iteration 12	2	1	11	38
Iteration13	2	1	27	38
Iteration14	2	2	38	38
Iteration 15	2	3	45	38
Iteration 16	3	0	11	38
Iteration 17	3	1	27	38
Iteration 18	3	2	38	38
Iteration 19	4	0	11	38
Iteration 20	4	1	27	38
Iteration 21	5	0	11	38

9.9 Sorting characters and strings

In the previous sections, we have studied various sorting and searching methods where many example programs dealt with numbers. In this section, we will focus on sorting strings and characters. String sorting is useful in applications such as sorting the names of students in class or university. If there are 1000 students in a university, sorting all the names manually may take from several hours to days, but a program in C++ may take few milliseconds or microseconds to perform such a task. In this section, we will study some methods to sort characters and strings.

Character sorting

As we know, each character is represented by an integer value internally. To understand the various codes for characters, one can refer to ASCII character set. The

lowercase letters are bigger than **uppercase** letters. This means that the character 'a' is greater than character 'A'. The character 'B' is greater than 'A', and so on. The characters can be compared as we compare integers, since characters are internally represented as numbers. Remember that each character in the array must enclose within single quotes (' '). Program 9.6 illustrates various characters sorting using bubble sort method.

Here, list[9] is an array of characters. The Array_Length is the length of the array, which is equal to 9.

```
// Program Number 9.6
// Bubble sort Program to sort characters
#include<iostream>
using namespace std;
#define  Array_Length 9
int main()
{
    char list[9] = {'a','B','A','Z','f','F','1','-','&'};
    int i,j;
    char temp;

    for (i = 0; i < Array_Length-1; i++)
    {
        for (j = 0; j < Array_Length-1-i; j++)
        {
        if (list[j+1] < list[j])
            {
                temp = list[j];
                list[j] = list[j+1];
                list[j+1] = temp;
            }
        }
    }
    cout << "The list of items in ascending order" << endl;
    for(i = 0; i < Array_Length; i++)
    {
        cout<< list[i] <<" ";
    }
    return 0;
}
```

The result of Program 9.6 is as follows:

```
The list of characters in ascending order
&-1 A B F Z a f
```

Sorting strings

In the previous section, we have studied about the sorting of characters. Thecharacters can be compared in a similar manner as integers. The operators like, >=, <,<=, and == can be applied to characters. In other way, these operators cannot be applied to strings because strings are array of characters. Before proceeding further to understand sorting strings, let us first understand the ways of comparing two strings using the following example:

```
char a[] = "CHINA";
char b[] = "china";
if(strcmp(a, b) < 0)
    cout<<"String "<<a<<" is smaller than String "<<b<<endl;
else
    cout<<"String "<<b<<" is smaller than String "<<a<<endl;
```

An example to understand strcmp() method is illustrated in Program 9.7.

```
// Program 9.7
// Program to compare two strings
#include <iostream>
#include <cstring>
using namespace std;

int main()
{
    char a[] = "CHINA";
    char b[] = "china";
    if(strcmp(a, b) < 0)
        cout<< "String " << a <<" is smaller than String " << b <<endl;
    else
        cout<< "String " << b <<" is smaller than String " << a <<endl;

    return 0;
}
```

The result of Program 9.7 is as follows:

```
String CHINA is smaller than String china
```

The strings are case sensitive, so string china is greater than string CHINA. The strcmp () method returns a value of 0 if both the strings are equal. It returns a value less than 0 if string a is less than string b and returns a value greater than 0 if string a is greater than string b. Program 9.8 illiterates the use of strcmp() method.

```
// Program 9.8
// Program understand strcmp() method
#include <iostream>
#include <cstring>
using namespace std;

int main()
{
    char a[] = "hello";
    char b[] = "Hello";
    int code;
    if(strcmp(a, b) < 0)          // if string a is less than string b
            code = 1;
    else if(strcmp(a, b) == 0)    //if string a is equal to string b
            code = 2;
    else
            code = 3;             //if string a is greater than string b
    switch(code)
    {
            case 1:   cout << "String a is less than string b" << endl;
                      break;
            case 2:   cout << "String a is equal to string b" << endl;
                      break;
            case 3:   cout << "String a is greater than string b" << endl;
                      break;
            default: cout << "invalid string comparison" << endl;
    }
    return 0;
}
```

The result of Program 9.8 is as follows:

```
String a is greater than String b
```

Let us look at the following example to understand sorting of strings. In this example, the names of the students in a class are listed for sorting.

```
Mary, Jack, Zhang, Rai, Ann, Lee, Liu, Bai, Devi, Shiela
```

Now to sort the above ten names, we will make use of an array of strings, that is,

```
char list[10][10]  =
{"Mary","Jack","Zhang","Rai","Ann","Lee","Liu","Bai","Devi","Shiela"};
```

In this example, the list[10][10] is a two-dimensional array of characters. Program 9.9 illustrates the sorting of the above strings using bubble sort technique.

```cpp
// Program 9.9
// Program to sort array of strings
#include <iostream>
#include <cstring>
using namespace std;
#define  Array_Length 10

int main()
{
    char list[10][10]  =

    {"Mary","Jack","Zhang","Rai","Ann","Lee","Liu","Bai","Devi","Shiela"};
    char temp[10];
    int i,j;

    for (i = 0; i < Array_Length-1; i++)
    {
        for (j = 0; j < Array_Length-1-i; j++)
        {
            if (strcmp(list[j+1], list[j]) < 0)
            {
                strcpy(temp,list[j]);
                strcpy(list[j],list[j+1]);
                strcpy(list[j+1],temp);
            }
        }
    }
    cout << "The Student's names in ascending order: " << endl;

    for(i = 0;i < Array_Length; i++)
    {
        cout << list[i] << endl;
    }
    return 0;
}
```

The result of Program 9.9 is as follows:

```
The Student's names in ascending order:
Ann
Bai
Devi
Jack
Lee
Liu
Mary
Rai
Shiela
Zhang
```

9.10 Review questions

1. What is searching? Explain linear search and binary search methods.
2. Compare the advantages and disadvantages of linear search and binary search methods.
3. What is sorting? Explain the selection, insertion, and bubble sorting algorithms.
4. How do you compare characters and strings? List the difference between character and strings.
5. Write a program to search number 189 in the following unsorted list using binary search method. Hint: first sort the list using any sorting method and then apply the binary search method.

   `67,90,34,2,56,78,189,45,788,69,99,100`

6. Enter the marks of ten students of your class and arrange the marks in descending order using insertion sort method and find the maximum marks and average marks.
7. Write a program to generate the following output from the given input.

   ```
   Input: 1 2 3 4 5 6 7 8 9 10
   Output: Eight, Five, Four, Nine, One, Seven, Six, Ten, Three, Two
   ```

8. Write a program to generate the following output from the given input using multidimensional arrays

   Input

56	67	89	99	78	57	80	76	75	88
Mary	Jack	Zhang	Rai	Ann	Lee	Liu	Bai	Devi	Shiela

   Output

78	76	75	67	57	80	56	99	88	89
Ann	Bai	Devi	Jack	Lee	Liu	Mary	Rai	Shiela	Zhang

10 Functions

Though bitter, good medicine cures illness.
    Though it may hurt, loyal criticism will have beneficial effects.
  – Sima Qian

10.1 Introduction

In this chapter, we will study about importance of functions in C++. The general
advantage of using functions is to make the program modular and to avoid repetition
of code. Any piece of code that is used repeatedly in a program is likely to be a candidate
for being a function. It is a common practice to divide the program into manageable
pieces of code and make it as a function when the program size grows bigger. This is also
one of the major principles behind **top-down** and **structured programming** concepts.
The functions allow structuring programs in segments of code to perform individual
tasks. As we have seen in previous chapters, every C++ program has at least one
function, which is main(). In C++, a function is a group of statements that is given a
name, and which can be called from some point of the program. A programmer has the
flexibility to divide his code into separate functions. While using function, we have to
consider function declaration, function definition, and function call. The function is
called when necessary, and the control returns back after the execution of function to
main(). A function declaration tells the compiler about a function's name, return type,
and parameters. A function definition provides the actual body of the function. The term
function is interpreted in different languages, for example, the terms such as subroutine
and procedure also carry the same meaning as functions.

Functions are the small modules of the program that perform specified operations, and they are executed when they are called. There are several benefits of
using functions. First, they are easier to code and understand. Second, the debugging of a large program is easier, and this makes maintenance simple. Third, they
support reusability of code. Finally, by using functions a programmer can write a
program for complex programs by structuring them into different submodules.
There are two types of functions: **user-defined functions** and **built-in functions**
(Fig. 10.1). Built-in functions are also known as **library functions**. The user-defined
functions are designed by the user, and user has the flexibility to name and use
them as per the program requirement. However, built-in functions are already
defined in C++ language, and they provide flexibility to use them without understanding the code beneath. So, we need not to declare and define these functions as
they are already written in the C++ libraries such as iostream and cmath. To use
built-in functions, we must include the appropriate header file within the program.
Majority of sections in this chapter discuss about the user-defined functions,
whereas Section 10.10 provides an overview of built-in functions in C++.

https://doi.org/10.1515/9783110593846-010

```
                    ┌──────────────────┐
                    │    Functions     │
                    └──────────────────┘
                              │
               ┌──────────────┴──────────────┐
               ▼                             ▼
      ┌──────────────────┐        ┌──────────────────┐
      │  User-defined    │        │  Built-in        │
      │  functions       │        │  functions       │
      └──────────────────┘        └──────────────────┘
```

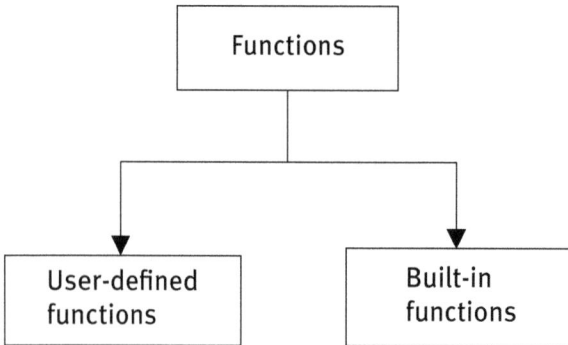

Fig. 10.1: Types of functions in C++.

10.2 Defining a function

Before understanding the functions in detail, let us understand the importance of `main()` function. The `main()` function is the starting point for execution of a program. In C++, the `main()` returns a value of type int to the operating system. Therefore, the functions that have a return value should use `return` statement for termination. So, the definition of `main()` function in C++ would look like as follows:

```
int main()
{
    ......
    ......
    // main program statements
    ......
    ......
    return 0;
}
```

The user-defined function in C++ has the following general structure:

```
<return-type> function-name (parameter-list)
{
    // function body
    // local variables
    ......
    ......
    // statements to perform a particular task

    ......
    ......
    // return statement;
}
```

A function declaration informs the compiler about a function's name, return type, and parameters. A function definition provides the actual body of the function. As mentioned earlier, a function may return a value. The return-type is the data type of the value the function returns. Some functions perform the desired operations without returning a value. In this case, the return type is the void. The function-name is the actual name of the function or the identifier by which the function can be called. The **function name** and the parameter-list together constitute the **function signature**. A parameter is similar to a placeholder. When a function is invoked, we pass a value to the parameter. This value is referred to as **actual parameter** or **argument**. The parameter list refers to the type, order, and number of the parameters of a function. Parameters are optional, that is, a function may contain no parameters. The function body contains a collection of statements that define the activity of the function.

As shown above, the return type statement is optional. However, if there is no return type, we declare the return type as void. The void function indicates that the function does something, but returns nothing to main() function. We will understand the significance of return statement with the help of few examples. First, let us consider Program 10.1 with void function. This is a simple program, where the main() function calls a user-defined function names print_message(), and after printing the statements on the screen, the control automatically returns to main(). Moreover, the rules governing the function names are similar to any valid C++ variables.

```
// Program 10.1
// Demonstration of void function ()
#include <iostream>
using namespace std;

void print_message()
{
    cout << " This is print_message function " << endl;
}

int main ()
{
    cout << " This is main() function" << endl;
    print_message();
    cout << " Statement after function execution  " << endl;
    return 0;
}
```

The result of Program 10.1 is as follows:

```
This is main() function
This is print_message function
Statement after function execution
```

The `main()` acts as an entry point of the program. Once the program execution begins, the control is transferred to the `print_message()` function after the first cout statement in the `main()`. Inside the `print_message()`, it prints the statement on the terminal, and the control returns to the `main()` function. After the function call the program execution will continue where the function call was executed. The statements inside the function body are surrounded by braces {}, which specify the activity of the function.

As can be seen in Program 10.1, the function code is written before `main()`. Now, just for a change, let us see what happens if we write the code after the main function definition, as shown in Program 10.2.

```
// Program 10.2
// Demonstration of void function()
#include <iostream>
using namespace std;

int main ()
{
    cout << " This is main() function" << endl;
    print_message();
    cout << " Statement after function execution " << endl;
    return 0;
}

void print_message()
{
    cout << " This is print_message function " << endl;
}
```

Surprisingly, this program generates errors while compiling as follows:

```
error C2065 : 'print_message'  : undeclared identifier
error C2373 : 'print_message'  : redefinition; different type modifiers
```

This clearly shows that there is a difference between placing the function code before and after `main()`. This is because `main()` is not aware of the function code – if it is placed after `main()` – because there is no exclusive statement to guide the main about function. So, it is a usual practice to place the function code before `main()`, so that readers can look for the `main()` statement. However, we can also compile and execute above program successfully by adding a prototype statement as shown in Program 10.3.

```
// Program 10.3
// Demonstration of void function()
#include <iostream>
```

```
using namespace std;

void print_message(); //function prototype

int main ()
{
    cout << " This is main() function" << endl;
    print_message();
    cout << " Statement after function execution  " << endl;
    return 0;
}
void print_message()
{
    cout << " This is print_message function " << endl;
}
```

Program 10.3 generates the same result as Program 10.1. As it is shown, the statement, void print_message(); called **prototype statement**, now guides the compiler about the existence of function with same name, so that the program runs successfully. Thus, in C++, a prototype has to be declared before a function is used. A function prototype is information to the compiler about the return type of a function and the parameter types that a function expects. Usually, all function prototypes are declared at the start of a program.

A **function declaration** guides the compiler about a function name and how to call the function. The actual body of the function can be defined separately. Function declaration is required when we define a function in one source file and call that function in another file. In such cases, we should declare the function at the top of the file calling the function. While creating a C++ function, we provide a definition of what the function has to perform. To use a function, we will have to call or invoke that function. When a program calls a function, program control is transferred to the called function. A called function performs defined task and when its return statement is executed or when its function ending closing brace is reached, it returns program control back to the main program. To call a function, we simply need to pass the required parameters along with function name, and if function returns a value, then we can store returned value.

10.3 Arguments and parameters

In the previous programs, we used only functions of type void. That means, these functions do not return anything to main(), instead they perform the task required. However, this is not the case while using functions in general. Usually, functions return a value after performing some operations. Program 10.4 illustrates an example function with parameters and return value.

```
// Program 10.4
// Function with parameters
#include <iostream>
using namespace std;

int find_square(int temp)
{
    return temp * temp;
}

int main()
{
    int num,  square_num;
    cout << " Enter a number to be squared  " << endl;
    cin >>num;
    square_num = find_square(num);
    cout << " Square of " << num << " is equal to "
        << square_num << endl;
    return 0;
}
```

The result of Program 10.4 is as follows:

```
Enter a number to be squared
18
Square of 18 is equal to 324
```

Program 10.4 is an example function where the function returns an integer to the main(). In this program, the objective is to compute the square of number (num) using a function with name find_square(), and returning the computed square to main(). In this case, the parameter used in the function code is temp, which is of integer type. When a function is declared the number of arguments passed to the function and their names must also be indicated. The name chosen for an argument is called its **formal parameter** name. Formal parameters must be declared inside a function before they are used in the function body. Always note that variables defined inside a function are known as **automatic variables** since they are automatically created each time the function is called and are destroyed once the function is executed. Their values are **local** to the function; they can be accessed only inside the function in which they are defined and not by other functions.

In Program 10.4, the num variable in the main() is called **argument**, and the temp in find_square() is called as **parameter**. Some authors use parameters and arguments interchangeably. However, the arguments are values passed into a function call, and parameters are variables defined in the function to receive them. In some sources, there are definitions for **actual argument** and **formal parameter**. The formal parameter is what is in the function declaration/definition/

prototype; the actual argument is what is passed when calling the function, an instance of a formal parameter. In program shown in Fig. 10.2, the num is the actual argument, and the temp is the formal parameter. Each parameter consists of a type followed by an identifier, with each parameter being separated from the next by a comma. Each parameter looks very much like a regular variable declaration (for example: int x), and in fact acts within the function as a regular variable that is local to the function. The purpose of parameters is to allow passing arguments to the function from the location where it is called from.

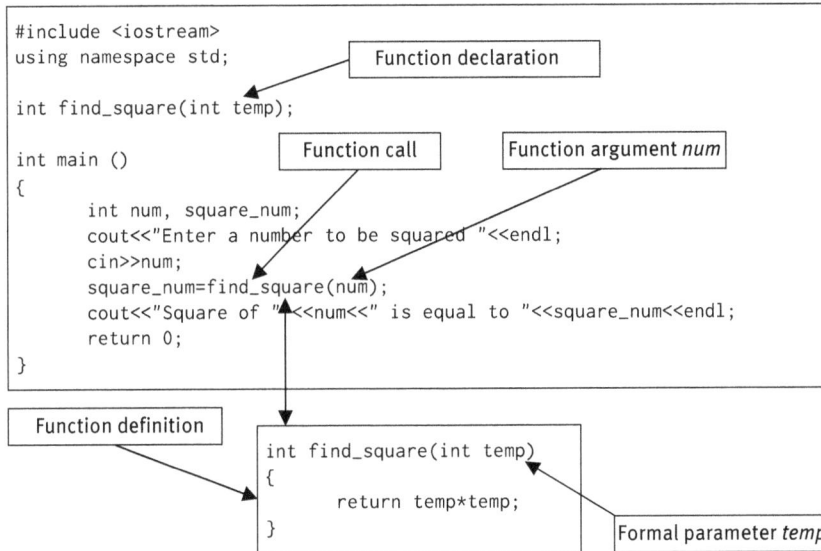

```
#include <iostream>
using namespace std;                    Function declaration

int find_square(int temp);

int main ()              Function call      Function argument num
{
        int num, square_num;
        cout<<"Enter a number to be squared "<<endl;
        cin>>num;
        square_num=find_square(num);
        cout<<"Square of "<<num<<" is equal to "<<square_num<<endl;
        return 0;
}
```

Function definition

```
int find_square(int temp)
{
        return temp*temp;
}                                    Formal parameter temp
```

Fig. 10.2: Terminologies related to functions.

It is very important to remember that arguments and parameters must match with the data type, and more than one argument or parameters can be separated by commas. When functions return a value to the calling routine, a return() statement needs to be used in the called function. Also, when the function is declared we must declare the return type. In the above program, the value returned by the find_square() is stored in the variable square_num in the calling program. One can call a function from anywhere within a program. The best use of functions is to organize a program into distinct parts. The function main() can only contain calls to the various functions. The actual work of the program is performed in the functions following main(). Moreover, the return type of the function must be same as the data type of value returned, for example, in this case, the int return type in function find_square(). This is similar to the data type of temp*temp.

10.4 Scope of function variables

In this section, we will consider some complex examples related to functions. One of the main benefits of function is that they can be called number of times, if necessary, and also a function can in turn call another function, and so on. If there is more than one function, sometimes, it may be necessary to use the same variable throughout the functions. So, we have to consider the scope of **local** and **global** variables.

The variables related to the function can be declared in different regions of the program. The scope in general is a region where a variable holds its value. In C++, a variable can be declared in three places: (a) inside a function or a block, which is called local variables; (b) in the definition of function parameters, which is called formal parameters; and (c) outside of all functions, which is called global variables. In this section, we will describe the importance of local and global variables.

Local variables

Local variables are local to a function, which are declared inside a function or block. They are created every time a function is called and destroyed on returning from that function. These variables cannot be accessed outside a function or block of code. Program 10.5 demonstrates the application of local variables.

```cpp
// Program 10.5
// Demonstration of local variables
#include <iostream>
using namespace std;

void fun(int t1,  int t2)
{
    int a, b;   //local variables within function
    a = t1;
    b = t2;
    cout << " Inside function : a  =  " << a
        << ", b = " << b << endl;
}

int main()
{
    int a, b;// local variables within main()
    a = 2;
    b = 3;
    fun(a,  b);
    cout << " Inside main : a  = " << a << ", b  =  " <<b << endl;
    a = 4;
```

```
    b = 5;
    fun(a,  b);
    cout << " Inside main : a  =  " << a << ", b  =  " << b << endl;
    return 0;
}
```

The result of Program 10.5 is as follows:

```
    Inside function : a  =  2,   b  =  3
    Inside main : a  =  2,   b  =  3
    Inside function : a  =  4,   b  =  5
    Inside main : a  =  4,   b  =  5
```

In Program 10.5, there are local variables declared within main(), as well as inside the function fun() as a, and b, which are integer variables. Although they share the same name in main() and fun(), they are totally different variables because their scope is limited to main() and fun(),respectively. So, this can be proved by calling the function again, as shown in the Program 10.5. In this program, the integer variables t1 and t2 are called formal parameters because they act as temporary locations to copy the values supplied from main through fun(). In this case, t1 and t2 obtain variables a and b, respectively, from main through fun(a, b).

As mentioned earlier, the variables defined inside a block are also called local variables. One may wonder the meaning of block in this context. How they are different from functions? Program 10.6 provides an example of local variables within a block, where local variables have automatic duration, which means that they are created at the point of definition and destroyed when the block they are defined in is exited. This is the reason why local variables are also termed as variables having block scope. Variables defined inside nested blocks are destroyed as soon as the inner block ends. Variables defined inside a block can only be seen within that block. Because each function has its own block, variables in one function cannot be seen from another function:

```
// Program 10.6
// Demonstration of local variables
#include <iostream>
using namespace std;

int main()
{
    int a,   b;//local variables within main()
    a = 2;
    b = 3;
    cout << " Inside main : a  =  " << a << ", b  =  " << b << endl;
    {    //block begins
        int a, b; //local variables within this block
```

```
        a = 4;
        b = 5;
        cout << " Inside block : a  =  " << a
             << ", b  =  " << b << endl;

    }    //block ends
    cout << " Inside main : a  =  " << a << ",    b  =  " << b << endl;
    return 0;
}
```

The result of Program 10.6 is as follows:

```
    Inside main : a  =  2,   b  =  3
    Inside block : a  =  4,   b  =  5
    Inside main : a  =  2,   b  =  3
```

As shown in Program 10.6, the variables a and b are declared twice; once within `main()` and another within a block enclosed within braces. The variables declared within `main ()` and within the block have entirely different scope. As soon as new block begins, the variables created gain a new scope, and their scope ends once the block ends.

Global variables

The purpose of global variables is to facilitate a mechanism, so that all functions and blocks can use the same variable when necessary. They are defined outside of all functions, usually on top of the program. In contrast to the local variables, the global variables hold their values throughout the lifetime of program after they are declared. They can be accessed by any function. Program 10.7 shows an example of using global variables.

```
// Program 10.7
// Demonstration of global variables
#include <iostream>
using namespace std;

int a , b; //global variables,   a & b

void fun(int t1,   int t2)
{
    a = t1;
    b = t2;
    cout << " Inside function : a  =  " << a
         << ",   b  =  " << b << endl;
}
```

```
int main()
{
    a = 2;
    b = 3;
    cout << " Inside main : a  =  " << a << ",    b  =  " << b << endl;
    {   a = 4;
        b = 5;
        cout << " Inside block : a  =  " << a
        << ",    b  =  " << b << endl;
    }
    fun(a,  b); //calling to function fun()
    cout << " Inside main : a  =  " << a << ",    b  =  " << b << endl;
    return 0;
}
```

The result of Program 10.7 is as follows:

```
Inside main : a  =  2,    b  =  3
Inside block : a  =  4,    b  =  5
Inside function : a  =  4,    b  =  5
Inside main : a  =  4,    b  =  5
```

As it is very clear from Program 10.7, the global variables hold value throughout the program, including functions and blocks. That means, only the copy of variables a and b is created in this program, and whenever the values of a and b change, they acquire new values as the program progresses.

10.5 Static variables

So far, we have studied about the role of local and global variables. There is a keyword in C++, static, which is used to give special characteristics to an element. Only once in a program lifetime, static elements are allocated storage in static storage area and they have a scope till the **program lifetime**. They can be used with static variable in functions, static class objects, static member variable in class, and static methods in class. However, as we have not covered the classes and objects, we limit our discussion only to static variables in this chapter.

Static variables are declared by prefixing the keyword static to a variable declaration. Unlike local variables these are not destroyed on return from a function, however, they continue to exist and retain their value. These variables can be accessed upon reentering a function. Program 10.8 demonstrates an example of the static variables without static keyword.

```
// Program 10.8
// Demonstration of static variables
#include <iostream>
using namespace std;

void fun()
{
    int temp = 0;
    cout << temp << endl;
    temp++;
}

int main()
{
    int i;
    for (i = 0; i < 5; i++)
    {
        fun();
    }
    return 0;
}
```

The result of Program 10.8 is as follows:

```
0
0
0
0
0
```

The results shown above serve no purpose, as it is clear that the variable temp is initialized to zero each time when it is called from main(); it is natural to have all the values as zeroes. This shows the variable temp is a local variable, and it is unable to retain the incremented value through temp ++;. Now, lets us change the variable temp as static, as shown in Program 10.9.

```
// Program 10.9
// Demonstration of static variables
#include <iostream>
using namespace std;

void fun()
{
    static int temp = 0;
    cout << temp << endl;
    temp++;
}
```

```
int main()
{
    int i;
    for (i = 0; i < 5; i++)
    {
        fun();
    }
    return 0;
}
```

The result of Program 10.9 is as follows:

```
0
1
2
3
4
```

When used inside function, static variables are initialized only once, and from there onward they hold the value even through function calls again. These static variables are stored on static storage area and not in stack. If we do not use `static` keyword, the variable `count` is reinitialized every time when `fun()` function is called and gets destroyed each time when `fun()` functions ends. However, if we make it `static`, once initialized, `count` will have a scope till the end of `main()` function and it will carry its value through function calls too. Moreover, if we do not initialize a `static` variable, it is by default initialized to zero.

10.6 Scope resolution operator

The scope resolution operator (::) is used when we want to use a global variable that also has a local variable with same name. This is also used to define a function outside of a class, which we will discuss in the next chapters. The scope resolution operator helps to identify and specify the context to which an identifier refers. However, in many cases it is used to access a global variable when there is a local variable with same name. Program 10.10 shows a simple example of using scope resolution operator.

```
// Program 10.10
// Demonstration of scope resolution operator
#include <iostream>
using namespace std;

int a = 2; //global variables,    a & b
```

```
int main()
{
    int a = 1;
    cout << " Inside main : local variable : a  =  " << a << endl;
    cout << " Inside main : global variable : a  =   "
         << ::a << endl;
    return 0;
}
```

The result of Program 10.10 is as follows:

```
        Inside main : local variable : a  =  1
        Inside main : global variable : a  =  2
```

As shown in the program, the variable with same name a is declared both as global and local variable. The global variable holds the value 2, and the local variable holds the value 1. Now, using scope resolution operator (::), we can access the global variable with same name. Program 10.11 is another example of using scope resolution operator along with functions.

```
// Program 10.11
// Demonstration of scope resolution operator
#include <iostream>
using namespace std;

int a = 6,   b = 7; //global variables,   a & b

void fun()
{
    int a = 4,  b = 5;
    cout << " Inside function,  local variables : a  =  "
         << a << ",    b  =  " << b << endl;
    cout << " Inside function : global variables : a  =   "
         << ::a << ",  b  =  " << ::b << endl;
}

int main ()
{
    int a = 1,  b = 2;
    cout << " Inside main : local variables : a  =  "
         << a << ",  b  =  " << b << endl;
    cout << " Inside main : global variables : a  =  "
         << ::a << ",  b  =  " << ::b << endl;
    fun();          // calling to function fun()
    return 0;
}
```

The result of Program 10.11 is as follows:

```
Inside main : local variables : a  =  1,   b  =  2
Inside main : global variables : a  =  6,   b  =  7
Inside function,   local variables : a  =  4,   b  =  5
Inside function : global variables : a  =  6,   b  =  7
```

10.7 Functions and pointers

It is important to remember that a function can return only one value. However, using pointers we can change the value of more than one variable within a function. This can be done by passing the pointers to the function, so that the function will not alter the pointer but the contents of the pointer. Program 10.12 shows an example where two integer pointers a and b are passed to a function called fun().Whenever we are calling a function that expects a pointer as one of its arguments, we have to pass the address of a variable to it. So, in the program address x(i. e. &x) and y(i. e. &y) are passed as arguments to function fun().

```cpp
// Program 10.10
// Function using pointers
#include <iostream>
using namespace std;

void fun(int *a,  int *b)
{
    int temp;
    temp  =  *b;
    *b  =  *a;
    *a  =  temp;
}

int main()
{
    int x  =  10,   y  =  20;
    cout << " Value of x before function call  =  " << x << endl;
    cout << " Value of y before function call  =  " << y << endl;
    fun(&x,  &y);
    cout << " Value of x after function call  =  " << x << endl;
    cout << " Value of y after function call  =  " << y << endl;
    return 0;
}
```

The result of Program 10.12 is as follows:

```
Value of x before function call  =  10
Value of y before function call  =  20
Value of x after function call   =  20
Value of y after function call   =  10
```

However, when we send an array to a function as parameter, we do not have to specify the address operator because the name of the array itself is the address of the first element in the array. Consider Program 10. 13 as an example, where an entire array with five integer elements is passed as an argument. However, in this case, we have passed the array contents to another array with name temp.

```cpp
// Program 10.13
// Function using arrays
#include <iostream>
using namespace std;

void fun(int temp[])
{
    int i;
    cout << " Values of array inside function  " << endl;
    for (i = 0; i < 5; i++)
        cout << temp [i] << " ";
    cout << endl;
}

int main()
{
    int arr[5] = {10, 15, 12, 11, 8};
    int i;
    cout << " Values of array inside main  " << endl;
    for (i = 0; i < 5; i++)
        cout << arr[i]<< " ";
    cout << endl;
    fun(arr);

    return 0;
}
```

The result of Program 10.13 is as follows:

```
Values of array inside main
10 15 12 11 8
Values of array inside function
10 15 12 11 8
```

We can also use function fun() in alternative way to obtain the array elements as shown:

```cpp
void fun(int *temp)
{
```

```
    int i;
    cout << " Values of array inside function  " << endl;
    for (i = 0; i < 5; i++)
        cout << temp[i] << " ";
    cout << endl;
}
```

In the previous examples, we studied the functions using pointers. We can also create function pointers in C++, just like normal data types such as int, float, or char. A function pointer can be declared as:

```
<return-type-of-function> (*<name-of-pointer>)(type-of-function-arguments);
```

For example: int (*fptr)(int, int)

The above line declares a function pointer 'fptr' that can point to a function whose return type is 'int' and takes two integers as arguments. Program 10.14 shows an example of using function pointers.

```
// Program 10.14
// Function pointers
#include <iostream>
using namespace std;

int fun (int a,   int b)
{
    cout << "a  =  " << a << endl;
    cout << "b  =  " << b << endl;
    return 0;
}

int main()
{
    int (*fptr) (int,  int);    // Function pointer
    fptr  =  fun;               // Assign address to function pointer
    fun (6,  9);
    fptr (7,  8);
    return 0;
}
```

The result of Program 10.14 is as follows:

```
        a  =  6
        b  =  9
        a  =  7
        b  =  8
```

In Program 10.14, function 'fun' is defined and takes two integers as input and returns an integer. In the main() function, function pointer 'fptr' is declared and then assigned a value. The name of the function can be treated as starting address of the function so we can assign the address of function to function pointer using function's name. So from the output we can see that calling the function through function pointer produces the same output as calling the function from its name.

10.8 Recursive functions

As already mentioned, a main() function can call a function and in turn that function can call another function. This seems surprising as one might think is it possible to make a function which can call to itself? In C++, a **recursive function** is such function that can call itself. We can demonstrate the applications of recursive functions, especially in carrying out operations, which follow the similar procedures in their subsequent steps. This means, a recursive call can substitute iteration statements (such as for, while, and do-while). Generally speaking, recursive solutions are simpler than iterative solutions. However, recursive solutions are slightly less efficient than the iterative ones.

Recursive functions are functions calling themselves repeatedly until a certain condition is met. Recursion involves two conditions. First, the problem must be written in a recursive form and second, the problem should have a terminating statement. If the terminating statement is missing, then the function goes into an endless loop. The most common example of a program demonstrating recursion is calculation of factorial of an integer number. The definition for finding the factorial of a number n is as follows:

```
n! = n×(n-1)×(n-2)×.....3×2×1
```

First, let us understand a program for finding a factorial of an integer number without using recursion, using the above definition.

```cpp
// Program 10.15
// Factorial of a number using iteration
#include <iostream>
using namespace std;

int fact(int n)
{
    int i = 0,  f = 1;
    while(i < n)
    {
        i++;
        f = f*i;
```

```
    }
    return f;
}

int main()
{
    int num = 0,    result;
    cout << " Enter a number ";
    cin >> num;
    result = fact(num);
    cout << " Factorial of number " << num << " " = " " << result << endl;
    return 0;
}
```

A sample result of Program 10.15 is as follows:

```
    Enter a number 4
    Factorial of number 4  =  24
```

In Program 10.15, the iterative statement while is used for calculating the factorial of a number. We can easily compute the factorial of a number n. However, in this case the fact() function is called only once from main(). Now, let us modify the definition of factorial as follows:

```
    n! = n×(n-1)×(n-2)×.....3×2×1
    n! = n×(n-1)!
    n! = n×(n-1)×(n-2)!
    n! = n×(n-1)×(n-2) ×.....3!
    n! = n×(n-1)×(n-2)×.....3×2!
    n! = n×(n-1)×(n-2)×.....3×2×1!
```

With this analysis, we can arrive at the following recursive definition:

```
    n! = n×(n-1)!,   for all values of n>0
    n! = 1, for n = 0
```

If we represent n! as fact(n), then the above definition transforms as follows:

```
    fact(n) = n × fact(n-1)!,   for all values of n>0
    fact(n) = 1,   for n = 0
```

Now, let us rewrite the same program for performing the same task using recursive function fact() as shown in Program 10.16. The only precondition to this program is that the value of n must be either greater or equal to 0.

```
// Program 10.16
// Factorial of a number using recursion
#include <iostream>
using namespace std;

int fact(int n)
{
    if(n == 0)
        return 1;
    else
        return n*fact(n-1);
}

int main()
{
    int num = 0,    result;
    cout << " Enter a number ";
    cin >> num;
    result = fact(num);
    cout << " Factorial of number " << num << "  =  " << result << endl;
    return 0;
}
```

A sample result of Program 10.16 is as follows:

```
Enter a number 5
Factorial of number 5 = 120
```

Now, let us understand how to design a recursive program in general. In the design of a recursive program, we usually follow a sequence of steps. First, we need to identify the basic cases and determine how they are solved. For example, in the case of factorial, the only basic case used in the function is n = 0. Similarly, we could have considered a more general basic case (i.e. n ≤ 1). In both the cases, the function should return 1. The second step is to determine how to resolve the nonbasic cases in terms of the basic cases, which we assume can be solved. In the case of a factorial, we know that the factorial of a number n greater than zero is n*fact(n-1). Finally, we must make sure that the parameters of the call move closer to the basic cases at each recursive call. This should guarantee a finite sequence of recursive calls that always termi-nates. In the case of a factorial, n-1 is closer to 0 than n. Therefore, we can guarantee that this function will terminate.

Let us consider the sequence of program execution for num = 3. If we enter num = 3, the statement result = fact(num), becomes result = fact(3), and the sequence of program control jumps to fact() function, where the formal parameter n becomes 3. After that the program continues its execution as shown in Fig. 10.3, where we can see the successive fact() functions with parameters. In this diagram, the values of

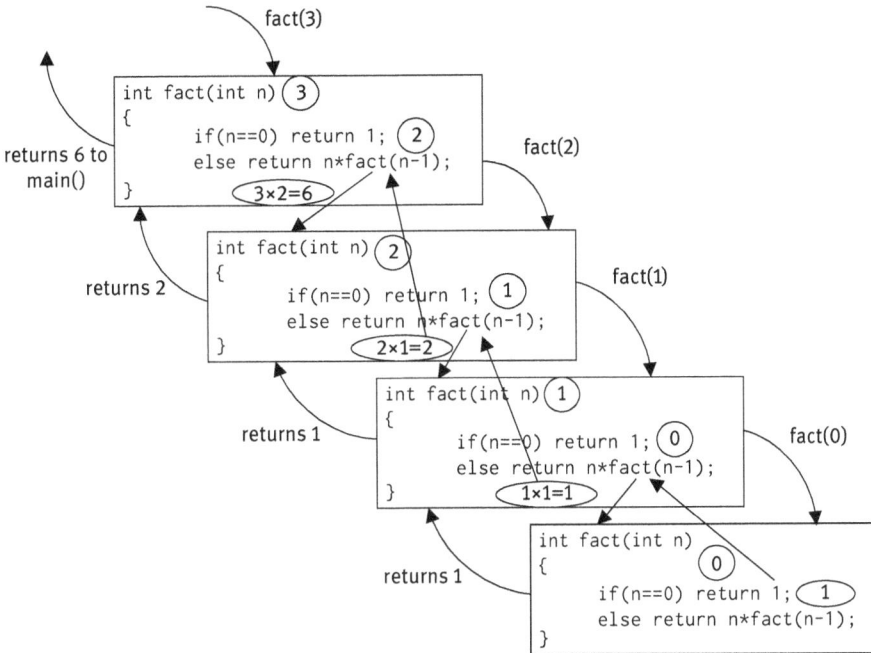

Fig. 10.3: Diagram shows the sequence of execution of a recursive factorial function `fact()` with parameter 3.

formal parameter *n* is shown within the circles, whereas the return values from each factorial function is shown within ellipses. We can derive many conclusions with this. First, each time a function is called, a new instance of the function is created, as shown in the Fig. 10.3; each box indicates a new instance of factorial function with different parameter. Moreover, as soon as the function returns a value, the instance is destroyed. Second, the creation of a new instance only requires the allocation of memory space for data, including parameters and local variables. Finally, the instances of a function are destroyed in reverse order of their creation, that is, the last in first out (LIFO) order, where instance created first will be destroyed last and vice versa. The recursion can also be used for implementing other programs such as generation of Fibonacci numbers and solving the Tower of Hanoi program.

Generating Fibonacci numbers using recursion

The series of the form 1, 1, 2, 3, 5, 8, 13, 21,... and so on are called Fibonacci numbers. as every number after the first two is the sum of the two preceding ones. In other words, an arbitrary number F_n in the series is defined by

$$F_n = F_{n-1} + F_{n-2}$$

with $F_1 = 1$ (or 0 sometimes) and $F_2 = 1$ as initial values. Program 10.17 shows the code to generate Fibonacci series using recursion, where for a given number n, it returns the Fibonacci number of order n. The precondition in this program is that the value of n should be greater than or equal to 0. The basic case is when the value of n is either equal to 0 or 1, the program returns 1.

```
// Program 10.17
// Fibonacci series using recursion
#include <iostream>
using namespace std;

int fib(int n)
{
    if(n <=  1)
        return 1;
    else
        return fib (n -2) + fib(n -1);
}
int main()
{
    int num = 0,  i;
    cout << " Enter a number ";
    cin >> num;
    cout << " Fibonacci series for num  =  " << num << endl;
    for (i = 0; i < num; i++)
    {
        cout << fib(i)<< " ";
    }
    cout << endl;
    return 0;
}
```

A sample result of Program 10.17 is as follows:

```
Enter a number 10
Fibonacci series for num  =  10
1 1 2 3 5 8 13 21 34 55
```

We can analyze this program considering the number of calls made for sample input, num = 5. In this case, the fib(5) is called once, fib(4) is called once, fib(3) called twice, fib(2) called three times, fib(1) called five times, and fib(0) is called three times. Figure 10.4 shows the sequence of calls.

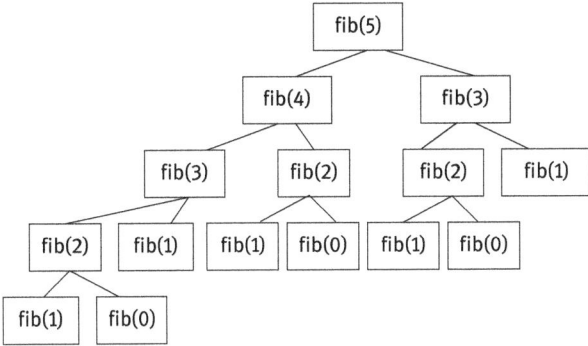

Fig. 10.4: Diagram showing the sequence of execution of a recursive Fibonacci series function `fib()` with parameter 5.

Tower of Hanoi program using recursion

The Tower of Hanoi is a mathematical puzzle widely popular among programmers. In this puzzle, there are three posts (A, B, C), as shown in the Fig. 10.5. The objective is to move the disks in the post A to C using the intermediate post B. The disks in the posts

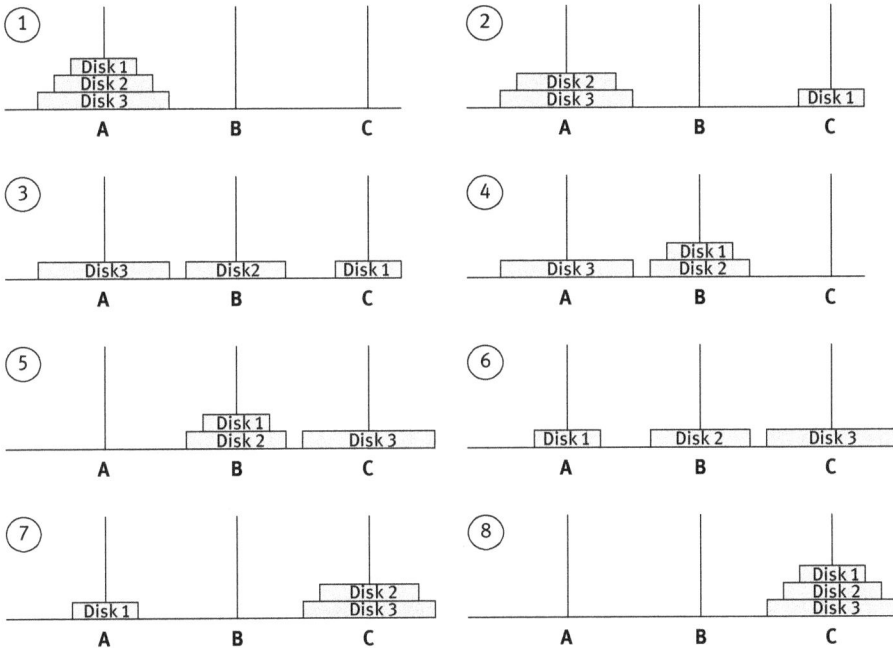

Fig. 10.5: Sequence of steps to move the disks from post A to post C in Tower of Hanoi program.

are organized in ascending order, that is, the small disk is placed above the bigger one. So, while moving these disks to C from A, one needs to follow few rules. First, only one disk can be moved at a time. Second, during each movement only upper disk from a stack can be removed, and placed on top of another post. Finally, no bigger disk may be placed on top of a smaller disk.

If we have just three disks, the puzzle can be solved in seven moves. The minimal number of moves required to solve a Tower of Hanoi puzzle is 2^n-1, where n is the number of disks. This puzzle dates back to an ancient story about an Indian temple with large room consisting of 64 golden discs. This puzzle is also known as the Tower of Brahma puzzle. As per this ancient puzzle, if the priests were able to move the disks at a rate of one per second, using the smallest number of moves, it would take them $2^{64}-1$ s or roughly 585 billion years or 18, 446, 744, 073, 709, 551, 615 turns to finish. Figure 10.5 shows the sequence of moving three disks from one post to another. Program 10.18 shows the implementation of Tower of Hanoi puzzle using recursion.

```cpp
// Program 10.18
// Tower of Hanoi program using recursion
#include <iostream>
using namespace std;

void towers(int n,  char frompeg,  char topeg,  char auxpeg)
{
    if(n == 1)
    {
        cout << endl << " Move Disk 1 from Post "
            << frompeg << " to Post " << topeg;
        return;
    }
    towers(n-1,  frompeg,  auxpeg,  topeg);
    cout << endl << " Move Disk " << n << " from Post "
        << frompeg << " to Post " << topeg;
    towers(n-1,  auxpeg,  topeg,  frompeg);
}

int main()
{
    int n;
    cout << " Enter the number of disks  : ";
    cin >> n;
    cout << " The Tower of Hanoi involves following moves  : "
        << endl << endl;
    towers(n,  'A',  'C',  'B');
    cout << endl << endl << " End of the Program " << endl;
    return 0;
}
```

A sample result of Program 10.18 is as follows:

```
Enter the number of disks  : 3
The Tower of Hanoi involves following moves  :

Move Disk 1 from Post A to Post C
Move Disk 2 from Post A to Post B
Move Disk 1 from Post C to Post B
Move Disk 3 from Post A to Post C
Move Disk 1 from Post B to Post A
Move Disk 2 from Post B to Post C
Move Disk 1 from Post A to Post C

End of the Program
```

10.9 Inline functions

When using functions, few questions might arise: It is worth using functions at all times? Are they fast? When we use a function, we come across calling function and called function. After the execution of function code is over, the control returns back to the calling function. It is obvious to imagine that these procedures are time consuming. Is there any way of making the programs run faster? Inline functions provide one simple solution in this context. They replace the function calls with the code of the function itself. However, one of the disadvantages is that this method greatly increases the size of the program. So, the **inline functions** are introduced as an optimization technique used by the compilers especially to reduce the execution time.

The inline functions are a C++ enhancement feature to increase the execution time of a program. The inline functions are also used along with C++ classes (the classes will be discussed in next chapters). This means, when the function is inline the compiler places a copy of the code of that function at each point where the function is called at compile time. Compiler replaces the definition of inline functions at compile time instead of referring function definition at runtime. To make a function inline, we have to use the inline keyword before the name of a function. Program 10.19 shows a simple example of using inline function.

```cpp
// Program 10.19
// Inline function example
#include <iostream>
using namespace std;

inline void print_message()
{
    cout << " This is inline function " << endl;
}
```

```
int main()
{
    cout << " This is main() function " << endl;
    print_message();
    return 0;
}
```

The result of Program 10.19 is as follows:

```
This is main() function
This is inline function
```

10.10 Built-in functions

As mentioned in the Introduction section, the C++ standard library provides several built-in stand-alone functions that can be used for various general purposes, such as I/O, string and character handling, mathematical operations, time, date, localization, and dynamic memory allocation. For example, function strcat() to concatenate two strings, function memcpy() to copy one memory location to another location, and many more functions. The function library in C++ is inherited from C and incorporates all the Standard C libraries as well, with small additions. The C++ standard library provides a large number of library functions under different header files for performing common tasks. Some of the C++ header files and their descriptions are provided in Table 10.1 Built-in functions, however, are declared in header files using the #include directive

Table 10.1: C++ standard header files.

Header File Name	Description
cmath	Declares functions for mathematical operations
cstdlib	For general purpose functions
iostream	Functions for standard I/O
cstring	Functions to manipulate C-style string
cctype	Functions to classify and transform individual characters
csignal	To handle signals
clocate	Internationalization support task such as date/time formatting
cwctype	For classifying and transforming individual wide characters
cstdio	C Standard Input and Output Library
cwchar	To work with C wide string
cuchar	Convert between multibyte characters and UTF-16 or UTF-32
csetjmp	Bypass the normal function call and return discipline
cfenv	Access floating point environment
ctime	Functions to work with date and time

on the top of the program file, for example, for common mathematical calculations, we include the file cmath with the #include <cmath> directive that contains the function prototypes for the mathematical functions in the cmath library. Appendix A provides list of some of the commonly used built-in functions in C++.

For example, to write mathematical programs involving floating point calculations and so on, we will undoubtedly require access to the mathematics library. The functions and associated macros are defined in the include file <cmath>. In Table 10.2, x and y are of type double, n is an int, and all functions return double. Angles for trigonometric functions are expressed in **radians** rather than degrees.

Table 10.2: Example math functions in C++.

Math Function	Description
sin(x)	Sine of x
cos(x)	Cosine of x
tan(x)	Tangent of x
exp(x)	Exponential function e^x
log(x)	Natural logarithm ln(x), x>0.
log10(x)	Base 10 logarithm $\log_{10}(x)$, x>0
pow(x, y)	x^y, a domain error occurs if x = 0 and y<= 0, or if x<0 and y is not an integer
sqrt(x)	Square root of x, x≥ 0.
ceil(x)	Smallest integer not less than x, as a double
floor(x)	Largest integer not greater than x, as a double
fabs(x)	Absolute value |x|

Program 10.20 shows an example of using mathematical built-in functions in C++.

```
// Program 10.20
// Built-in functions example
#include <iostream>
#include <cmath>
using namespace std;

int main()
{
    double x = 1.0,  y = 2.0,  z = -3.45;
    cout << " Math-sin example : " << sin(22.0/42.0) << endl;
    cout << " Math-cos example : " << cos(0.0) << endl;
    cout << " Math-tangent example : " << tan(22.0/28) << endl;
    cout << " Math-exp example : " << exp(x) << endl;
    cout << " Math-log(base e) example : " << log(2.718212) << endl;
    cout << " Math-log(base 10) example : " << log10(100.0) << endl;
    cout << " Math-power example : " << pow(4,y) << endl;
    cout << " math-square root example : " << sqrt(y) << endl;
```

```
    cout << " Math-ceil example : " << ceil(z) << endl;
    cout << " Math-floor example : " << floor(z) << endl;
    cout << " Math-absolute value example : " << fabs(z)<< endl;

    return 0;
}
```

The result of Program 10.20 is as follows:

```
Math-sin example : 0.500183
Math-cos example : 1
Math-tangent example : 1.00063
Math-exp example : 2.71828
Math-log(base e) example : 0.999974
Math-log(base 10) example : 2
Math-power example : 16
math-square root example :1.41421
Math-ceil example : -3
Math-floor example : -4
Math-absolute value example : 3.45
```

10.11 Review questions

1. Describe a function? How user-defined functions are different from `main()` function?
2. How user-defined functions are different from built-in functions? Discuss.
3. Describe these terms related to functions: function name, function signature, return type, function prototype, actual parameter, formal parameter, and function arguments.
4. Describe the general format of function in C++.
5. Write a program in C++ to demonstrate user-defined function.
6. Write an executable program to demonstrate passing arguments from `main()` to a function.
7. Explain the following keywords using an example with relation to functions: (a) `main`, (b) `return` (c) `void`, and (d) `inline`.
8. What is the meaning of scope of function variables? Describe the role of global and static variables in C++ functions.
9. What is recursion? Write a C++ program to demonstrate recursion.
10. Write a C++ program to find a factorial of a number using recursion.

11. Write a C++ program to generate n Fibonacci numbers using recursion.
12. Write a C++ program to demonstrate Tower of Hanoi program using recursion.
13. Write a program in C++ to describe inline functions.
14. List at least five mathematical functions available in C++, and write a program to demonstrate their application.

11 Structures and Unions

Only wisdom and virtue can truly win men's devotion.
– Liu Bei

11.1 Introduction

A structure is a user-defined data type that defines a list of variables under one name in a block of memory, allowing different variables to be accessed through a single variable. A structure can be defined by using struct keyword in C++. So far, we have understood how the variables are used to store information of different data types. However, all these variables store a single type of information, such as an integer, a floating-point number, or a character. On the other hand, the arrays store more than one elements of same data type. However, in reality, we deal with different data types, and hence cannot use same data type for everything. For example, let us consider contact details of a person, which includes:(a) his/her name that is an array of characters or a string; (b) the address that is also an array of characters; (c) the phone number that is of integer type rather than characters. Hence, to store the contact details of a person, we have to consider the use of multiple data types under a single name, such as address. We can consider another example of an item in a grocery store. Each item in the store comprises of different types of information such as item name, price, manufacturer name, and item number. The item number is usually a unique number used for billing information. All the information about an item does not belong to same data type. The item name is an array of characters; the price is a floating-point number; the dates include integers; and the item number is also an integer. The following statements show how we can individually declare these details in C++ by using different data types.

```
char item_name[10];     // for example biscuit named "SweetBest"
float price;            // for example 7.5 RMB
char manufacturer[40];  // for example Qingdao Biscuits Ltd.
int item_no;            // for example 9341
```

Even though all this information is related to one specific item, we have still declared the information in different statements. However, if we use structures, all these statements can be declared under a single name. In C++, the arrays allow us to define variables that combine several data items of the same kind, but structure is another user-defined data type that allows us to combine data items of different kinds. In the next section, we will understand the ways of defining structures in C++.

https://doi.org/10.1515/9783110593846-011

11.2 Defining structures

A structure can be considered as a template used for defining a collection of variables under a single name. Structures help a programmer in grouping elements of different data types into a single logical unit. Unlike structures, arrays permit a programmer to group the elements of same data type only. To define a structure, we must use the struct keyword. The struct keyword defines a new data type that has more than one member. The format to define a structure is as follows:

```
struct [structure-tag]
{
    member definition;
    member definition;
    ...
    member definition;
} [one or more structure variables];
```

The structure tag is optional, and each member is defined as a normal variable is defined, such as int i; or float f; or any other valid variable. At the end of the structure's definition and before the final semicolon, we can specify one or more structure variables; but it is optional. Considering the previous example of an item, we can define a structure called item with four elements item_name, price, manufacturer, and item_no, as shown below:

```
struct item
{
    char item_name[10];
    float price;
    char manufacturer[40];
    int item_no;
};
```

The previous statement does not define any variables, but it does define a new type, and the name of the type is item. This means that when we first define a structure in a file, the statement simply tells the C++ compiler that a structure exists, but it does not allocate any memory to it. Memory allocation takes place only when a structure variable is declared. The struct keyword defines item as a structure, and the elements making up an object of this type are defined within the braces. Note that each line defining an element in the struct is terminated by a semicolon, and that a semicolon also appears after the closing brace. The elements of a struct can be of any type, except the same type as the struct being defined. A structure type is usually defined at the beginning of a program, usually just after the main() statement in a file. Thereafter, a variable of this structure type is declared and used in the program. For example:

```
struct item Biscuit;
```

We can also define a variable of struct item as shown below:

```
struct item
{
    char item_name[10];
    float price;
    char manufacturer[40];
    int item_no;
} Biscuit;
```

Similarly, to define more than one variables of struct item, we can use any of the following statements.

```
struct item Biscuit, Candy;
```

Or,

```
struct item
{
    char item_name[10];
    float price;
    char manufacturer[40];
    int item_no;
} Biscuit, Candy;
```

11.3 Initializing structures

The first way to assign values to members of a struct object is to define their initial values in the object definition. Suppose if we want to initialize an item to contain the data for one of your favorite biscuit names "SweetBest," with price tag 7.50 RMB, item number 9341, and manufactured by "Qingdao Biscuits Ltd." We can initialize the structure as follows:

```
struct item Biscuit =
{
    "SweetBest",
    7.5,
    "Qingdao Biscuits Ltd",
    9341
};
```

The initializing values appear in an initializer list in much the same way as for elements of an array. However, the sequence of initial values in an array needs to be the same as the sequence of the members of the struct in its definition. Each member of the Biscuit structure has a corresponding initial value assigned to it, as indicated in the comments. The syntax for initializing structure variables is different from that of standard variables. Since item_name and manufacturer members are character arrays or strings, simply using assignment statement will not work. The structure elements are accessed by using the **dot notation**. The individual elements, such as price and item_no are initialized as follows:

```
Biscuit.price = 7.5;
Biscuit.item_no = 9341;
```

One can initialize a structure either by initializing the individual elements as shown previously or by simply listing the element's value inside curly braces, with each value separated by a comma in a single line as shown below.

```
struct item Biscuit = {"SweetBest",7.5,"Qingdao Biscuits Ltd",9341};
```

Similar to initialization of arrays, partial initialization of a structure can be done as follows:

```
struct item Biscuit = {"SweetBest",7.5,"Qingdao Biscuits Ltd"};
```

In the previous case, the item_no element is initialized to 0.0. In the next section, we will study more about dot notation and how to access member structures.

11.4 Accessing structure members

In Section 11.3, we have studied defining structures and initializing their members. To access individual members of a struct, we use the member selection operator that is a period (.). This operator is sometimes referred to as the **member access operator**. To refer to a member, we write the variable name structure, followed by a period, followed by the name of the member. The member access operator is coded as a period between the structure variable name and the structure member that we wish to access. For example, to change the item_no to 1818, we can write as shown below:

```
Biscuit.item_no = 1818;
```

This sets the value of the item_no to 1818. In addition, we can use a member of a structure in exactly the same way as any other variable. To increase the member year by 4, for example, we can write:

```
Biscuit.item_no += 4;
```

Program 11.1 shows an example that summarizes previous descriptions. In the following program two structures Biscuit and Candy of type struct item are declared for structure Biscuit. We supply the value by initializing it. However, for structure Candy, we read the values from keyboard. Finally, the information is displayed on the screen.

```
// Program 11.1
// Understanding structures
#include <iostream>
using namespace std;

int main()
{
    struct item
    {
        char item_name[10];
        float price;
        char manufacturer[40];
        int item_no;
    };

    //Initialization of Biscuit structure variable

    struct item Biscuit = {
        "SweetBest",
        7.5,
        "Qingdao Biscuits Ltd",
        9341
    };

    struct item Candy;

    //Reading values for members of Candy
    cout << "Enter the item_name for Candy " << endl;
    cin >> Candy.item_name;
    cout << "Enter the price of candy " << endl;
    cin >> Candy.price;
    cout << "Enter the Manufacturer name " << endl;
    cin >> Candy.manufacturer;
    cout << "Enter the item number "<< endl;
    cin >> Candy.item_no;
```

```
//Displaying Biscuit information to screen
cout << endl << "Biscuit Information " << endl;
cout << "Biscuit Name: " << Biscuit.item_name << endl;
cout << "Biscuit Price: " << Biscuit.price << endl;
cout << "Biscuit Manufacturer: " << Biscuit.manufacturer << endl;
cout << "Biscuit Item Number: " << Biscuit.item_no << endl;

//Displaying Candy information to screen
cout << endl << "Candy Information " << endl;
cout << "Candy Name: " << Candy.item_name << endl;
cout << "Candy Price: " << Candy.price << endl;
cout << "Candy Manufacturer: " << Candy.manufacturer << endl;
cout << "Candy Item Number:  "<< Candy.item_no << endl;
return 0;
}
```

The result of Program 11.1 is shown below:

```
Enter the item_name for Candy
KidCandy
Enter the price of candy
18.6
Enter the Manufacturer name
HuangdaoSweets
Enter the item number
16321

Biscuit Information
Biscuit Name: SweetBest
Biscuit Price: 7.5
Biscuit Manufacturer: Qingdao Biscuits Ltd
Biscuit Item Number: 9341

Candy Information
Candy Name: KidCandy
Candy Price: 18.6
Candy Manufacturer: HuangdaoSweets
Candy Item Number: 16321
```

11.5 Using typedef keyword

As mentioned in Chapter 3, C++ allows a programmer to rename data types by using
the keyword typedef. For example:

```
typedef unsigned int Uint;
Uint price;
```

Here we have type-defined an unsigned integer as Uint so that we can use Uint in our program as any native data type and declare other variables with its data type. We can apply this to typedef structure as shown below.

```
typedef struct item
{
    char item_name[10];
    float price;
    char manufacturer[40];
    int item_no;
} Food_item;
```

The newly defined data type, then, can be used as given in the following example:

```
Food_item Biscuit;
Food_item Candy;
```

Program 11.2 shows an example of a typedef statement.

11.6 Nested structures

In Program 11.1, there are only four members for structure item. Let us consider another member of the item using the expiry_date variable. Usually a date includes a day, a month, and a year, which includes three additional members. In such situations, we can define a structure that in turn can contain another structure as one of its members. The example below describes an example for nested structures.

```
struct item
{
    char item_name[10];
    float price;
    char manufacturer[40];
    int item_no;
    item_date expiry_date;
};
```

The definition of expiry_date structure requires that an item_date structure be previously defined to the compiler, otherwise a compiler error is generated. So, we can define item_date structure as follows:

```
typedef struct date{
    int day;
```

```
      int month;
      int year;
}item_date;
```

Program 11.2 shows an example of using nested structures with the previously described structures.

```cpp
// Program 11.2
// Example of Nested Structures
#include <iostream>
#include <cstring>
using namespace std;

int main()
{
    typedef struct date
    {
        int day;
        int month;
        int year;
    }item_date;

    struct item
    {
        char item_name[10];
        float price;
        char manufacturer[40];
        int item_no;
        item_date expiry_date;
    } Biscuit;

    // Initializing the first three members of structure Biscuit
    strcpy(Biscuit.item_name, "SweetBest");
    Biscuit.price = 7.5;
    strcpy(Biscuit.manufacturer,"Qingdao Biscuits Ltd");
    Biscuit.item_no = 9341;

    // Initializing the nested structure expiry_date
    Biscuit.expiry_date.day = 11;
    Biscuit.expiry_date.month = 8;
    Biscuit.expiry_date.year = 2019;

    // Displaying Biscuit information to screen including expiry date
    cout << endl << "Biscuit Information " << endl;
    cout << "Biscuit Name: " << Biscuit.item_name << endl;
    cout << "Biscuit Price: " << Biscuit.price << endl;
    cout << "Biscuit Manufacturer: " << Biscuit.manufacturer << endl;
    cout << "Biscuit Item Number: " << Biscuit.item_no << endl;
    cout << "Biscuit Expiry Date: "
```

```
            << Biscuit.expiry_date.day << "/"
            << Biscuit.expiry_date.month << "/"
            << Biscuit.expiry_date.year << endl;
    return 0;
}
```

The result of Program 11.2 is shown below:

```
Biscuit Information
Biscuit Name: SweetBest
Biscuit Price: 7.5
Biscuit Manufacturer: Qingdao Biscuits Ltd
Biscuit Item Number: 9341
Biscuit Expiry Date: 11/8/2019
```

This example demonstrates the application of typedef keyword along with structures. Initially, the first four members of structure Biscuit of type struct item are initialized one by one by using membership operator or dot notation. As the first member item_name and third member manufacturer are character arrays, we have used the strcpy() function to assign the strings to them. The fourth member, expiry date, is the nested structure of type item_date. As expiry_date structure is inside the Biscuit structure, we should use periods, as shown in the following statements.

```
Biscuit.expiry_date.day = 11;
Biscuit.expiry_date.month = 8;
Biscuit.expiry_date.year = 2019;
```

11.7 Structures containing arrays

In the structure item defined in Program 11.2, both members item_name and manufacturer are arrays of characters. Hence, it is quite possible that there can also be structures containing arrays as its elements, however, extra care should be taken while initializing them. Let us consider an example of a structure containing both characters and integer arrays.

```
struct Science_Scores
{
    char student_name[20];
    int student_number;
    char subject_name[4][15];
    int student_score[4];
```

```
    };
```

```
    struct Science_Scores FirstYearStudent;
```

In the previous structure FirstYearStudent, there are four members, where three of them are arrays. The arrays student_name and student_score are one dimensional, and the array subject_name is two dimensional. Consider an example of score card of a student "Dong Chao," where her student number is 911212:

Table 11.1: Example score card of science student

Student Name	Dong Chao	
Student Number	911212	
	SCORE CARD	
	Subject Name	Marks Obtained
Subject 1	Physics	86
Subject 2	Chemistry	97
Subject 3	Mathematics	81
Subject 4	Biology	91

The score card shown in Table 11.1 has four subjects, all of them are character arrays. Hence, we have defined array of strings: char subject_name[4][15]. Since there are four subjects, there is a need of an integer array with a minimum length of four to display the scores of each subject. Program 11.3 demonstrates this example of displaying the score-card information mentioned in Table 11.1, and shows how the structures are useful in manipulating data that contains different types of arrays.

```
// Program 11.3
// Example of structures containing arrays
#include <iostream>
#include <cstring>
using namespace std;

int main()
{
    struct Science_Scores
    {
        char student_name[20];
        int student_number;
        char subject_name[4][15];
        int student_score[4];
    };
```

```
      struct Science_Scores FirstYearStudent;
      strcpy(FirstYearStudent.student_name, "Dong Chao");
      FirstYearStudent.student_number = 911212;

      strcpy(FirstYearStudent.subject_name[0], "Physics");
      strcpy(FirstYearStudent.subject_name[1], "Chemistry");
      strcpy(FirstYearStudent.subject_name[2], "Mathematics");
      strcpy(FirstYearStudent.subject_name[3], "Biology");

      FirstYearStudent.student_score[0] = 86;
      FirstYearStudent.student_score[1] = 97;
      FirstYearStudent.student_score[2] = 81;
      FirstYearStudent.student_score[3] = 91;

      //Displaying Student information to screen
      cout<<"Student Score Information " << endl << endl;
      cout<<"Student Name: " << FirstYearStudent.student_name << endl;
      cout<<"Student Number: " <<FirstYearStudent.student_number<< endl;
      cout<< "Subject 1 :" <<FirstYearStudent.subject_name[0]
          <<", Marks: " << FirstYearStudent.student_score[0] << endl;
      cout<< "Subject 2 :" << FirstYearStudent.subject_name[1]
          <<", Marks: " << FirstYearStudent.student_score[1] << endl;
      cout<<"Subject 3 :" << FirstYearStudent.subject_name[2]
          << ", Marks: " << FirstYearStudent.student_score[2] << endl;
      cout<<  "Subject 4 :" << FirstYearStudent.subject_name[3]
          << ", Marks: " << FirstYearStudent.student_score[3] << endl;
      return 0;
}
```

The result of Program 11.3 is shown below:

```
      Student Score Information

      Student Name: Dong Chao
      Student Number: 911212
      Subject 1 :Physics, Marks: 86
      Subject 2 :Chemistry, Marks: 97
      Subject 3 :Mathematics, Marks: 81
      Subject 4 :Biology, Marks: 91
```

We can simplify the procedure of initializing all the members of FisrtYearStudent structure as shown below. This is not only easy to understand but also provides information about assigning structures containing arrays. Program 11.4 is same as Program 11.3, the only exception is that Program 11.4 is easier to understand, and the values to the FisrtYearStudent structure are initialized by initializing the whole structure, rather than initializing it member by member.

```
    struct Science_Scores FirstYearStudent=
    {
        {'D','o','n','g',' ','C','h','a','o'},
        911212,
        {"Physics", "Chemistry","Mathematics","Biology"},
        {86,97,81,91}
    };
```

```
// Program 11.4
// Example of structures containing arrays
#include <iostream>
using namespace std;

int main()
{
    struct Science_Scores
    {
        char student_name[20];
        int student_number;
        char subject_name[4][15];
        int student_score[4];
    };

    // Whole structure initialization
     struct Science_Scores FirstYearStudent=
    {
        {'D','o','n','g',' ','C','h','a','o'},
        911212,
        {"Physics", "Chemistry","Mathematics","Biology"},
        {86,97,81,91}
    };

    cout << "Student Score Information " << endl << endl;
    cout << "Student Name: " << FirstYearStudent.student_name << endl;
    cout << "Student Number: " << FirstYearStudent.student_number
         << endl;
    cout << "Subject 1 :" << FirstYearStudent.subject_name[0]
        << ", Marks: " << FirstYearStudent.student_score[0] << endl;
    cout << "Subject 2 :" << FirstYearStudent.subject_name[1]
        << ", Marks: " << FirstYearStudent.student_score[1] << endl;
    cout << "Subject 3 :" << FirstYearStudent.subject_name[2]
        << ", Marks: " << FirstYearStudent.student_score[2] << endl;
    cout << "Subject 4 :" << FirstYearStudent.subject_name[3]
        << ", Marks: " << FirstYearStudent.student_score[3] << endl;
    return 0;
}
```

The result of Program 11.4 is shown below:

```
Student Score Information

Student Name: Dong Chao
Student Number: 911212
Subject 1 :Physics, Marks: 86
Subject 2 :Chemistry, Marks: 97
Subject 3 :Mathematics, Marks: 81
Subject 4 :Biology, Marks: 91
```

11.8 Arrays of structures

Let us have a look on another kind of table that is much different from Table 11.1, where information about only one student Dong Chao, and her scores in physics, chemistry, mathematics, and biology are displayed. How about more than one student? How to process their scores by using structures? Table 11.2 shows another scenario, where four students' information is displayed.

Table 11.2: Example results of multiple science students

Student Name	Student Number	Physics	Chemistry	Mathematics	Biology	Average Score
Dong Chao	911212	86	97	81	91	88.75
Lianhua An	913418	81	90	82	85	84.5
Zhaopeng Deng	917890	85	82	90	82	84.5
Xieyu Yan	916745	89	80	82	78	82.25

Table 11.2 displays records of more than one student. To process these records, we need to make use of more than one structure. In Program 11.3, we have used only structure, because the program satisfies the requirements. To process more than one structure, we make use of arrays of structures. Please note that arrays containing structures are different from arrays of structures. An array of structures is highly useful in processing information as shown in Table 11.2. For example, the following statement defines an array called FirstYearStudent that has 10 elements. Each element inside the array will be of type struct Science_Scores.

```
struct Science_Scores FirstYearStudent[10];
```

Referencing an element in an array is simple and straightforward. The following statement assigns student number in the second element in the array (as the array index starts from 0) FirstYearStudent.

```
FirstYearStudent[1].student_number = 913418;
```

Similarly, initialization of structure arrays is similar to initialization of multidimensional arrays. Program 11.5 demonstrates the use of array of structures to process the information available in Table 11.2. In addition, the program also displays the average score for each student.

```cpp
// Program 11.5
// Example of array of structures
#include <iostream>
using namespace std;

int main()
{
    struct Science_Scores
    {
        char student_name[20];
        int student_number;
        char subject_name[4][15];
        int student_score[4];
        float average_score;
    };

    // Whole array of structure declaration and initialization
    struct Science_Scores FirstYearStudent[4] =
    {
        {
            "Dong Chao",
            911212,
            {"Physics", "Chemistry","Mathematics","Biology"},
            {86,97,81,91}
        },
        {
            "Lianhua An",
            913418,
            {"Physics", "Chemistry","Mathematics","Biology"},
            {81,90,82,85}
        },
        {
            "Zhaopeng Deng",
            917890,
            {"Physics", "Chemistry","Mathematics","Biology"},
            {85,82,90,82}
        },
        {
            "Xieyu Yan",
            916745,
            {"Physics", "Chemistry","Mathematics","Biology"},
```

```
            {89,80,82,78}}
      };

   int i;
   cout << "Student Score Information " << endl << endl;
   for(i = 0; i < 4; i++)
   {
       cout << "Student Name: "
            << FirstYearStudent[i].student_name << endl;
       cout << "Student Number: "
            << FirstYearStudent[i].student_number << endl;
       cout << "Subject 1 :" << FirstYearStudent[i].subject_name[0]
            << ", Marks: " << FirstYearStudent[i].student_score[0]
          <<endl;
       cout <<"Subject 2 :" << FirstYearStudent[i].subject_name[1]
            <<", Marks: " << FirstYearStudent[i].student_score[1]
            <<endl;
       cout <<"Subject 3 :" << FirstYearStudent[i].subject_name[2]
            <<", Marks: "<< FirstYearStudent[i].student_score[2]
            <<endl;
       cout << "Subject 4 :" << FirstYearStudent[i].subject_name[3]
            << ", Marks: " << FirstYearStudent[i].student_score[3]
            <<endl;

       //Calculating average score of four subjects for each student
       FirstYearStudent[i].average_score=
             (       FirstYearStudent[i].student_score[0]+
                     FirstYearStudent[i].student_score[1]+
                     FirstYearStudent[i].student_score[2]+
                     FirstYearStudent[i].student_score[3]
             )/4.0;
       cout << "Average Score: "
            << FirstYearStudent[i].average_score << endl;
       cout << endl;

   }
     return 0;
}
```

The result of Program 11.5 is shown below:

```
   Student Score Information

   Student Name: Dong Chao
   Student Number: 911212
   Subject 1 :Physics, Marks: 86
   Subject 2 :Chemistry, Marks: 97
   Subject 3 :Mathematics, Marks: 81
```

```
Subject 4 :Biology, Marks: 91
Average Score: 88.75

Student Name: Lianhua An
Student Number: 913418
Subject 1 :Physics, Marks: 81
Subject 2 :Chemistry, Marks: 90
Subject 3 :Mathematics, Marks: 82
Subject 4 :Biology, Marks: 85
Average Score: 84.5

Student Name: Zhaopeng Deng
Student Number: 917890
Subject 1 :Physics, Marks: 85
Subject 2 :Chemistry, Marks: 82
Subject 3 :Mathematics, Marks: 90
Subject 4 :Biology, Marks: 82
Average Score: 84.75

Student Name: Xieyu Yan
Student Number: 916745
Subject 1 :Physics, Marks: 89
Subject 2 :Chemistry, Marks: 80
Subject 3 :Mathematics, Marks: 82
Subject 4 :Biology, Marks: 78
Average Score: 82.25
```

Note that in Program 11.5, we have not supplied initial value for `average_score`, because the program computes after processing scores of all four subjects. However, if a variable is not initialized, it is initialized by 0 by default. We have also made use of `for` loop to process the information of all four students, including the statement that calculates their respective average scores. This shows that we can write complex programs such as processing customer information, preparing students score cards, and sorting names in particular order, and so on by using arrays of structures.

11.9 Structures and pointers

As we have discussed in Chapter 8, a pointer is a variable that holds the address of another variable. We can define pointers to a structure as we define pointers to any other variable. We can declare a pointer to a structure and assign the beginning address of a structure to it. The following piece of code explains this concept.

```
struct item
{
    char item_name[10];
    float price;
    char manufacturer[40];
    int item_no;
};
```

Then, a pointer can be defined as pointing to a variable as follows:

```
struct item *ptrBiscuit;
```

We can store the address of a structure variable in the previously defined pointer variable as shown below.

```
ptrBiscuit=&Biscuit;
```

The character "*" is used in front of *ptrBiscuit to specify that ptrBiscuit is a pointer, and the character "&" is used in front of Biscuit to pass its address to ptrBiscuit rather than its value.

Another important concept one must learn is the usage of the -> operator in conjunction with a pointer variable pointing to a structure. This operator is used to access the member of a structure using pointer to that structure. This is shown below.

```
ptrBiscuit->item_name
```

Program 11.6 demonstrates how to use pointers along with structures. In this example program, we have displayed the results using membership (.) operator as well as -> operator. While accessing the members by using period operator, we make use of the structure variable, however while using -> operator, we make use of the pointer variable. Program 11.6 displays the member values by using both ways.

```
// Program 11.6
// Structures and pointers
#include <iostream>
using namespace std;

int main()
{
    struct item
    {
        char item_name[10];
        float price;
```

```
      char manufacturer[40];
      int item_no;
   };

   //Declaration and initilization of the strucure
   struct item Biscuit = {"SweetBest",7.5,"Qingdao Biscuits Ltd",9341};

   //Pointer to structure
   struct item *ptrBiscuit;
   ptrBiscuit = &Biscuit;

   //Displaying Biscuit information
   cout << endl << "Biscuit Information "<< endl;
   cout << "Biscuit Name: " << Biscuit.item_name << endl;
   cout << "Biscuit Price: " << Biscuit.price << endl;
   cout << "Biscuit Manufacturer: " << Biscuit.manufacturer<< endl;
   cout << "Biscuit Item Number: " << Biscuit.item_no << endl;

   //Displaying Biscuit information using pointer
   cout << endl << "Biscuit Information (using pointer) " << endl;
   cout << "Biscuit Name: " << ptrBiscuit->item_name << endl;
   cout << "Biscuit Price: "<< ptrBiscuit->price << endl;
   cout << "Biscuit Manufacturer: "<< ptrBiscuit->manufacturer
       << endl;
   cout << "Biscuit Item Number: " << ptrBiscuit->item_no << endl;
   return 0;
}
```

The result of Program 11.6 is shown below:

```
   Biscuit Information
   Biscuit Name: SweetBest
   Biscuit Price: 7.5
   Biscuit Manufacturer: Qingdao Biscuits Ltd
   Biscuit Item Number: 9341

   Biscuit Information (using pointer)
   Biscuit Name: SweetBest
   Biscuit Price: 7.5
   Biscuit Manufacturer: Qingdao Biscuits Ltd
   Biscuit Item Number: 9341
```

11.10 Structures and functions

Structures can be used along with functions just like other data types. Generally, functions use structures as parameters, where structures can be sent to functions as whole structure or address of structures. We can pass a structure as a function argument in very similar way as you pass any other variable or pointer. We can access structure variables in the similar way as we have accessed in previous examples of this chapter. In Program 11.7,a structure is passed as an argument.

```cpp
// Program 11.7
// Functions using structures
#include <iostream>
using namespace std;

struct item
{
    char item_name[10];
    float price;
    char manufacturer[40];
    int item_no;
};

//The function accept structure as parameter
void printItem( struct item Temp)
{
    cout << "Biscuit Name: " << Temp.item_name << endl;
    cout << "Biscuit Price: " << Temp.price << endl;
    cout << "Biscuit Manufacturer: " << Temp.manufacturer << endl;
    cout << "Biscuit Item Number: " << Temp.item_no << endl;
}

int main()
{
    //Declaration and initilization of the structure
    struct item Biscuit = {"SweetBest",7.5,"Qingdao Biscuits Ltd",9341};
    //Passing a structure as an argument
    printItem(Biscuit);
    return 0;
}
```

The result of Program 11.7 is shown below:

```
Biscuit Name: SweetBest
Biscuit Price: 7.5
Biscuit Manufacturer: Qingdao Biscuits Ltd
Biscuit Item Number: 9341
```

As shown in Program 11.7, the structure Biscuit is sent as an argument to function printItem(). In function printItem(),temp is a formal parameter that has the matching structure type struct item. It is important to note that struct item should be declared before referencing the same either in main or function. Program 11.8 shows another similar example of using structures along with functions, with exception of pointers. In this example, address of a structure is passed as an argument to function printItem(). As the address of the structure is passed as an argument, the function accepts the pointer to the structure as a formal parameter. As shown in Program 11.6, we can make use of the -> operator to display the values of structure members.

```cpp
// Program 11.8
//Function accepting pointer to structure
#include <iostream>
using namespace std;

struct item
{
    char item_name[10];
    float price;
    char manufacturer[40];
    int item_no;
};

//The function accept pointer to structure as parameter
void printItem( struct item *ptrItem )
{
    //Printing Biscuit information using pointer
    cout << "Biscuit Name: " << ptrItem->item_name << endl;
    cout << "Biscuit Price: " << ptrItem->price << endl;
    cout << "Biscuit Manufacturer: " << ptrItem->manufacturer << endl;
    cout << "Biscuit Item Number: " << ptrItem->item_no << endl;
}

int main()
{
    //Declaration and initilization of the structure
    struct item Biscuit = {"SweetBest",7.5,"Qingdao Biscuits Ltd",9341};
    //Passing address of structure
    printItem(&Biscuit);
    return 0;
}
```

The result of Program 11.8 is shown below:

```
Biscuit Name: SweetBest
Biscuit Price: 7.5
Biscuit Manufacturer: Qingdao Biscuits Ltd
Biscuit Item Number: 9341
```

11.11 Unions

Unions and structures are very similar, with an exception that a union uses a single memory location to hold more than one variable. A **union** is a user-defined variable that may hold members of different sizes and types. Let us consider some cases where unions may be preferable over structures.

1. A program with two variables, for example, var1 and var2 of two different data types, may use var1 for some time, and when its purpose is over, the same memory location of var1 can be allocated to var2.
2. Sometimes, it is not possible to find what type of data should be passed to a function. In such cases, we can pass union that contains all possible data types.

So, a union is a user-defined type in which all members share the same memory location, and at any given time a union can contain no more than one object from its list of members. It also means that no matter how many members a union has, it always uses only enough memory to store the largest member. Unions can be useful for conserving memory when we have a lot of objects and/or limited memory. However, it requires an extra care to ensure that we always access the last written member. The syntax for declaring a union is similar to that of a structure; the only exception is that the keyword union is used instead of struct. Union-tag is the name given to a union and its member definitions, collectively. The general format of union declaration is as follows:

```
union [union-tag]
{
      member definition;
      member definition;
   ...
      member definition;
} [one or more union variables];
```

The following example defines a union called tempNum and a variable called intDouble. Here, tempNum is the name of the variable, and it acts in the same way as a tag for the structure. Members of a union can be accessed in same way as members of a structure are accessed.

```
union tempNum
{
    int number;
    double floatnumber;
} intDouble;
```

As unions allocate memory for single-member variable, the allocation is always done according to the variable that needs largest memory. In the previous example, as the floatnumber requires more memory than number, the memory allocation is done for the space required to store double instead of int. Program 11.9 summarizes the difference between unions and structures, and it also demonstrates the use of unions in C++.

```cpp
// Program 11.9
// Understanding unions and structures
#include <iostream>
using namespace std;

int main()
{
    union tempNum1
    {
        int number1;
        double floatnumber1;
    };
    struct tempNum2
    {
        int number2;
        double floatnumber2;
    };

    union tempNum1 TN1 = {3.00};
    struct tempNum2 TN2 = {24,3.14};
    cout<< "Size of union TN1 = " << sizeof(TN1) << endl;
    cout<< "Size of structure TN2 = " << sizeof(TN2) << endl;
    cout<< "Union member number1 = " << TN1.number1 << endl;
    cout<< "Union member floatnumber1 = " << TN1.floatnumber1 << endl;
    cout<< "Structure member number1 = " << TN2.number2 << endl;
    cout<< "Structure member floatnumber1 = "<< TN2.floatnumber2 << endl;
    return 0;
}
```

The result of Program 11.9 is shown below:

```
Size of union TN1 = 8
Size of structure TN2 = 16
Union member number1 = 3
Union member floatnumber1 = 1.4822e-323
Structure member number1 = 24
Structure member floatnumber1 = 3.14
```

In Program 11.9, there is one structure and one union, both with same number and type of data members. Initially, the program makes use of sizeof() operator to find the length of memory address allocated for both unions and structures. As shown in the result, the union is allocated only 8 bytes, as compared to 16 bytes allocated to the structure. Since unions can store only one value at a time, it is not possible to initialize both of its members at the same time. Hence, only one member of union is initialized. On the other hand, we can initialize all the members of structures at the same time. A union is initialized with a floating-point number; because we are displaying the integer member value first, the corresponding integer value of the floating-point number is displayed successfully. However, if we try to print the value stored in the same memory location as double, a strange value displayed. Unions can also be used as members of structure. Program 11.10 shows an example of using a two-member union as a member of a structure.

```cpp
// Program 11.10
// Union as member of a structure
#include <iostream>
#include <cstring>
using namespace std;

int main()
{
    union id
    {
        char name[40];
        int number;
    };
    struct {
        float salary;
        union id description;
    } employee;

    strcpy (employee.description.name,"Jessica");
    cout<< "Employee Name :" << employee.description.name << endl;
    employee.description.number = 1729;
    cout<< "Employee Number :" << employee.description.number << endl;
    employee.salary = 18700.25;
    cout<< "Employee Salary :" << employee.salary << endl;
    return 0;
}
```

The result of Program 11.10 is shown below:

```
Employee Name :Jessica
Employee Number :1729
Employee Salary :18700.3
```

In the previous example, it is worth noting that 40 bytes of memory is allocated for union, because the largest member is an array of characters. A character occupies 1 byte of memory, however, for 40 characters it would be 40 bytes. The second member of union, which is an integer of size less than 40 bytes, the size of union is 40. The program carefully uses both the member variables by assigning values at different times and displaying them on the screen as required.

11.12 Review questions

1. What is a structure? How is a structure different from an array? Explain with an example.
2. Write a program to explain structures in C++.
3. Define and initialize a structure? Describe with an example.
4. What is the meaning of dot notation? Explain two ways of initializing structure members with examples.
5. What is the use of `typedef` keyword? Explain with an example in relation to structures.
6. Write an executable C++ program to demonstrate nested structures.
7. Write a C++ program to demonstrate an array of structures.
8. Write a C++ program to demonstrate structures containing arrays.
9. What is a union? How are unions different from structures? Explain.
10. Write a program to demonstrate unions in C++.

12 Exception Handling

> There is no greater weapon than a prepared mind.
> – Zhuge Liang

12.1 Introduction

Exception handling is one of the most useful features of C++ programming language. A program may encounter problems, such as runtime errors, when it executes. These problems may occur without the knowledge of the programmer during coding, and may stop the normal flow of execution. The program may be compiled without any errors, but the execution may stop at some section of code, without executing further. These problems are called **exceptions**. An exception is a problem or an error that occurs when a program is running. These problems are not in control of the program. In such circumstances, exceptions provide special functions called exception handlers as a way to respond to such exceptional situations. C++ provides powerful mechanisms to handle these exceptions. This chapter focuses on exception-handling methods to understand the importance of exceptions. For example, let us consider Program 12.1.

```
// Program 12.1
// A program with no exception mechanism
#include<iostream>
using namespace std;

int main()
{
    int a = 1,b = 0;
    cout << a/b << endl;
    return 0;
}
```

Even if we compile the program without any errors, the results remain unpredictable while executing the program. In fact, the previous program may force you to stop the execution as it tries to run indefinitely. This is because the value of a is non-zero and value of b is zero. Theoretically, a/b is equal to **infinity**, however, it is not possible to express infinity as a fixed value in this program. We will consider another simple example through Program 12.2, where the user has a choice to select different values for a and b.

```
// Program 12.2
// A program with no exception mechanism
```

https://doi.org/10.1515/9783110593846-012

```
#include<iostream>
using namespace std;

int main()
{
    int a,  b;
    cout << "Enter two integers for division" << endl;
    cin >> a >> b;
    cout << a << " divided by "<< b << " = " << a/b << endl;
    return 0;
}
```

In Program 12.2, if we enter non-zero integers as input, the program provides output without any problems. For example, consider these results.

Case 1:

```
        Enter two integers for division
        4 2
        4 divided by 2 = 2
```

Case 2:

```
        Enter two integers for division
        4 8
        4 divided by 8 = 0
```

In both cases, the results are as expected for integer division. The result is 0 in case 2, because both 4 and 8 are integers, and in integer division, the result truncates to 0 instead of 0.5. However, in the same program, if we enter a as non-zero and b as zero, the results will have same consequences as shown in Program 12.1. In these circumstances, we use **exception handling** statements in C++ to avoid the values of b becoming zero unexpectedly. Program 12.3 shows the ways of using exception mechanism in C++ to deal with previously mentioned situations. Program 12.2 is modified here, so that the **"divide by zero"** problem can be dealt with exception handling mechanisms.

```
// Program 12.3
// A program with exception mechanism
#include<iostream>
using namespace std;

int main()
{
    int a,  b;
    cout << "Enter two integers for division" << endl;
```

```
    cin >> a >> b;
    try
    {
        if(b == 0)
            throw "There is an exception";
        else
            cout << a << " divided by " << b << " = " << a/b << endl;
    }
    catch (const char* msg)
    {
        cout << msg << endl;
    }

    return 0;
}
```

Sample results of Program 12.3 are as follows:

Case 1:

```
    Enter two integers for division
    18 2
    18 divided by 2 = 9
```

Case 2:

```
    Enter two integers for division
    0 1
    0 divided by 1 = 0
```

Case 3:

```
    Enter two integers for division
    0 0
    There is an exception
```

Case 4:

```
    Enter two integers for division
    2 0
    There is an exception
```

Hence, it is clear from the previous example that the normal flow of execution may stop, or it may generate exceptions. As shown in Program 12.3, several keywords, such as try, catch, and throw are used to handle the "**divide by zero**" exception. In the next section, we will study how to handle exceptions using exception handling mechanism in C++.

12.2 Handling exceptions

The objective of exception handling mechanism is to provide ways to detect and report an "exceptional circumstance," so that appropriate action can be taken at the right time. In general, the exception handling mechanism handles these tasks: (a) find the problem with a possibility of exception, (b) inform that an error has occurred or throw an exception, (c) receive the error information or catch the exception, and finally (d) take the corrective actions or handle the exceptions. When an exceptional circumstance arises within a block, an exception is thrown that transfers the control to the exception handler. If no exception is thrown, the code continues normally and all handlers are ignored. An exception is thrown by using the throw keyword from the inside of the try block. Exception handlers are declared with the keyword catch that must be placed immediately after the try block. Hence, in C++, the exception handling mechanism is handled by using three keywords, namely try, catch, and throw. The brief details of these three are described below.

try: In try block, the part of program or code that may generate exceptions is included, and it is followed by catch block. The block is enclosed by braces ({}). When an exception is generated within this block, it is thrown and the control is transferred to an exception handler. If no exception is thrown, the program code continues its execution normally and all handlers are ignored.

catch: The purpose of catch keyword is to catch an exception where the data type of the catch argument matches with exception type. The catch block must be placed immediately after the try block. When an exception is caught, the code in the catch block is executed. The catch block catches the exception "thrown" by the throw statement in the try block.

throw: As mentioned earlier, a program throws an exception during exceptional circumstances. The exceptions are thrown by using the throw keyword, and they can be thrown anywhere within a code. The type of the exception is also determined by the throw statement. The general format of handling exceptions in C++ is shown as follows:

```
try
{
    //Statements that may throw an exception
}

catch (type argument)
{
    //Statements to handle exception Type
}
```

Program 12.4 shows a simple example to use the try-catch block, where an integer number is thrown and is processed by the catch block.

```
// Program 12.4
// Try-catch Example
#include<iostream>
using namespace std;

int main()
{
    int a = 100;
    try
    {
        throw a;
    }
    catch (int temp)
    {
        cout << "Exception Example :caught integer number "
        << temp << endl;
    }

    return 0;
}
```

Sample results of Program 12.4 are as follows:

```
Exception Example: caught integer number 100
```

12.3 Multiple catch statements

In Program 12.4, the throw statement uses an integer number (in this case it is equal to 100), which is declared with catch keyword, and passed as an argument to the exception handler. It is clear from the example that the type of parameter thrown (which is int here) should match with the data type in the catch block. We can also have multiple catch statements during exception handling. This is important in situations where a program segment has more than one conditions that throw an exception. The general format is as follows:

```
try
{
    // Statements that may throw an exception
}

catch (type1 argument)
{
    // Statements to handle exception Type 1
}
```

```
catch (type2 argument)
{
    // Statements to handle exception Type 2
}

....

catch (typeN argument)
{
    // Statements to handle exception Type N
}
```

Program 12.5 shows an example of multiple catch statements with two throw statements.

```
// Program 12.5
// Multiple catch statements
#include<iostream>
using namespace std;

int main()
{
    int a =100;
    float b = 3.14f;

    try
    {
        throw a;
        throw b;
    }
    catch (int temp1)
    {
        cout << "Exception Example :caught integer number "
            << temp1 << endl;
    }
    catch (float temp2)
    {
        cout << "Exception Example :caught floating point number "
            << temp2 << endl;
    }

    return 0;
}
```

Result of Program 12.5 is as follows:

```
Exception Example: caught integer number 100
```

In Program 12.5, the first throw is executed, and the second throw statement remains unreachable. However, Program 12.6 shows a modified version of Program 12.5, where multiple catch statements are effectively used.

```
// Program 12.6
// Multiple catch statements
#include<iostream>
using namespace std;

int main()
{
    int a;
    float b;
    cout << "Enter the values of a and b" << endl;
    cin >> a >> b;

    try
    {
        if (a == 100) throw a;
        else if(b == 3.14f) throw b;
        cout << "No exception is thrown!" <<endl;
    }
    catch (int temp1)
    {
        cout << "Exception Example :caught integer number "
            << temp1 << endl;
    }
    catch (float temp2)
    {
        cout << "Exception Example :caught floating point number "
            << temp2 << endl;
    }

    return 0;
}
```

Sample results of Program 12.6 are as follows:

Case 1:

```
Enter the values of a and b
1 2
No exception is thrown!
```

Case 2:

```
Enter the values of a and b
100 200
Exception Example :caught integer number 100
```

Case 3:

```
Enter the values of a and b
1 3.14
Exception Example :caught floating point number 3.14
```

Case 4:

```
Enter the values of a and b
100 3.14
Exception Example :caught integer number 100
```

12.4 Exceptions within functions

In all the programming examples shown earlier, the exceptions are thrown within function. However, this not the case when the program size becomes larger. Generally, several functions are created to read programs with bigger code size. Hence, some functions may throw an exception instead of main function. Program 12.7 shows that whenever the function fun() throws an exception, the appropriate exception block is executed within the main().

```
// Program 12.7
// Functions invoking exceptions
#include<iostream>
using namespace std;

void fun()
{
    int a;
    float b;
    cout << "Enter the values of a and b" << endl;
    cin >> a >> b;
    if (a == 100)    throw a;
    else if(b == 3.14f) throw b;
    cout << "No exception is thrown!" << endl;
}

int main()
{
    try
    {
        fun();
    }
    catch (int temp1)
```

```
    {
        cout << "Exception Example :caught integer number "
        << temp1 << endl;
    }
    catch (float temp2)
    {
        cout << "Exception Example :caught floating point number "
        << temp2 << endl;
    }
    return 0;
}
```

A typical result of Program 12.7 is shown below:

```
Enter the values of a and b
23 3.14
Exception Example :caught floating point number 3.14
```

12.5 C++ standard exceptions

The C++ standard library provides a list of **standard exceptions** that are defined in
<exception> header. These standard exceptions can be used in programs, and they
are arranged in base-class and derived-class hierarchy. The base class of the standard
library is designed to declare objects to be thrown as exceptions. The hierarchical
chart of C++ standard exceptions is shown in Fig. 12.1. Header <exception> defines
two generic exception types that can be inherited by custom exceptions to report
errors: logic_error and runtime_error. All exceptions thrown by the components of

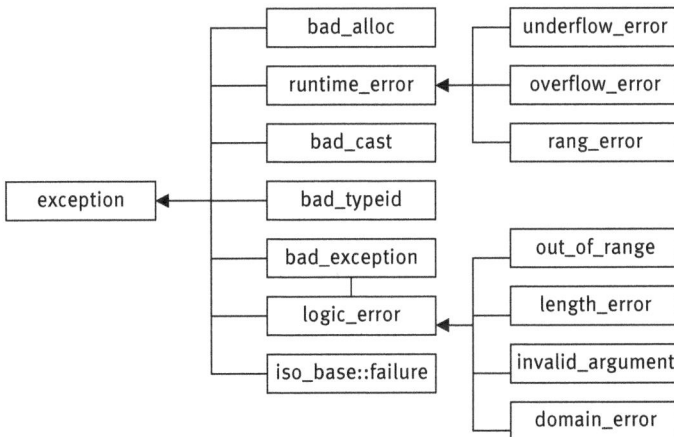

Fig. 12.1: Hierarchy in C++ standard exception.

C++ standard library belong to this exception class. The exceptions logic_error and runtime_error are standard exception classes. We can use the base classes from which we can derive our own types of exceptions. The exception classes derived from logic_error are: domain_error, invalid_argument, length_error, out_of_range, bad_cast, and bad_typeid, whereas those derived from runtime_error are: range_error, overflow_error, and bad_alloc.

Table 12.1 lists some of the C++ standard exceptions and their brief descriptions.

Table 12.1: Standard C++ exceptions and their descriptions

exception	It is the parent class of all the standard C++ exceptions. This is the base class for all the exceptions thrown by the C++ standard library. Function what() can be used to retrieve the optional string with which the exception was initialized.
bad_alloc	Reports a failure to allocate storage.
bad_cast	This can be thrown by dynamic_cast for executing an invalid dynamic_cast expression in runtime type identification.
bad_exception	This is useful device to handle unexpected exceptions in a C++ program.
bad_typeid	This can be thrown by typeid. It reports a null pointer p in an expression typeid(*p).
logic_error	It is an exception that can theoretically be detected by reading a code. It is derived from exception, and reports program logic errors that could presumably be detected by inspection.
domain_error	This exception is thrown when a mathematically invalid domain is used. It reports violations of a precondition.
invalid_argument	This exception is thrown due to invalid arguments, and indicates an invalid argument to the function from which it is thrown.
length_error	This is thrown when a too big std::string is created, and indicates an attempt to produce an object whose length is greater than or equal to npos (the largest representable value of context's size type, usually std::size_t).
out_of_range	This can be thrown by the method, for example, a std::vector and std::bitset<>::operator[](). It reports an out-of-range argument.
runtime_error	It is an exception that theoretically cannot be detected by reading the code. It reports runtime errors that can presumably be detected only when the program executes.
overflow_error	This exception is thrown if a mathematical overflow occurs. It reports an arithmetic overflow.
range_error	This exception occurs when one tries to store a value which is out of range. It reports violation of a postcondition.
underflow_error	This exception is thrown if a mathematical underflow occurs.

One of advantages of having the knowledge of standard C++ exceptions is that we can define our own exceptions by inheriting and overriding exception class functionality. Program 12.8 uses an exception class to implement the programmer's own exception. In this program, what() is a public method provided by exception class, which has been overridden by all the child exception classes.

```cpp
// Program 12.8
// Defining our own exceptions
#include <iostream>
using namespace std;

struct NewException : public exception
{
    const char * what () const throw ()
    {
        return "C++ Exception";
    }
};

int main()
{
    try
    {
        throw NewException();
    }
    catch(NewException& EX)
    {
        cout << "New Exception caught" << endl;
         cout<< EX.what() << endl;
    }
    return 0;
}
```

The result of Program 12.8 is shown below:

```
New Exception caught
C++ Exception
```

12.6 Review questions

1. What is the meaning of "divide-by-zero" problem? Discuss.
2. What is an exception? How it is different from errors?
3. Write a program in C++ with try, catch, and throw keywords.
4. What is the main role of exception handlers in C++?
5. Write a note on try, catch, and catch keywords in connection to exceptions.
6. Write a C++ program with multiple catch statements.
7. Write a program to demonstrate exceptions within functions.
8. Write a note on the hierarchy of C++ standard exceptions.
9. What is the meaning of standard exceptions in C++? Describe them with an example.
10. Write a program to define new exceptions.

13 Basic I/O and File Handling

A virtuous man concentrates on his own work, not that of others.
– Zengzi

13.1 Introduction

This chapter describes basic input and output along with I/O streams in C++. It also focuses on dealing with file handling operations and some stream classes. The input is data going into a program and the output is data going out of a program as shown in Fig. 13.1. A **stream** is a sequence of data moving from a source to a destination. An input stream is a source and an output stream is a destination. These streams handle the data moving from the source or to the destination. A **buffer** is a block of memory that is used along with streams. The idea is that data flows from one part of the computer to another and from one program to another. As shown in Fig 13.1, an input from keyboard is read by a program, and the results will be displayed on computer screen.

The input and output streams, `cin` and `cout` are actually C++ objects. For example, `istream` is actually a type name for a class, and `cin` is the name of a variable of type `istream`. Hence, we can say that it is an instance or an object of the class `istream`. A stream provides a connection between the process that initializes it and an object, such as a file, which may be viewed as a sequence of data. In the simplest view, a stream object is simply a sequenced view of that object. We think of data as flowing in the stream to the process, which can remove data from the stream as desired. The data in the stream cannot be lost by "flowing past" before the program has a chance to remove it. The stream object provides the process with an "interface" to the data.

The C++ standard libraries provide an extensive set of I/O capabilities, and in this chapter we will discuss some basic and most common I/O operations required for C++ programming. As mentioned, C++ I/O occurs in streams that are sequences of bytes. If bytes flow from a device such as a keyboard, a disk drive, a network connection, or so forth to main memory, this process is called input operation and if bytes flow from main memory to a device such as a display screen, a printer, a disk drive, a network connection, or so forth, this process is called output operation.

13.2 Standard input and output

We have extensively used `cin` and `cout` in many earlier programs. To use `cin` and `cout`, we have to include `iostream`. In C++, three library header files are important to manage I/O operations: `iostream`, `iomanip`, and `fstream`. The `iostream` file

https://doi.org/10.1515/9783110593846-013

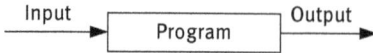

Fig. 13.1: A program with input and output data as source and destination.

defines the cin, cout, cerr, and clog objects that correspond to the standard input stream, the standard output stream, the unbuffered standard error stream, and the buffered standard error stream, respectively. The iomanip file declares services useful for performing formatted I/O or parameterized stream manipulators, such as setw and setprecision. The fstream file declares services for user-controlled file processing.

The standard output stream (cout)

The basic data type for I/O in C++ is streams. There are several stream types in C++, and most common stream types are the standard I/O streams. The cin is a built-in input stream variable that is by default connected to keyboard. Similarly, cout is another built-in output stream variable that is by default connected to console. In addition, C++ also supports all the I/O mechanisms that were included in C language. In addition, C++ streams provide all the I/O capabilities of C, with substantial improvements.

To get information out of a file or a program, we need to explicitly instruct the computer to output the desired information. One way of accomplishing this in C++ is by using of an output stream. In order to use the standard I/O streams, we must have the pre-compiler directive #include <iostream> in our program. In order to output on to the screen, we merely use a statement, such as:

```
cout << " Value = "  << value;
```

where, value is the name of a variable or constant that we want to write to the screen. The << is called **insertion operator** that points in the direction of the data flow.

The predefined object cout is an instance of ostream class. The cout object is said to be "connected to" the standard output device that is usually the display screen. The cout is used in conjunction with the stream insertion operator that is written as << (two less than signs). The C++ compiler also determines the data type of the variable to be output and selects the appropriate stream insertion operator to display the value. The << operator is overloaded to output data items of built-in types integer, float, double, strings, and pointer values. The insertion operator << may be used more than once in a single statement as shown previously, and endl is used to add a new-line at the end of a line.

The standard input stream (cin)

To get information into a file or a program, we need to explicitly instruct the computer to acquire the desired information. One way of accomplishing this in C++ is by using an input stream. As with cout, the program must use the pre-compiler directive #include <iostream> for cin as well. In order to input, we use a statement, such as:

```
cin >> value;
```

where, value is the name of a variable the value of which will be read from the keyboard. The >> operator is called **extraction operator**; it points in the direction of data flow.

The predefined object cin is an instance of istream class. The cin object is said to be attached to the standard input device, which usually is the keyboard. The cin is used in conjunction with the stream extraction operator, which is written as >> (two greater than signs), as shown in the following example. The C++ compiler also determines the data type of the entered value and selects the appropriate stream extraction operator to extract the value and store it in the given variables. The stream extraction operator >> may be used more than once in a single statement.

The standard error stream (cerr)

The predefined object cerr is an instance of ostream class. It is said to be attached to the standard error device, which is also a display screen, however, the object cerr is unbuffered, and each stream insertion to cerr causes its output to appear immediately. It is also used in conjunction with the stream insertion operator.

The standard log stream (clog)

The predefined object clog is an instance of ostream class. It is said to be attached to the standard error device, which is also a display screen, however, the object clog is buffered. This means that each insertion to clog can cause its output to be held in a buffer until the buffer is filled or flushed. The clog is also used in conjunction with the stream insertion operator. In general, it is a good practice to display error messages by using cerr stream, and to display other log messages by using clog. Program 13.1 shows an example with cout, cin, err, and clog.

```
// Program 13.1
// Input and output
#include<iostream>
using namespace std;
```

```
int main( )
{
    char st_err[] = "Error in the Program!";
    char st_log[] = "Log Details!";
    char st_input[50];
    cout << "Enter a String :" << endl;
    cin >> st_input;
    cout << "Entered String = :" << st_input<<endl;
    cerr << "Displaying Error Message : " << st_err << endl;
    clog << "Displaying Log Message : " << st_log << endl;
    return 0;
}
```

The result of Program 13.1 is shown below:

```
Enter a String :
Qingdao
Entered String = :Qingdao
Displaying Error Message : Error in the Program!
Displaying Log Message : Log Details!
```

13.3 File I/O

Reading from and writing into files are very useful during the development of many applications related to manipulating text information. So far, we have been using the iostream standard library that provides cin and cout methods for reading from standard input and writing to standard output, respectively. In this section, we will learn about how to read from and write into a file. This requires another standard C++ library called fstream that defines three new data types: ofstream, ifstream, and fstream. To perform file processing in C++, header files <iostream> and <fstream> must be included in C++ source file. C++ provides the following classes to perform output and input of characters to/from files:

ofstream: This is a stream class to write on files. This data type represents the output file stream, and is used to create files and write information into those files.

ifstream: This is a stream class to read from files. This data type represents the input file stream, and is used to read information from files.

fstream: This is a stream class to both read from and write into files. This data type generally represents the file stream, and has the capabilities of both ofstream and ifstream. This means that it can create files, write information into files, and read information from files.

These classes are derived directly or indirectly from the classes istream and ostream. We have already used objects whose types were these classes: (a) cin is an object of class istream and (b) cout is an object of class ostream. Therefore, we have already been using classes that are related to our file streams. We can use our file streams in the same way by using cin and cout, with the only difference that we have to associate these streams with physical files. Program 13.2 creates a file called output.txt, and inserts a sentence "Hello!, This is how we use file in C++!" by using the file stream myfile.

```
// Program 13.2
// Basic file operations example
#include <iostream>
#include <fstream>
using namespace std;

int main ()
{
  ofstream myfile;
  myfile.open ("output.txt");
  myfile << "Hello!, This is how we use file in C++!"<<endl;
  myfile.close();
  return 0;
}
```

Once the program is successfully compiled, the output.txt file can be found in the same folder that of the program, and the contents of the file are as shown below:

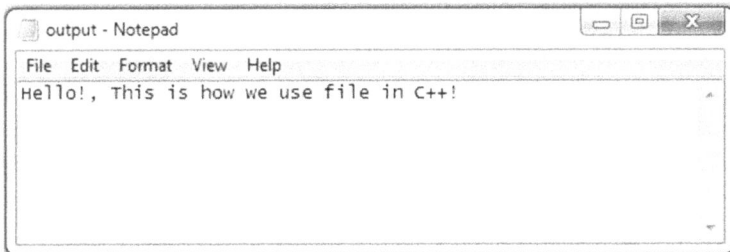

Streams for file I/O

C++ provides stream types for reading from and writing into files stored on a disk. For the most part, these operate in exactly the same way as the standard I/O streams cin and cout. For basic file I/O operations, we must include the statement #include <fstream>. There are no predefined file stream variables, so a programmer who needs to use file streams must declare file stream variables:

```
ifstream inFile;     // input file stream object
ofstream outFile;    // output file stream object
```

The file stream objects ifstream and ofstream are C++ stream classes designed to be connected to input or output files. File stream objects have all the member functions and manipulators possessed by the standard streams, cin and cout.

Connecting streams to files

A file stream is not connected to anything by default. In order to use a file stream, a programmer must establish a connection between the file stream and a file. This can be done in two ways.(1) using open() member function, (2) using ifstream, and outsream classes. We may use the open() member function associated with each stream object as follows:

```
inFile.open("input.data");
outFile.open("output.data");
```

This sets up the file streams to read data from a file called "input.data" and write output to a file called "output.data." For an input stream, if the specified file does not exist, it will not be created by the operating system, and the input stream variable will contain an error flag. This can be checked by using the member function fail(). For an output stream, if the specified file does not exist, it will be created by the operating system. We may also connect a file stream variable to a file when the stream variable is declared as follows:

```
ifstream inFile("input.data");
ofstream outFile("output.data");
```

This also sets up the file streams to read data from a file called "input.data" and write output to a file called "output.data." The only difference between this approach and using the open() function is compactness. If we are to use a string constant (or variable) to store the file name, we must add a special conversion when connecting the stream:

```
string   inputFileName = "input.data";
ifstream inFile(inputFileName.c_str());
```

Opening a file

An open file is represented within a program by a stream, that is, an object of one of these classes. In Program 13.2, this was myfile, and any input or output operation performed on this stream object will be applied to the physical file associated to it. In order to open a file with a stream object, we use its member function open as follows:

```
open (filename, mode);
```

Where filename is a string representing the name of the file to be opened, and mode is an optional parameter with a combination of flags shown in Table 13.1. A file must be opened before you can read from it or write into it. Either ofstream or fstream object may be used to open a file for writing, and ifstream object is used to open a file for reading purpose only. Following is the standard syntax for open() function, which is a member of fstream, ifstream, and ofstream objects.

```
void open(const char *filename, ios::openmode mode);
```

Here, the first argument specifies the name and location of the file to be opened; and the second argument of the open() member function defines the mode in which the file should be opened.

Table 13.1: File mode flags and their description.

Mode Flag	Description
ios::app	It is called append mode. It means that all output to a file is to be appended to the end. That is, all output operations are performed at the end of the file, appending the content to the current content of the file.
ios::ate	Open a file for output and move the read/write control to the end of the file. This is used to set the initial position at the end of the file. If this flag is not set, the initial position is the beginning of the file.
ios::in	Open a file for reading or input operations.
ios::out	Open a file for writing or output operations.
ios::trunc	If the file already exists, its contents will be truncated before opening the file. This means, if the file is opened for output operations and it already exists, its previous content is deleted and replaced by the new one.
ios::binary	Open in binary mode.

We can combine two or more of these values performing OR operation on them together. For example, if we want to open a file in write mode and truncate it in case it already exists, following will be the syntax:

```
ofstream outfile;
outfile.open("file.dat", ios::out | ios::trunc );
```

Similarly, we can open a file for reading and writing purpose as follows:

```
fstream afile;
afile.open("file.dat", ios::out | ios::in );
```

File streams opened in **binary mode** perform input and output operations independently of any format considerations. Non-binary files are known as **text files,** and some translations may occur due to formatting of some special characters such as newline and carriage return characters. Table 13.2 shows that each of the open member functions of classes ofstream, ifstream, and fstream has a default mode that is used if the file is opened without a second argument.

Table 13.2: Default mode parameters of ofstream, ifstream, and fstream classes.

Class	Default Mode Parameter
ofstream	ios::out
ifstream	ios::in
fstream	ios::in | ios::out

For ifstream and ofstream classes, ios::in and ios::out are automatically assumed, respectively, even if a mode that does not include them is passed as a second argument to the open member function (the flags are combined). For fstream, the default value is only applied if the function is called without specifying any value for the mode parameter. If the function is called with any value in that parameter, the default mode is overridden, not combined. To check if a file stream was successful opening a file, we can do it by calling is_open member function that returns a **bool** value of true in case the stream object is associated with an open file or returns false otherwise:

```
if (myfile.is_open()) { /* ok, proceed with output */ }
```

Closing a file

When a C++ program terminates, it automatically flushes all the streams, releases all the allocated memory, and close all the opened files. But it is always a good practice that a programmer should close all the opened files before terminating the program.

Following is the standard syntax for `close()` function that is a member of `fstream`, `ifstream`, and `ofstream` objects.

```
void close();
```

As mentioned earlier, when a program does not need a file anymore, it must close the file by using the `close()` member function that is associated with each file stream variable:

```
inStream.close();
outStream.close();
```

Calling `close()` member function notifies the operating system that your program is done with the file, and that the system should flush any related buffers, update file security information, and so forth. It is always best to close files explicitly, even though by the C++ standard, files are closed automatically whenever the associated file stream variable goes out of scope.

When we have completed our input and output operations on a file, we should close it so that the operating system is notified and its resources become available again. For this purpose, we call the stream's member function `close ()`. This member function flushes the associated buffers and closes the file. Once this member function is called, the stream object can be reused to open another file, and the file becomes available again to be opened by other processes. In case an object is destroyed while still associated with an open file, the destructor automatically calls the member function `close ()`.

Text files

Text file streams are those that do not include `ios::binary` flag in their opening mode. These files are designed to store text. Hence, all values that are input or output from/to them can suffer some formatting transformations, which do not necessarily correspond to their literal binary value. Writing operations on text files are performed in the same way we operate with `cout`.

Writing to a file

In C++ programming, we write information into a file from a program by using the stream insertion operator (`<<`) just as we use that operator to output information on the screen. The only difference is that we use an `ofstream` or `fstream` object instead of the `cout` object.

```cpp
// Program 13.3
// Writing on a text file
#include <iostream>
#include <fstream>
using namespace std;

int main ()
{
    ofstream myFile("output.txt");
    if (myFile.is_open())
    {
        myFile << "This is a first line."<< endl;
        myFile << "This is second line line." << endl;
        myFile <<  "This is the last line in this file " << endl;
        myFile.close();
    }
    else
        cout << "Unable to open file";
    return 0;
}
```

Once the program is successfully compiled, the **output.txt** file can be found in the same folder as that of the program. The contents of the **output.txt** file are shown below:

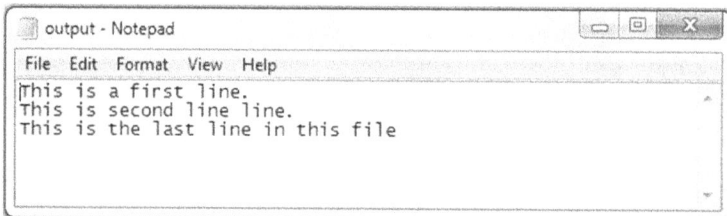

```
output - Notepad
File  Edit  Format  View  Help
This is a first line.
This is second line line.
This is the last line in this file
```

Reading from a file

We can read information from a file into our program by using the stream extraction operator (>>) just as we use that operator to input information from the keyboard. The only difference is that we use an ifstream or fstream object instead of the cin object. Program 13.4 shows how the contents of text file **input.txt** are read and displayed to screen, provided that the **input.txt** file exists in the same folder as the program file. We have created a while loop that reads the file line by line by using function getline(). The value returned by getline() is a reference to the stream object itself, which when evaluated as a Boolean expression in this while loop is (a) true if the stream is ready for more operations, and (b) false if either the end of the file has been reached or if some other error occurred.

```
// Program 13.4
// Reading a text file
#include <iostream>
#include <fstream>
#include <string>
using namespace std;

int main ()
{
    string readline;
    ifstream myFile ("input.txt");
    if (myFile.is_open())
    {
        while ( getline (myFile,readline) )
        {
            cout << readline << endl;
        }
        myFile.close();
    }
    else
        cout << "Unable to open file" << endl;
    return 0;
}
```

The result of Program 13.4 is shown below:

```
Hello, this is input.txt file.
This is a text file.
The contents will be displayed to screen!
Happy Programming!
```

Checking state flags

Several member functions exist to check for specific states of a stream and all of them return a bool value as shown in Table 13.3.

Table 13.3: Functions to check the states of streams and their description.

Functions	Description
bad()	Returns true if a reading or a writing operation fails. For example, in case we try to write to a file that is not open for writing or if the device where we try to write has no space left.
fail()	Returns true not only in same cases as bad() but also in the case if a format error occurs, for example, when an alphabetical character is extracted while we are trying to read an integer number.

(continued)

Table 13.3 (Continued)

Functions	Description
eof()	Returns true if a file that is open for reading has reached the end.
good()	It is the most generic state flag. It returns false in cases in which calling any of the previous functions would return true.
clear()	This can be used to reset the state flags.

Program 13.5 shows an example of a file that is opened for reading and writing mode. During its execution, the program asks the user to input information that is stored in **input.txt**. Then, the program reads the information from the file and outputs on the screen.

```
// Program 13.5
// Reading and writing to a file
#include <fstream>
#include <iostream>
using namespace std;

int main()
{
    char indata[100];
    // Open a file in write mode.
    ofstream outfile;
    outfile.open("input.dat");

    cout << "Writing to the file:input.dat" << endl;
    cout << "Enter the name of your city: ";
    cin.getline(indata, 100);

    // Write inputted data into the file.
    outfile << indata << endl;

    outfile.close();

    // Open a file in read mode.
    ifstream infile;
    infile.open("input.dat");

    cout << endl << "Reading from the file:input.dat" << endl;
    infile >> indata;

    // Write the data at the screen.
    cout << indata << endl;
```

```
    // Close the opened file.
    infile.close();

    return 0;
}
```

The result of Program 13.5 is shown below:

```
Writing to the file:input.dat
Enter the name of your city: Beijing
Reading from the file:input.dat
Beijing
```

13.4 Review questions

1. Explain the following: (a) input stream (b) output stream, and (c) buffer.
2. Write a brief note on (a) cin, (b) cout, (c) cerr, and (d) clog.
3. Describe the following classes that are related to files: (a) ofstream, (b) ifstream, and (c) fstream.
4. Discuss the difference between binary files and text files.
5. Write a program to read information from a file, input.txt, and write contents to another file with name output.txt.
6. Write a program to input two text files and merge the contents to an output file.

   input1.txt

   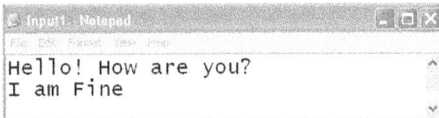

   input2.txt

   output.txt

   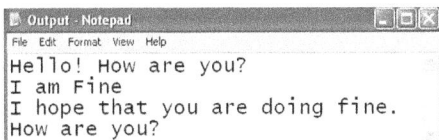

14 Classes and Objects

> If one extends knowledge to the utmost, one will have wisdom.
>   Having wisdom, one can then make choices.
> – Cheng Yi

14.1 Introduction

In this chapter, we will study the most important part of object-oriented programming, that is, classes and objects. The most common **object-oriented programming
(OOP)** languages are C++ and Java. Languages such as C, PASCAL, FORTRAN, and so
forth are usually called procedure-oriented or structured programming languages. In
recent years, many programmers have found OOP to be a better approach than
procedure-oriented programming.

Software is basically a collection of many interrelated programs that in turn
consist of **data** and **methods**. In traditional programming languages, data and
methods are loosely tied together. Hence, it is difficult to find which data belong to
which function? In addition, traditional procedure-oriented languages are not able to
represent real-time entities or situations. A few examples of real-time entities are:
bank, customer, university, and student. OOP solves all these problems by providing
an effective way to represent real-time entities through **objects** and **classes**, two
most important concepts in object-oriented programming. Every reader or programmer must be aware of these concepts.

14.2 Object definition

What is an object?

Object is the key feature of OOP. If we see around us, we may notice many real-world
objects such as dog, bag, computer, pen, telephone, and so forth. These objects may
be both tangible and intangible. If we analyze all these objects, we notice that they
share two common characteristics such as **data** and **behavior**. Let us take an
example of a dog object. The data related to this object are name, age, height, and
weight. Other than these data, a dog may exhibit some behaviors, such as walking,
running, barking, biting (sometimes!), eating, and so forth.

In general, every object has two fundamental features called data and behavior.
The data of an object is basically represented by data type, and related behavior is
represented by a method in OOP. The object is a software entity with both data and
methods.

https://doi.org/10.1515/9783110593846-014

How objects are useful in software development?

We may wonder about a question: How is the concept of an object useful in software development? To answer this question, we must understand the applications of software. Today, software is designed for various applications, such as student data management, banking applications, customer transactions, railway reservation, and so on. All these softwares use entities, such as customer, bank, transaction, reservation, and so forth. All these real-time entities are represented as objects. Hence, it is very easy to write a program with an easy understanding about both programmers and customers.

14.3 Class definition

What is a class?

In Section 14.2, we have analyzed the meaning of an object. A **class** is a generic term used to create objects. A class in OOP represents real-world entities through both data and behavior under single name. For example Mr. Chen is a student, this means that Mr. Chen belongs to class student. In this example, Mr. Chen is an object and student is a class. A class may have many objects. Let us look at the following sentence:

Mr. Chen, Ms. Fang, and Mr. Bruce are all students.

What do we infer from the previous statement? It indicates that Chen, Fang, and Bruce belong to student class. This clearly shows that one class is responsible for creating one or more objects. Now, let us compare the following statements:

```
int Chen_Weight, Fang_Weight, Bruce_weight;
Student Chen, Fang, Bruce;
```

If we compare the previous two statements, it looks similar. In the first statement, all three variables are integers. In the second statement, all three objects belong to the **class** Student. Hence, class is just like a template or model for creating many objects. Usually an object is called an instance of a class. In Section 14.2, we have studied that an object has data and methods or behavior. A class is used to define data and methods. As we know that Chen, Fang, and Bruce all are students who share many characteristics that are expressed as data and methods, and are defined in the class. Hence, class is used to define data and methods that are common to all of its objects. So, a C++ class is a collection of data and methods (functions) that creates a new data type that is used for creating objects of this class. In general, the syntax of a class definition is shown as follows:

```
classclass_name
{
    public:
            <variable declaration>  // for data members
            <method declaration>    // member functions
    private:
            <variable declaration>  // for data members
            <method declaration>    // member functions
    protected:
            <variable declaration>  // for data members
            <method declaration>    // member functions
};
```

As shown in the syntax, there are three different keywords used as **access specifiers** in C++: public, private, and protected. They guide the rules for accessing the members of a class, such as functions (methods) or data within the class, outside of a class, and within a program. The private access specifier supports to achieve the data hiding feature of OOP. The private members of a class can only be accessed within the class itself. On the other hand, public members can be accessible outside of the class as well. These access specifiers are followed by a colon. If no access specifier is mentioned, then by default all the member functions or data become private. Further details about the same are provided in Section 14.7. A class definition ends with a semicolon. To understand class and objects, let us define a Student class.

```
class Student
{
    public:
            int student_number;
            char name[20];
            int marks;
            char university_name[40];

            void get_name_number()
            {
                cout << "Student Number=" << student_number  << endl;
                cout << "Student Name="   << name << endl;
            }

            void get_marks()
            {
                cout << "Student Marks=" << marks << endl;
            }
};
```

A class must be defined before its objects are created. This means that the class definition acts as a template for creating objects later. For example, the following statement creates an object of type Student. As explained earlier, every object is an instance of the class. This means that

```
Student Fang;
```

statement declares an object Fang of type Student. Here, Fang is an instance of class Student. We can also create multiple objects of type Student as follows:

```
Student Fang, Wang;
```

Each object is allocated separate memory for their members. Hence, we can store different values for members of each object.

How to access data and methods?

In the previous example, **class** Student student_number, name, marks are called data members of the class, and get_name_number() and get_marks() are called method members of the class. To use these data and method members, we make use of .(**dot** or **period**) operator. The following statement assigns 18976587 to student_number data of Fang object:

```
Fang.student_number = 18976587;
```

Similarly, we can call method member of the Fang object:

```
Fang.get_marks();
```

The previous statement calls the get_marks() method of Fang object.

Program 14.1 completely summarizes the previous description, class and objects, and also uses both data and method members. The class definition is always written before the definition of main() function. This is because, an object must be defined before being used within the main. Definition of class is written after main leads to errors.

```
// Program 14.1
// Program to understand class and object
#include <iostream>
#include <cstring>
using namespace std;

class Student
{
```

```
    public:
        int student_number;
        char name[20];
        int marks;
        char university_name[40];

        void get_name_number()
        {
            cout << "Student Number=" << student_number << endl;
            cout << "Student Name=" << name << endl;
        }

        void get_marks()
        {
        cout  << "Student Marks=" << marks << endl;
        }
};

int main()
{
    Student Fang;
    Fang.student_number = 18976587;
    strcpy(Fang.name,"Xiaong Dong Fang");
    Fang.marks = 87;
    Fang.get_name_number();
    Fang.get_marks();
    return 0;
}
```

The result of Program 14.1 is shown below:

```
    Student Number=18976587
    Student Name=Xiaong Dong Fang
    Student Marks=87
```

Comparing a OOP program to non-OOP program in C++

Programs 14.2 and 14.3 demonstrate the ways of writing a program without using objects (or classes) and with using objects (or classes). It is useful to understand the difference between an OOP program and a non-OOP program. Program 14.2 is a simple program that is written to add two numbers without objects.

```
// Program 14.2
// Program to add two numbers without using object
#include<iostream>
using namespace std;
```

```
int main()
{
    int a = 99,b = 88;
    int c = a + b;
    cout << "Result=" << c << endl;
    return 0;
}
```

The result of Program 14.2 is shown below:

```
Result=187
```

Now, we will rewrite Program 14.2 as Program 14.3 by using objects and classes in C++. Here we need to write a class, and later we need to create an object of that class. Program 14.3 looks as follows:

```
// Program 14.3
// Program to add two numbers using classes and objects
#include<iostream>
using namespace std;

class Add_Two
{
    public:
        int a,b,c;
    void Result()
    {
        c = a + b;
        cout << "Result=" << c <<endl;
    }
};

int main()
{
    Add_Two TWOADD;
    //set the fields
    TWOADD.a = 99;
    TWOADD.b = 88;
    TWOADD.Result();
    return 0;
}
```

The result of Program 14.3 is shown below:

```
Result=187
```

14.4 Overloaded methods

A class may have many methods, and each method has zero or more parameters. Is it possible to write more than one method with same name? The answer is Yes. A class may have multiple methods with same name. This concept is called **method over-loading**. To overload a method, the following conditions must be satisfied:
1. The name of the method should be the same.
2. The method should have different parameter list or signature.
3. The method can be in the same class or sub class.

The signature of a method is determined by the method name and the number of data type parameters. The following three methods have three different signatures:

```
void oneMethod(int a, int b);
void oneMethod(int a, float b);
void oneMethod(int a, float b,long c);
```

If multiple methods have the same name but different signatures, we say that the method is overloaded, and call these methods overloaded methods. Program 14.4 illustrates an example of this.

```
// Program 14.4
// Program to understand Overloaded Methods
#include<iostream>
using namespace std;

class Overload
{
    public:
        int add(int a,int b)
        {
            return (a+b);
        }
        float add(float a,float b)
        {
            return (a+b);
        }
        double add(double a,double b)
        {
            return (a+b);
        }
};

int main()
{
```

```
        Overload SAME;
        int a = 10;
        int b = 20;
        float c = 23.75F;
        float d = 78.987F;
        double e = 23456.879;
        double f = 33445.789645;
        cout << "Integer Addition : a + b = " << SAME.add(a,b) << endl;
        cout << "Float Addition   : a + b = " << SAME.add(c,d) << endl;
        cout << "Double Addition  : a + b = " << SAME.add(e,f) << endl;
        return 0;
}
```

The result of Program 14.4 is shown below:

```
        Integer Addition: a + b = 30
        Float Addition:   a + b = 102.737
        Double Addition:  a + b = 56902.7
```

14.5 Multiple objects

So far we studied about creating one object and using it. Usually an object-oriented program may have many objects and classes. Program 14.5 illustrates how to write a program with multiple objects.

```
// Program 14.5
// Program with multiple objects

#include<iostream>
using namespace std;

class Student
{
    public:
        int rollNumber;
        int marks;
        char grade;
        void printRollNo()
        {
            cout << "rollNumber = " << rollNumber  << endl;
        }
        void printMarks()
        {
            cout << "Marks = "  << marks << endl;
        }
```

```
        void printGrade()
        {
            cout << "Grade = "  << grade << endl;
        }
};

int main()
{
    Student s1,s2;
    s1.rollNumber = 9;
    s1.marks = 90;
    s1.grade = 'A';
    s1.printRollNo();
    s1.printMarks();
    s1.printGrade();
    s2.rollNumber = 10;
    s2.marks = 99;
    s2.grade = 'A';
    s2.printRollNo();
    s2.printMarks();
    s2.printGrade();
    return 0;
}
```

The result of Program 14.5 is shown below:

```
        rollNumber = 9
        Marks = 90
        Grade = A
        rollNumber = 10
        Marks = 99
        Grade = A
```

14.6 Array of objects

In many software applications, we may have to create a program with many objects of
the same type. In such cases, we will use array of objects, that is, only one class and
an array, which is used to create many similar objects. In this section, we will explore
further arrays of objects. To illustrate the processing of an array of objects, we will use
Person class in the following example.

```
class Person
{
    public:
        int Age;
        char Gender;
```

```
        char Name[20];
        void setName(char *name)
        {
            strcpy(Name,name);
        }
        void setAge(int age)
        {
            Age = age;
        }
        void setGender(char gender)
        {
            Gender = gender;
        }
        void getName()
        {
            cout << "Name="  << Name  << endl;
        }
        void getAge()
        {
            cout << "Age=" << Age << endl;
        }
        void getGender()
        {
            cout << "Gender=" << Gender << endl;
        }
};
```

Now let us study how we can create and manipulate an array of Person objects. An array of objects is declared and created just like an array of primitive data types. The following is the declaration and creation of an array of Person objects.

```
    Person person[20];
```

Program 14.6 creates two objects as members of an array, initializes the members of these objects, and displays the initialized values to screen.

```
// Program 14.6
// Program to understand array of objects
#include <iostream>
#include <cstring>
using namespace std;

class Person
{
    public:
        int Age;
        char Gender;
        char Name[20];
```

```
        void setName(char *name)
        {
            strcpy(Name,name);
        }
        void setAge(int age)
        {
            Age = age;
        }
        void setGender(char gender)
        {
            Gender = gender;
        }
        void getName()
        {
            cout << "Name= "  << Name << endl;
        }
        void getAge()
        {
            cout << "Age= "  << Age << endl;
        }
      void getGender()
        {
            cout << "Gender= "  << Gender  <<endl;
        }
};

int main()
{
    Person person[20];

    // Initializing the data members of the first object in the array
    person[0].setName("Jackie");
    person[0].setAge(40);
    person[0].setGender('M');

    // Initializing the data members of the second object in the array
    person[1].setName("Suchi");
    person[1].setAge(28);
    person[1].setGender('F');

    // Calling the method members of the first object in the array
    person[0].getName();
    person[0].getAge();
    person[0].getGender();

    // Calling the method members of the second object in the array
    person[1].getName();
    person[1].getAge();
    person[1].getGender();
```

```
        return 0;
}
```

The result of Program 14.6 is shown below:

```
        Name= Jackie
        Age= 40
        Gender= M
        Name= Suchi
        Age= 28
        Gender= F
```

14.7 Access modifiers

As we have discussed earlier, OOP is useful to represent real-time applications by using several objects and classes. For example, in a school data-management application, there are several classes, such as school, management, teachers, students, account, grading, and so forth. Sometimes many of these classes may share common data and methods. Moreover, data belonging to one class may be used by some other class. In such situations, **access modifiers** are used to effectively solve this problem in C++ by providing various keywords such as `public`, `private`, `protected`, and default (no modifier). They use data effectively and provide more security to C++ applications.

The most commonly used modifiers are `public` and `private`. If data member is declared as `public`, then any outside method can access it using the **dot** (.) notation. The data members and member methods that are declared public become available everywhere and can be accessed by other classes too. But if the data member is declared `private`, then any outside method cannot access it. Declaring the data members as `private` ensures the integrity of the class. This means that no one can access those class members outside that class. An access modifier can be used along with class, data, and methods. For example:

```
public class test
{
    public int student_number;
    public String name;
    private int marks;
    public String university_name;

    public void get_name_number()
    {
        cout<< "Student Number = " + student_number);
        cout<< "Student Name= " + name);
    }
```

```
    private void get_marks()
    {
        cout << "Student Marks = " + marks);
    }
};
```

In this example, the class test is defined as public class; student_number, name, and university_name are public data members of the class; and marks is a private data member. Similarly, get_name_number() is a public method and get_marks() is a private method. If data or method is declared private, it is accessible only inside the class. The public data can be accessed everywhere. The protected keyword is further explained in Chapter 16. Program 14.7 illustrates the use of private as well as public data and method members in a class.

```
// Program 14.7
// Program to understand private and public members
#include<iostream>
using namespace std;

class Student
{
    public:
        int rollNumber;
    private:
        int marks;
    public:
        char grade;
    private:
        void printRollNo()
        {
            cout << "rollNumber = " << rollNumber << endl;
        }
    public:
        void printMarks()
        {   marks = 90;
            cout << "Marks = " << marks << endl;
        }
        void printGrade()
        {
            cout << "Grade = " << grade << endl;
        }
};

int main()
{
    Student s1;
```

```
        s1.rollNumber = 9;
        // s1.marks = 90; Not possible because private
        s1.grade = 'A';
        // s1.printRollNo(); Not possible because private
        s1.printMarks();
        s1.printGrade();
        return 0;
}
```

The result of Program 14.7 is shown below:

```
        Marks = 90
        Grade = A
```

Program 14.8 illustrates the use of only public method data members in a class.

```
// Program 14.8
// Program with only public data and methods
#include<iostream>
using namespace std;

class Student
{
    public:
        int rollNumber;
        int marks;
        char grade;
        void printRollNo()
        {
            cout << "rollNumber = " << rollNumber << endl;
        }
        void printMarks()
        {
            cout << "Marks = " << marks << endl;
        }
        void printGrade()
        {
            cout << "Grade = " << grade << endl;
        }
};

int main()
{
    Student s1;
    s1.rollNumber = 9;
    s1.marks = 90;
    s1.grade = 'A';
```

```
    s1.printRollNo();
    s1.printMarks();
    s1.printGrade();
    return 0;
}
```

The result of Program 14.8 is shown below:

```
    rollNumber = 9
    Marks = 90
    Grade = A
```

14.8 Review questions

1. Why is object-oriented programming relevant in software development? Justify your answer.
2. Explain the following in relation with OOP: (a) object, (b) class, (c) method, and (d) data.
3. Write a program to add three numbers by using objects and classes.
4. What is method overloading? Explain with an example.
5. Explain with an example how to declare an array of objects.
6. What is access modifier? What are the different types of access modifiers?
7. Explain the difference between `private` and `public` access modifiers with an example.

15 Constructors and Destructors

> If you stop and confine yourself to one place, you will develop prejudices.
> – Guo Xiang

15.1 Introduction

The constructors are one of the most powerful features of object-oriented languages. They are used for initializing objects during their creation. Initialization of data members is necessary when we deal with multiple objects of same class. A **constructor** is a special method that is executed when an object of that class is created. The name of the constructor must be the same as the class. To understand constructors, we will first write a program without a constructor, and later convert the same program with constructor. Program 15.1 illustrates a class without constructor.

```
// Program 15.1
// Program to initialize and print values without constructor
#include<iostream>
using namespace std;

class day
{
    public:
        int date,month,year;
        void setValues()
        {
            date = 1;
            month = 1;
            year = 2018;
        }
};

int main()
{
    day TODAY;
    TODAY.setValues();
    cout << "Date is   :" << TODAY.date << endl;
    cout << "Month is  :" << TODAY.month << endl;
    cout << "Year is   :" << TODAY.year << endl;
    return 0;
}
```

https://doi.org/10.1515/9783110593846-015

The result of Program 15.1 is shown below:

```
Date is   :1
Month is  :1
Year is   :2018
```

In Program 15.1, the call to setValues() method is explicitly made with TODAY. setValues() statement. The setValues() method is used here to initialize or set some values of the data members of the class. There may be cases where we need to create many instances of class day, such as,

```
day TODAY;
day TOMM;
day YESTERDAY;
day SUNDAY;
```

In such situations, we also need to call setValues() method along with the associated objects.

```
TODAY.setValues();
TOMM.setValues();
YESTERDAY.setValues();
SUNDAY.setValues();
```

This seems to be a time-consuming and repetitive process. We use constructors to avoid these problems. A constructor will initialize the objects when they are created. Hence, an explicit call to the initializing method (here setValues()) is avoided. The initial settings of all objects are easily done along with their creation without calling any other methods. The main purpose of a constructer is to initialize the objects of a particular class with supplied initial values. Sometimes, this is also called **automatic initialization** of objects.
The general syntax of a constructor is as follows:

```
<class-name> (<parameters>)
{
    <statements>
}
```

In the previous example, class-name is the name of the class to which this constructor belongs. The constructors are declared in the public section, and are invoked automatically when the object is created. They do not have any return types including void. Moreover, they cannot be inherited; however, a derived-class constructor can call the base class constructor. Program 15.1 is rewritten as Program 15.2 to illustrate the use of constructors.

```
// Program 15.2
// A program to demonstrate constructors
#include<iostream>
using namespace std;

class day
{
    public:
        int date,month,year;
        day()
        {
            date = 1;
            month = 1;
            year = 2018;
        }
};

int main()
{
        day TODAY;
        cout << "Date is   :"  << TODAY.date   << endl;
        cout << "Month is  :"  << TODAY.month  << endl;
        cout << "Year is   :"  << TODAY.year   << endl;
        return 0;
}
```

The result of Program 15.2 is shown below:

```
Date is:1
Month is:1
Year is:2018
```

Here the day() is a constructor in day class. Whenever TODAY object is created, the constructor is automatically called and data members are initialized.

15.2 Default constructors

In C++, a constructor with no parameters is called a **default** constructor. Moreover, if no constructor is defined, the C++ compiler will include a default constructor. Program 15.3 illustrates this, as it makes no difference whether we include student(){} constructor within the program or not.

```
// Program 15.3
// Default constructor, Example 1
#include<iostream>
```

```
using namespace std;

class student
{
    public:
        int marks;
        student()
        {

        }
};

int main()
{
    student JACK;
    return 0;
}
```

Program 15.4 illustrates another default constructor; however, there are two state-ments inside the constructor's body in this program.

```
// Program 15.4
// Default constructor, Example 2

#include<iostream>
using namespace std;

class student
{
    public:
        int marks;
        student()
        {
            marks = 90;
            cout << "Default Constructor :"  << marks  << endl;
        }
};

int main()
{
    student JACK, JILL;
    return 0;
}
```

The result of Program 15.4 is shown below:

```
        Default Constructor :90
        Default Constructor :90
```

Notice that a default constructor has no parameters. In the previous example, student() is a default constructor without any parameters. A default constructor is called immediately after memory allocation and initialization of objects.

15.3 Constructors with parameters

In Program 15.4, we have noticed that a default constructor initializes the data members. It is the same for multiple objects of same class. Here, both JACK and JILL objects use the marks variable with value equals to 90. In practice, it may be necessary to initialize different objects of same class with different values. In such applications, we make use of constructors with parameters when it is possible to pass different values to members of different objects of same class. Program 15.5 illustrates the use of constructors with parameters. JACK and JILL are two objects of class student. JACK object is created with 89 as an argument to constructor student (int m), whereas JILL object is created with value 90. Different objects in the program are created with different arguments to constructor.

```cpp
// Program 15.5
// Constructor with Parameters
#include<iostream>
using namespace std;

class student
{
    public:
        int marks;
        student(int m)
        {
            marks = m;
            cout  << "Constructor :"  << marks  << endl;
        }
};

int main()
{
    student JACK(89),JILL(90);
    return 0;
}
```

The result of Program 15.5 is shown below:

```
Constructor:  89
Constructor:  90
```

In Program 15.5, the constructor is as follows:

```
student(int m)
{
    marks = m;
    cout  << "Constructor :"  << marks  << endl;
}
```

Notice that once the previous constructor is defined, we will not be allowed to create a student object as follows:

```
student JACK;
```

It is not possible to do so because no matching constructor is defined for the class. However, it is possible to define multiple constructors for a class, so that the programmer can create a new instance of the class in different ways. In the next section, we will study about multiple constructors of same class. Similarly, we can rewrite the code for parameterized constructor (Program 15.5) as shown in Program 15.6:

```
// Program 15.6
// Constructor with Parameters
// Constructor definition is outside of the class definition
#include<iostream>
using namespace std;

class student
{
    public:
        int marks;
        student(int m);
};

student::student(int m)
{
    marks = m;
    cout  << "Constructor :"  << marks  << endl;
}

int main()
{
    student JACK(89),JILL(90);
    return 0;
}
```

Program 15.6 also generates the same result as Program 15.5. Please note that the parameterized constructor also provides a new mechanism to initialize the fields. Program 15.7 also generates the same result.

```
// Program 15.7
// Constructor with Parameters
// Constructor definition with initialization
#include<iostream>
using namespace std;

class student
{
    public:
        int marks;
        student(int m);
};

student::student(int m): marks(m)
{
    cout  << "Constructor :"  << marks  << endl;
}

int main()
{
    student JACK(89),JILL(90);
    return 0;
}
```

In this program, the following constructor of Program 15.6:

```
student::student(int m)
{
    marks = m;
    cout  << "Constructor :"  << marks  << endl;
}
```

is modified as follows, where colon (:) is used for initializing the marks variable with m.

```
student::student(int m): marks(m)
{
    cout  << "Constructor :"  << marks  << endl;
}
```

Program 15.8 shows the initialization of multiple members along with constructor definition. In this program, the traditional way of initializing multiple members, that is,

```
student::student(int a,int m, char g)
{
```

```
        age = a;
        marks = m;
        grade = g;
        cout << "Age:"  << age  << endl;
        cout << "Marks:"  << marks  << endl;
        cout << "Grade:"  << grade  << endl;
}
```

is changed as follows:

```
student::student(int a,int m, char g):age(a),marks(m),grade(g)
{
        cout << "Age:"  << age  << endl;
        cout << "Marks:"  << marks  << endl;
        cout << "Grade:"  << grade  << endl;
}
```

The complete Program 15.8 is as follows:

```
// Program 15.8
// Constructor with Parameters
// Constructor definition with multiple initializations
#include<iostream>
using namespace std;

class student
{
    public:
        int age;
        int marks;
        char grade;
        student(int a,int m, char g);
};

student::student(int a, int m, char g):age(a),marks(m),grade(g)
{
        cout << "Age:"  << age  << endl;
        cout << "Marks:"  << marks  << endl;
        cout << "Grade:"  << grade  << endl;
}

int main()
{
        student JACK(20,70,'B'),JILL(19,90,'A');
        return 0;
}
```

The result of Program 15.8 is shown below:

```
Age:20
Marks:70
Grade:B
Age:19
Marks:90
Grade:A
```

15.4 Multiple constructors

In Program 15.5, we have seen that the two objects JACK and JILL created with integer form an argument to the constructor. In practice, it may be necessary to use many constructors in same class with different data types as arguments to constructor. C++ supports declaration of multiple constructors in the same class. This is quite useful while dealing with several members of different data types. For example, if we want the programmers to create a new instance either as:

```
student JACK;
or
student JACK(89);
```

Hence, we can simply define two constructors for the same class. There will be no problems in defining multiple constructors, as shown in Program 15.9, as long as the constructors defined for a class have either of the two: different number of parameters or different data types for the parameters, in case the number of parameters is the same.

```
// Program 15.9
// Multiple Constructors
#include<iostream>
using namespace std;

class student
{
    public:
        int marks;
        char grade;

        student()
        {
            marks = 0;
            cout  << "Default Constructor :"  << marks  << endl;
        }
}
```

```
        student(int m)
        {
            marks = m;
            cout  << "Constructor with One Parameter :"
                    << marks  << endl;
        }
        student(int m,char g)
        {
            marks = m;
            grade = g;
            cout  << "Constructor with Two Parameters :"
                    << marks  << " "  << grade  << endl;
        }
};

int main()
{
    student JACK,JILL(89),JOHN(90,'A');
    return 0;
}
```

The result of Program 15.9 is shown below:

```
        Default Constructor        :0
        Constructor with One Parameter   :89
        Constructor with Two Parameters :90 A
```

The main purpose of a constructor is to initialize an object. To achieve this, we have to define a constructor in a class and initialize the data members in the method body of the constructor.

15.5 Copy constructor

In C++, there is special kind of constructor that is called copy constructor. It is used where a constructor can accept a reference to its own class as a parameter. In other words, a copy constructor is one that initializes an object by using the values of another object passed to it as a parameter. The main purpose of a copy constructor is to declare and initialize an object from another object. Program 15.10 shows an example of the copy constructor.

```
// Program 15.10
// Program to demonstrate Copy Constructor
#include<iostream>
using namespace std;
class student
```

```
{
    public:
        int marks; char grade;

        student(int m, char g)
        {
            marks = m;
            grade = g;
        }

        student (student &x)
        {
            marks = x.marks;
            grade = x.grade;
        }
        void displayResults(void)
        {
            cout  << "Marks= "  << marks  << endl;
            cout  << "Grade= "  << grade  << endl;
        }
};

int main()
{
    student JACK(90,'A'); // Object creation and initialization
    student JILL(JACK);   // Calling copy constructor
    JACK.displayResults();
    JILL.displayResults();
    return 0;
}
```

In this example, initially an object named JACK is created with values 90 and 'A'. These values are initialized to marks and grade, respectively, through parameterized constructor of object JACK. The statement student JILL(JACK); makes a copy of these values and assigns to another object named JILL through copy constructor. After the program is executed, values of marks and grade in both the objects are same. This can be verified by calling displayResults() of JACK and JILL objects.

The result of Program 15.10 is shown below:

```
Marks= 90
Grade= A
Marks= 90
Grade= A
```

We can also call the copy constructor by using assignment operator instead of student JILL(JACK); as follows:

```
student JILL = JACK;
```

15.6 Destructors

A **destructor** is a special member function that is used to destroy the objects that have been created by a constructor. A destructor will have the exact same name as the class prefixed with a tilde (~) and it can neither return a value nor take any parameters. For example, the destructor for class student can be defined as shown below:

```
~student () {}
```

Destructors are useful for releasing resources such as memory by the compiler upon exit from the program to clean up the storage that is no longer accessible. This makes the released memory available so that it can be used by other programs in future. A destructor is invoked when an object's scope is over. Program 15.11 shows an example of a destructor with a constructor and other member functions, all of which are defined inside class definitions.

```cpp
// Program 15.11
// Program to demonstrate Destructors
#include<iostream>
using namespace std;

class student
{
    public:
        int marks;
        char grade;

        // Parameterized Constructor
        student(int m, char g)
        {
            cout << "The Constructor is called "  << endl;
            cout << "The Object is being created"  << endl;
            marks = m;
            grade = g;
            cout << endl;
        }

        // Member Function
        void displayResults(void)
        {
            cout << "The Member Function is called "  << endl;
            cout << "Marks= "  << marks  << endl;
            cout << "Grade= "  << grade  << endl;
            cout << endl;
        }
```

```
        // Destructor declaration and definition
        ~student()
        {
            cout  << "The Destructor is called "  << endl;
            cout  << "The Object is being deleted"  << endl;
        }
};

int main()
{
    student JACK(90,'A'); // Object creation and initialization
    JACK.displayResults();
    return 0;
}
```

The result of Program 15.11 is shown below:

```
    The Constructor is called
    The Object is being created

    The Member Function is called
    Marks= 90

    Grade= A
    The Destructor is called
    The Object is being deleted
```

15.7 Review questions

1. What is a constructor? Explain with the help of a program.
2. Describe the special features of constructors.
3. What is a default constructor? How it is different from constructors with parameters.
4. Describe the meaning of parameterized constructors with an example program.
5. Describe the meaning of a copy constructor with an example program.
6. Describe the meaning of a destructor with an example program.
7. Can constructors be public or private? Discuss with an example.

16 Inheritance

> A finger points at the moon, but the moon is not at the tip of the finger.
>   Words points at the truth, but the truth is not in words.
> – Huineng

16.1 Introduction

Inheritance is a very important feature in object-oriented programming. It plays a major role in writing large programs. Inheritance property is highly required when we deal with many similar classes with minor changes. It enables us to define a new class based on an existing class definition, for example, if book is a class, then notebook is a subclass. This means that many characteristics of notebook are derived from book, such as size, pages, cover, and so forth. With inheritance we can implement an **is-a** relationship. For example, notebook **is a** book, textbook **is a** book, and so forth. Here, we call the class book as a **parent** class (or **super** class or **base** class) and the class notebook as **child** class (or **subclass** or **derived** class).

Fig. 16.1 shows the concept of inheritance. Here, we create or derive a new class similar to that of the existing class, but it will have some new characteristics. This is very useful when we are making modifications to an existing program. For example, Program A needs some modifications to be changed to Program B, a new program. In such cases, instead of developing Program B from scratch, we can derive the existing features from Program A. This makes the programming task very easier. The main advantage of inheritance is **code reuse**. In this chapter, we will study the use of inheritance and its importance in programming.

16.2 Single inheritance

As discussed in the Section 16.1, the class that is used to create a new class is called a parent class (or super class or base class), and the class that is derived from a base class is called child class (or subclass or derived class). In single inheritance, a derived class is inherited from a single base class, as shown in Fig. 16.1. C++ also allows a subclass to inherit from multiple base classes. This is called **multiple inheritance**. This means that a derived class can inherit data and functions from multiple classes. However, Java, another popular OOP language, does not support multiple inheritance.

A child class is almost like a parent class with some added features. To create a child class, we should first create a parent class. Remember that the **inheritance is between classes and not between objects**. It is not possible to inherit features from one object to another. Hence, we apply all the inheritance principles only to classes,

https://doi.org/10.1515/9783110593846-016

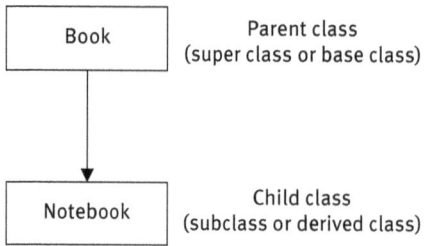

Fig. 16.1: Inheritance in book object.

and not to objects. Please note that in this Chapter we will make use of terms base class and subclass for our convenience.

To create a **subclass** from an existing base class, we make use of colon (:) in the definition of subclass as follows:

```
class subclass-name: access-specifier baseclass-name
{
    // members of child class
    // new features of child class
};
```

As shown previously, the access specifier is public, private, or protected. The base-class-name is the name of the previously defined class, and subclass-name is the new class derived from base class or base classes. If the access specifier is omitted, it is private by default. The access specifier decides whether the features of the class are derived privately or publicly. To derive features from more than one class, we can use comma in between base classes. For example, the following format shows the ways of deriving a subclass from two base classes, baseclass-name1 and baseclass-name2.

```
class subclass-name: access-specifier baseclass-name1, access-specifier baseclass-
name2
{
    // members of child class
    // new features of child class
};
```

Program 16.1 illustrates the concept of inheritance. It shows two classes: baseclass and subclass. The baseclass has one method, and subclass is derived from base-class. When we derive a baseclass, the subclass inherits all the methods and variables. Note that private variables and data are not inherited to subclass. Hence, it is possible to call the base method of baseclass by using an object of type subclass, since the subclass is derived from baseclass.

```
// Program 16.1
// A program to understand single inheritance
// Example for public inheritance
#include<iostream>
using namespace std;

class baseclass
{
    public:
        void basemethod()
        {
            cout << "Base class " << endl;
        }
};
class subclass: public baseclass
{
    public:
        void submethod()
        {
            cout << "Sub Class " << endl ;
        }
};

int main()
{
    baseclass base ;
    base.basemethod();
    subclass sub ;
    sub.basemethod();
    sub.submethod();
    return 0;
}
```

The result of Program 16.1 is shown below:

```
Base class
Base class
Sub Class
```

This is also an example of public inheritance, because the definition of subclass includes public access modifier preceding the baseclass. In public inheritance, public members of the base class become public members of the derived class. However, in case of private inheritance, public members of the base class become private members of the derived class. In such cases, these members are only accessed by the member functions of the derived class. Program 16.2 is an example for private inheritance. In this case, it is not possible to use sub.basemethod(); statement in main(), because the basemethod() becomes private in subclass, so it cannot be in objects of type subclass.

```
// Program 16.2
// A program to understand single inheritance
// Example for private inheritance
#include<iostream>
using namespace std;

class baseclass
{
    public:
        void basemethod()
        {
            cout << "Base class " << endl;
        }
};

class subclass: private baseclass
{
    public:
        void submethod()
        {
            cout << "Sub Class " << endl ;
        }
};

int main()
{
    baseclass base ;
    base.basemethod();
    subclass sub ;
    // sub.basemethod(); is not possible because it is private
    sub.submethod();
    return 0;
}
```

The result of Program 16.2 is shown below:

```
Base class
Sub Class
```

In addition, it is possible to derive many subclasses from a single base class. As we explained in Fig 16.1, notebook is a subclass of book. In the similar way, textbook is also a subclass of book. Hence, many subclasses can be derived from a base class as shown in Fig. 16.2.

Program 16.3 demonstrates the use of multiple subclasses.

```
// Program 16.3
// A program with multiple derived classes
#include<iostream>
```

```cpp
using namespace std;

class baseclass
{
    public:
        void basemethod()
        {
            cout << "Base Class " << endl;
        }
};
class subclass1: public baseclass
{
    public:
        void submethod()
        {
            cout << "Sub Class 1" << endl;
        }
};
class subclass2: public baseclass
{
    public:
        void submethod()
        {
            cout << "Sub Class 2" << endl ;
        }
};
int main()
{
    baseclass base;
    base.basemethod();
    subclass1 sub1;
    sub1.basemethod();
    sub1.submethod();
    subclass2 sub2;
    sub2.basemethod();
    sub2.submethod();
    return 0;
}
```

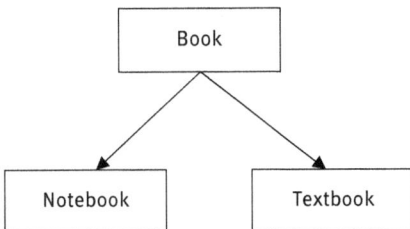

Fig. 16.2: Multiple subclasses.

The result of Program 16.3 is shown below:

```
Base Class
Base Class
Sub Class 1
Base Class
Sub Class 2
```

16.3 Multiple inheritance

In this section, we will study another kind of inheritance called multiple inheritance. In multiple inheritance, a subclass can be derived from multiple base classes. For example, a student may use his notebook that he has written during class, and read a textbook from library. After some studying, he may write a study book only for exam preparation, as shown in Fig. 16.3. In this example, the study book is derived from note book as well as textbook. Program 16.4 shows one such example of multiple inheritance. In the recent years, the idea of multiple inheritance is a very controversial topic, but it is still widely used in C++ programming. The main advantage of multiple inheritance is that the derived class has the benefits of inheriting different methods from different classes and combining these features to make it as an interesting class.

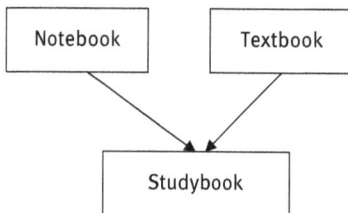

Fig. 16.3: Multiple inheritance example.

```
// Program 16.4
// Multiple Inheritance Example
#include<iostream>
using namespace std;

class notebook
{
    public:
        void notebookmethod()
        {
            cout << "Base Class: Note Book " << endl;
        }
};
```

```
class textbook
{
    public:
        void textbookmethod()
        {
            cout << "Base Class: Text Book " <<endl;
        }
};
class studybook: public notebook,public textbook
{
    public:
        void submethod()
        {
            cout << "Sub Class:  Study Book" << endl ;
        }
};

int main()
{
    notebook NB;
    textbook TB;
    studybook SB;
    NB.notebookmethod();
    TB.textbookmethod();
    SB.notebookmethod();
    SB.textbookmethod();
    SB.submethod();
    return 0;
}
```

The result of Program 16.4 is shown below:

```
Base Class: Note Book
Base Class: Text Book
Base Class: Note Book
Base Class: Text Book
Sub Class: Study Book
```

As the inheritance is public, the subclass studybook can access the methods of base classes notebook and textbook.

16.4 Multilevel inheritance

In Fig. 16.1, we have seen that notebook is derived from book. Here notebook is subclass and book is base class. In the similar way, science notebook is a class that may be derived from notebook (not from book!). Here science notebook is a derived class of notebook, and in this case notebook is the base class and science notebook is the subclass; Fig. 16.4 shows this.

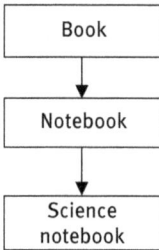

Book

Notebook

Science
notebook

Fig. 16.4: Inheritance extended to more than one level.

Program 16.5 illustrates the previous explanation. In this program, there are three classes, namely, baseclass, subclass, and lastclass. The subclass is derived from the baseclass and the lastclass is derived from the baseclass. Here we will see that lastclass includes all the two methods of its ancestors along with lastmethod(). Notice that subclass includes all methods and variables of its ancestor classes (except private members).

```cpp
// Program 16.5
// Example of Multilevel Inheritance
#include<iostream>
using namespace std;

class baseclass
{
    public:
        void basemethod()
        {
            cout << "Base Class " << endl;
        }
};
class subclass:public baseclass
{
    public:
        void submethod()
        {
            cout << "Sub Class of Base Class" << endl ;
        }
};
class lastclass:public subclass{
    public:
        void lastmethod()
        {
            cout << "Derived Class from Sub Class" << endl ;
        }
};

int main()
```

```
{
    baseclass base;
    base.basemethod();
    subclass sub;
    sub.basemethod();
    sub.submethod();
    lastclass last;
    last.basemethod();
    last.submethod();
    last.lastmethod();
    return 0;
}
```

The result of Program 16.5 is shown below:

```
Base Class
Base Class
Sub Class of Base Class
Base Class
Sub Class of Base Class
Derived Class from Sub Class
```

A subclass inherits variables and methods from its **superclass** and all of its ancestors, as Program 16.5 shows. Subclasses inherit those base class members declared as public or protected. (We will see protected keyword in next section.)

16.5 The protected keyword

As we studied in earlier sections, the private data or method cannot be inherited to subclasses, as it is accessible in the same class only. But, if we make the data or methods public, then they can be accessible everywhere. This is a typical problem we face when we deal with inheritance. In practice, a base class may want to inherit only some of its data and members to its subclasses, and not to other classes. In such cases, we make use of protected keyword. This keyword is an access specifier for data and members of a class. If we make a data or method protected, then it is visible only inside the same class, and in any subclass. In summary, when we derive from a protected base class, public and protected members of the base class become protected members of the derived class.

The example to understand protected data members is presented in Program 16.6. The subclass is derived from baseclass. The baseclass has three data and one basemethod(). The subclass is derived from baseclass and only data member a (int a), b (int b), and basemethod() can be derived to subclass. Remember that we cannot make use of c (int c) outside of baseclass, since it has a private access. In the main() method, we can access only a (int a) because it is declared public.

```
// Program 16.6
// Program with protected data members
#include<iostream>
using namespace std;

class baseclass
{
    public:
        int a;
    protected:
        int b;
    private:
        int c;
    public:
        void basemethod()
        {
            a = 20,b = 30,c = 40;
            cout << "Base Class" << endl;
            cout << a << endl;
            cout << b << endl;
            cout << c << endl;
        }
};
class subclass: public baseclass
{
    public:
        void submethod()
        {
            cout << "Sub Class" << endl;
            cout << a << endl;
            cout << b << endl;
            // cout<< c << endl; //Not possible, c is private
        }
};

int main()
{
    baseclass base;
    subclass sub;
    base.basemethod();
    sub.basemethod();
    sub.submethod();
    cout<< "MAIN FUNCTION" << endl;
    cout<< base.a <<endl;
    // cout<< base.b << endl; // Not possible, b is protected
    // cout<< base.c << endl; // Not possible, c is private
    cout << sub.a << endl;
    // cout<< sub.b << endl;  // Not possible, b is protected
    // cout<< sub.c << endl;  // Not possible, c is private
```

```
    return 0;
}
```

The result of Program 16.6 is shown below:

```
Base Class
20
30
40
Base Class
20
30
40
Sub Class
20
30
MAIN FUNCTION
20
20
```

In summary, a derived class can access all the members of a base class except those that are private. Hence, any private member of a class is not accessible outside of that class. Table 16.1 summarizes the visibility of access modifiers in C++.

Table 16.1: Inheritance and access control

Access	Default (No Access Specifier)	private	protected	public
Accessible inside the class	Yes	Yes	Yes	Yes
Accessible in derived classes	No	No	Yes	Yes
Accessible outside of classes	No	No	No	Yes

16.6 Overriding data and methods

As we have discussed earlier, a subclass can inherit methods and variables from base class and add its own code to it. What if the name of base class variables and methods is same as subclass variables and methods? In such cases subclasses do not inherit the member variables and methods of the base class. The member variables and methods in subclass override (hides) member variables and methods of base class. This is called **overriding**. A subclass method can completely rewrite the inherited base methods or add a new code to it. Remember that overridden methods must have the same name, argument list, and return type.

Program 16.7 illustrates overriding. The value is a member variable in baseclass, and fun() is a member method. In the same way, we have similar method and

variable with same name in subclass. The fun() and value of baseclass are overridden by the fun() and value of the subclass.

```cpp
// Program 16.7
// Program to Demonstrate Overriding
#include<iostream>
using namespace std;

class baseclass
{
    public:
        int value;
        void fun()
        {
            value = 10;
            cout << "Base Class :" << value << endl;
        }
};
class subclass:public baseclass
{
    public:
        int value;
        void fun()
        {
            value = 100;
            cout << "Sub Class :" << value << endl;
        }
};
int main()
{
    baseclass base;
    subclass sub;
    base.fun();
    sub.fun();
    return 0;
}
```

The result of Program 16.7 is shown below:

```
Base Class:10
Sub Class:100
```

16.7 Constructors and inheritance

We are aware that subclass methods and variables can be inherited from base class.
What about constructors? In this section, we will understand the relationship

between constructors and inheritance case by case. Initially, we will consider a case where the base classes include a constructor, but derived class does not. Program 16.8 shows this kind of example.

```
// Program 16.8
// Constructor and Inheritance
// Example1
#include<iostream>
using namespace std;

class baseclass
{
    public:
        baseclass()
        {
            cout << "Base Class Constructor" << endl;
        }
};
class subclass: public baseclass
{
};
int main()
{
    baseclass base;
    subclass sub;
    return 0;
}
```

The result of Program 16.8 is shown below:

```
        Base Class Constructor
        Base Class Constructor
```

This shows that base class constructor is inherited to subclass, and is invoked during the creation of objects of both base class and subclass. Program 16.9 shows another scenario, where both base class and subclass include constructors.

```
// Program 16.9
// Constructor and Inheritance
// Example2
#include<iostream>
using namespace std;

class baseclass
{
    public:
        baseclass()
```

```
        {
                cout << "Base Class Constructor" << endl;
        }
};
class subclass:public baseclass
{
    public:
        subclass()
        {
                cout<< "Sub Class Constructor" << endl;
        }
};
int main()
{
    baseclass base;
    subclass sub;
    return 0;
}
```

The result of Program 16.9 is shown below:

```
        Base Class Constructor
        Base Class Constructor
        Sub Class Constructor
```

This is because the subclass also inherits the base class constructor, and the base class constructor is executed first as compared to the subclass constructor during the creation of subclass object. This means, the order of execution is hierarchical. Program 16.10 shows an example, where two base classes include constructor, and one subclass is derived from these two base classes.

```
// Program 16.10
// Constructor and Inheritance
// Example3
#include<iostream>
using namespace std;

class baseclass_1
{
    public:
        baseclass_1()
        {
                cout << "Base Class 1: Constructor" << endl;
        }
};
class baseclass_2
{
```

```
    public:
        baseclass_2()
        {
            cout << "Base Class 2: Constructor" << endl;
        }
};
class subclass: public baseclass_1, public baseclass_2
{
    public:
        subclass()
        {
            cout << "Sub Class Constructor" << endl;
        }
};
int main()
{
    subclass sub;
    return 0;
}
```

The result of Program 16.10 is shown below:

```
    Base Class 1: Constructor
    Base Class 2: Constructor
    Sub Class Constructor
```

The results clearly show the order of execution. Similarly, Program 16.11 shows another example of multilevel inheritance and constructor.

```
// Number 16.11
// Constructor and Inheritance
// Example4
#include<iostream>
using namespace std;

class baseclass
{
    public:
        baseclass()
        {
            cout << "Base Class: Constructor" << endl;
        }
};
class subclass:public baseclass
{
    public:
        subclass()
        {
```

```
                cout << "Sub Class: Constructor" << endl;
        }
};
class lastclass:public subclass
{
    public:
        lastclass()
        {
                cout << "Last Class: Constructor" << endl;
        }
};
int main()
{
    baseclass base;
    subclass sub;
    lastclass last;
    return 0;
}
```

The result of Program 16.11 is shown below:

```
    Base Class: Constructor
    Base Class: Constructor
    Sub Class: Constructor
    Base Class: Constructor
    Sub Class: Constructor
    Last Class: Constructor
```

16.8 Review questions

1. What is inheritance? List the advantages of inheritance in software development.
2. What is single inheritance? How it is different from multiple inheritance?
3. What is multiple inheritance? Describe with an example program.
4. What is multilevel inheritance? Describe with an example program.
5. What is use of protected keyword in C++? Compare its advantages and disadvantages over public and private access modifiers.
6. Explain overriding with an example. How is overriding different from overloading (see Chapter 14)?
7. Write a note on constructors and inheritance with an example program.
8. Summarize of role of access modifiers in inheritance.

17 Polymorphism

> The world is like a great empty dream. Why should one toil away one's life?
> – Li Bai

17.1 Introduction

Polymorphism is one of the most essential features of an object-oriented programming. It makes writing programs simpler and reusable. **Polymorphism** means many forms (or many faces). For example, a person may be a father at home, an officer in the office, or a customer in a restaurant. Here, father, officer, and customer all refer to the same person. There are two kinds of polymorphism: **compile-time** polymorphism (or **static** polymorphism) and **run-time** polymorphism (or **dynamic** polymorphism). Typically, polymorphism occurs when there is a hierarchy of classes and they are related by inheritance. C++ polymorphism means that a call to a member function will cause a different function to be executed depending on the type of object that invokes the function. Fig. 17.1 shows the types of polymorphism. In this chapter, we will cover all these types with at least one example each.

17.2 Static polymorphism

Static polymorphism is also called compile-time polymorphism. There are two categories of static polymorphism: function overloading and operator overloading, as shown in Fig. 17.1. It is an **early binding** polymorphism, where memory will be allocated during compile time. The binding of functions is based on the number of arguments, data type, and sequence of arguments. During the program execution, the calls are already fixed to suitable functions. For example, let us consider these two statements.

```
void add(float ,  float);
void add(int ,  float);
```

When the add() function is invoked, the types of parameters already decide during compile time that which version of the function code will be executed.

Function overloading

In C++, an overloaded function is a function with same function name, but with different signature in the same scope. A function signature includes the number of arguments,

https://doi.org/10.1515/9783110593846-017

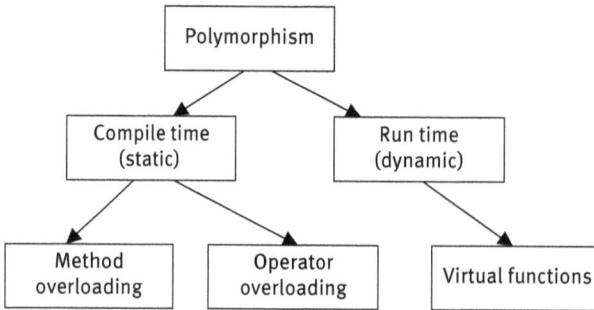

Fig. 17.1: Types of polymorphism.

type of arguments, and sequence of arguments. This means that the function definitions are different from each other by the data types and number of arguments in the argument list. When we call an overloaded function, the compiler will automatically determine most suitable function for execution. Program 17.1 shows an example of function overloading. In this program, the function add() is overloaded with different parameters for five times.

```cpp
// Program 17.1
// Example Program of Function Overloading
#include<iostream>
using namespace std;

class addNumbers
{
    public:
        void add(int a, int b)
        {
            cout << "Adding two integers, Result = " << a+b << endl;
        }
        void add(int a, int b, int c)
        {
            cout << "Adding three integers, Result = "
                << a+b+c << endl;
        }
        void add(float a,  float b)
        {
            cout << "Adding two floating point numbers, Result = "
                << a+b << endl;
        }
        void add(int a, float b)
        {
            cout << "Adding one integer and a floating point number, Result = "
                << a+b << endl;
        }
}
```

```
        void add(float a, float b, float c)
        {
            cout << "Adding three floating point numbers, Result = "
                    << a+b+c << endl;
        }
};

int main()
{
    addNumbers ADDTEST;
    ADDTEST.add(1,2);
    ADDTEST.add(1,2,3);
    ADDTEST.add(2.2f,3.1f);
    ADDTEST.add(2,3.14f);
    ADDTEST.add(1.5f,2.5f,6.4f);
    return 0;
}
```

The result of Program 17.1 is shown below:

```
    Adding two integers, Result = 3
    Adding three integers, Result = 6
    Adding two floating point numbers, Result = 5.3
    Adding one integer and a floating point number, Result = 5.14
    Adding three floating point numbers, Result = 10.4
```

Function overriding

Function overriding is another feature where functions share the same name during inheritance. In function overriding, a subclass function overrides the base class function, because they both have the function with same name and signature. This means that the base class function and subclass function have the same name, same parameter list, and same return type. Program 17.2 shows an example of function overriding.

```
// Program 17.2
// Example Program of Function Overriding
#include<iostream>
using namespace std;

class baseclass
{
    public:
        void  fname()
        {
```

```
                cout << "Base Class Function" << endl;
        }
};
class subclass: public baseclass
{
    public:
        void fname()
        {
                cout << "Sub Class Function" << endl;
        }
};

int main ()
{
    subclass SUB;
    SUB.fname();
    return 0;
}
```

Program 17.3 shows another example for function overriding, where the subclass overrides the base class function, but it uses the data member from base class (in this case it is variable y).

```
// Program 17.3
// Example Program of Function Overriding
#include<iostream>
using namespace std;

class baseclass
{
    public:
        int x,y;
        void getxy()
        {
            x = 10;
            y = 20;
        }

        void  add()
        {
            cout << "Base Class, Result = " << x+y << endl;
        }
};

class subclass: public baseclass
{
    public:
        void setx()
```

```
        {
            x = 30;
        }

        void add()
        {
            cout << "Subclass, Result = " << x+y << endl;
        }
};

int main()
{
    baseclass BASE;
    subclass SUB;
    BASE.getxy();
    BASE.add();
    SUB.getxy();
    SUB.setx();
    SUB.add();
    return 0;
}
```

The result of Program 17.3 is shown below:

```
        Base Class, Result = 30
        Subclass, Result = 50
```

Operator overloading

Operator overloading is another interesting feature of C++, which provide extending features for unary and binary operators. This means, various operators such as +, *, <=, +=, and so forth can be used not just with numbers but also with additional features. For example, if we want to write a program to find the sum of two linear equations (for example, EqA = $6x + 7y$, and EqB = $2x + 5y$), and to produce another linear equation (EqC = $8x + 12y$), then it is possible by using operator overloading to write a program, which looks like, EqC =EqA + EqB, by overloading operator "+." Similarly, by overloading "−" operator, we can also calculate EqD = EqA − EqB. Hence, the concept of providing additional meaning to C++ operators is called operator over-loading. The keyword **operator** is used for the symbol of the operator while writing overloaded operator functions. These overloaded functions are similar to normal func-tions, and also include return type and parameter list. Program 17.4 shows an example of operator overloading, where both addition (+) and subtraction (−) binary operators are overloaded to add two simple linear equations. In this case, Equation A = $6x + 7y$, and Equation B = $2x + 5y$. The Equations C and D represent the results after addition and subtraction, respectively.

```
// Program 17.4
// Example Program of Operator Overriding
#include<iostream>
using namespace std;

class Equation
{
    int coefx;      // coefficient of x
    int coefy;      // coefficient of Y
    public:
        Equation(){}  // constructor 1
        Equation(int cx, int cy)  // constructor 2
        {
            coefx = cx;
            coefy = cy;
        }

        Equation operator+(Equation);
        Equation operator-(Equation);
        void printResult(void);
};

// overloading + operator
Equation Equation :: operator+(Equation B)
{
    Equation temp;
    temp.coefx = coefx + B.coefx;
    temp.coefy = coefy + B.coefy;
    return (temp);
}

// overloading - operator
Equation Equation :: operator-(Equation B)
{
    Equation temp;
    temp.coefx = coefx - B.coefx;
    temp.coefy = coefy - B.coefy;
    return (temp);
}

void Equation::printResult(void)
{
    cout<< coefx << "x + " << coefy << "y" << endl;
}

// main function for the program
int main()
{
    Equation EqA(6,7); // A=6x+7y
```

```
    Equation EqB(2,5); // B=2x+5y
    Equation EqC,EqD;

    cout << "Equation A = ";
    EqA.printResult();
    cout << "Equation B = ";
    EqB.printResult();
    EqC = EqA + EqB;        //Adding two equations
    cout << "Equation C = ";
    EqC.printResult();
    EqD = EqA - EqB;        //Subtracting two equations
    cout << "Equation D = ";
    EqD.printResult();
    return 0;
}
```

The result of Program 17.4 is shown below:

```
    Equation A = 6x + 7y
    Equation B = 2x + 5y
    Equation C = 8x + 12y
    Equation D = 4x + 2y
```

17.3 Dynamic polymorphism

As we mentioned earlier, another type of polymorphism is called dynamic polymorphism or run-time polymorphism. As the name suggests, the dynamic aspect of resolution makes it different from static polymorphism. For example, in dynamic polymorphism, a function that exists in multiple forms is executed dynamically by calling appropriate calls during runtime. That means, the resolution that which function call is going to execute a particular instance is decided during program execution. That is why the dynamic polymorphism is called late-binding polymorphism, because function resolution happens at runtime, rather than compile time, as in static polymorphism. This interesting feature provides a flexibility of executing a function depending on the context. Dynamic polymorphism is implemented by using virtual functions.

For example, in Chapter 16, we have discussed about book and notebook. Here notebook is a subclass derived from base class book. It is also clear that notebook is also a book. So in C++, it is possible to make instance of subclass object as a type of base class. Here is an example:

```
    class book
    {
```

```
    public:
        void printName()
        {
            cout << "This is a Book" << endl;
        }
};

class notebook:public book
{
    public:
        void printName()
        {
            cout << "This is a NoteBook" << endl;
        }
};
```

We have already studied that the following statements are true

```
book myBook ;
notebook myNoteBook;
```

However, consider the following statements.

```
book *mybook;           // base class pointer
notebook NTBK;          // derived class object
mybook = &NTBK;         // making base class pointer to hold
                        // derived class object
mybook->printName();    // early binding
```

In the previous statements, we are making the base class pointer (mybook) hold the address of derived class object (NTBK) of notebook class. This is possible because notebook object is a type of book, moreover notebook class is derived from book. In summary, an object can be used as its own type or as an object of its base type. In Program 17.5, both superclass book and subclass notebook contain the same function printName() with same signature. So, when subclass object is used to call printName () function in subclass notebook, this leads to the execution of overriding the function in super class book.

```
// Program 17.5
// A program to understand polymorphism
#include<iostream>
using namespace std;

class book
{
```

```
    public:
        void printName()
        {
            cout << "This is a Book" << endl;
        }
};

class notebook: public book
{
    public:
        void printName()
        {
            cout << "This is a NoteBook" << endl;
        }

};

int main()
{
    book *mybook;
    notebook NTBK;
    mybook = &NTBK;
    mybook->printName();
    return 0;
}
```

However, when we run the program, the result is as shown below.

```
        This is a Book
```

We expected the result "This is a NoteBook" rather than the one shown previously. This is because the previous program still runs in the mode of early binding, rather than late binding. To make the program generate the expected output, we should make use of virtual functions. We can also test early binding in Program 17.6, another modified example.

```
// Program 17.6
// A program to understand polymorphism
#include<iostream>
using namespace std;

class book
{
    public:
        void printName()
```

```
        {
            cout << "This is a Book" << endl;
        }
};

class notebook: public book
{
    public:
        void printName()
        {
            cout << "This is a NoteBook" << endl;
        }
};

class textbook: public book
{
    public:
        void printName()
        {
            cout << "This is a TextBook" << endl;
        }
};

int main()
{
    book *mybook;
    notebook NTBK;
    mybook = &NTBK;
    mybook->printName();
    textbook TBK;
    mybook = &TBK;
    mybook->printName();
    return 0;
}
```

The result of Program 17.6 is shown below:

```
This is a Book
This is a Book
```

The user does not expect these results, because of early binding in both cases. The reason for the incorrect output is that the call of the function printName() is set once by the compiler as the version defined in the base class. This is called static resolution of the function call, or static linkage, that is, the function call is fixed before the program is executed. This is called **early binding** because the printName() function is set during the compilation of the program.

To solve this, we will make slight modification to Program 17.6, by adding virtual keyword preceding the declaration of printName() in the base class(book), as shown in Program 17.7.

```cpp
// Program 17.7
// A program to understand polymorphism
#include<iostream>
using namespace std;

class book
{
    public:
        virtual void printName()
        {
            cout << "This is a Book" << endl;
        }
};

class notebook:public book
{
    public:
        void printName()
        {
            cout << "This is a NoteBook" << endl;
        }
};

class textbook:public book
{
    public:
        void printName()
        {
            cout << "This is a TextBook" << endl;
        }
};

int main()
{
    book *mybook;
    notebook NTBK;
    mybook = &NTBK;
    mybook->printName();
    textbook TBK;
    mybook = &TBK;
    mybook->printName();
    return 0;
}
```

The result of Program 17.7 is shown below:

```
This is a NoteBook
This is a TextBook
```

Now, the results are as expected, because this time, the compiler looks at the contents of the pointer instead of its type. Hence, since addresses of objects of NTBK and TBK classes are stored in *book the respective printName() function is called. As we have seen in these examples, each of the child classes (notebook and textbook) has a separate implementation for the function printName(). This is how polymorphism is generally used. We have different classes with a function of the same name, and even the same parameters, but with different implementations.

A function in a base class becomes virtual function, if that is declared using the keyword virtual. If a base class function is defined as virtual, having similar implementation in derived class, then it guides the compiler that, we do not need static binding for this function. This dynamic linkage makes the selection of the function to be called at any given point in the program to be based on the kind of object for which it is called. This is also called **late binding**. A class which contains one or more virtual functions is known as a polymorphic class. This is also helpful to access the extra features of the derived class by making the base class pointer referring to a derived class object. The syntax for creating a virtual function is as follows:

```
virtual return-type function-  name(params-list)
{
    //Body of function
    ...
}
```

Program 17.8 demonstrates the ways of accessing derived class features by using virtual function.

```
// Program 17.8
// A program with Virtual Function
#include <iostream>
using namespace std;

class book
{
    protected:
        int Serial_No;
    public:
        virtual void Display()
        {
            cout << "Serial Number = " << Serial_No << endl;
        }
```

```
};

class textbook : public book
{
    protected:
        int Year;
    public:
        textbook(int Serial_No, int Year)
        {
            this->Serial_No = Serial_No;
            this->Year = Year;
        }
        void Display()
        {
            cout<< "Book Serial Number = " << Serial_No << endl;
            cout << "Book Year = " << Year << endl;
        }
};

int main()
{
    book *bptr;
    textbook objBook(30, 2016);
    bptr = &objBook;
    bptr->Display();
    return 0;
}
```

The result of Program 17.8 is shown below:

```
Book Serial Number = 30
Book Year = 2016
```

Although the programmers must be careful while using the virtual functions, there are several rules that must be remembered while working with virtual functions. Some of them are as follows: (a) virtual functions must be members of a class, (b) virtual functions must be created in public section so that objects can access them, (c) when a virtual function is defined outside the class, virtual keyword is required only in the function declaration, and not necessarily in the function definition, (d) virtual functions cannot be static members, (e) virtual functions must be accessed using a pointer to the object, (f) a virtual function cannot be declared as a friend of another class, (g) virtual functions must be defined in the base class even if they do not have any significance, (h) the signature of virtual function in base class and derived class must be the same, and (i) if a function is declared as virtual in the base class, it will be virtual in all its derived classes.

17.4 Pure virtual function and abstract classes

In Section 17.3, we have studied the role of virtual functions in polymorphism. As shown in Program 17.8, a virtual function Display() is defined in base class, but it is not actually used. This means that it is possible to include a virtual function in a base class, and redefine it in derived class to suit the objects of that class. It also means that we can make the virtual function that has no body or no meaningful definition in the base class. Such a virtual function is called **pure virtual function**.

A function can be made virtual by replacing the definition by =0 (an equal sign and a zero). For example, the following code shows a virtual function.

```
virtual void Display()
{
    cout << "Serial Number = " << Serial_No << endl;
}
```

The previous virtual function can be made pure by replacing its definition by =0, as shown below:

```
virtual void Display () = 0;
```

The =0 tells the compiler that the function has no body and the virtual function will be called pure virtual function. A class that contains at least one pure virtual function is considered an **abstract class**. Classes derived from an abstract class must implement the pure virtual function and too become abstract classes. Program 17.9 shows an example of implementation of a pure virtual function and abstract class.

```
// Program 17.9
// A Program with Pure Virtual Function
#include<iostream>
using namespace std;

class book
{
    protected:
        int Serial_No;
    public:
        virtual void Display() = 0;
};

class textbook : public book
{
    protected:
        int Year;
    public:
        textbook(int Serial_No, int Year)
```

```
        {
             this->Serial_No = Serial_No;
             this->Year = Year;
        }
        void Display()
        {
             cout<< "Book Serial Number = "<< Serial_No<< endl;
             cout<< "Book Year = "<< Year<< endl;
        }
 };
int main()
{
        book *bptr;
        textbook objBook(30, 2016);
        bptr = &objBook;
        bptr->Display();
        return 0;
}
```

The result of Program 17.9 is shown below:

```
    Book Serial Number = 30
    Book Year = 2016
```

The idea of abstract classes is to tell the users that all classes do not necessarily represent objects, because sometimes a class is insufficient to completely represent an object. Such classes are called as abstract classes. The abstract class does not fully represent an object, but it provides a partial description of objects. As these classes do not represent an object fully, they cannot be instantiated. This means that a statement shown below, in Program 17.9, can create an error.

```
    book BK;
```

To understand the reasons behind why abstract classes are not instantiated, we can take an example of a flower class. There are so many kinds of flower such as rose, jasmine, chrysanthemum, so on. We can create an instance of rose, however, we cannot create an instance of a flower! Because the term flower does not fully represent any flower. This shows that with abstract classes we can express general terms from which more specific classes are derived. As shown in Program 17.9, we cannot create an abstract class type, but we can use pointers and references to abstract class type.

17.5 Review questions

1. What is polymorphism? Explain with a program.
2. List the advantages of polymorphism in C++.

3. What is function overloading? Explain with an example program.
4. What is function overriding? Explain with an example program.
5. What is operator overloading? Explain with an example program.
6. List the differences between function overloading and function overriding.
7. List the difference between static polymorphism and dynamic polymorphism.
8. Which rules must be remembered while using virtual functions?
9. What is the difference between virtual function and pure virtual function?
10. Write a program to demonstrate pure virtual function.
11. Write a note on abstract classes in C++.

18 Templates

Success is not worth rejoicing over;
  Failure is not worth grieving over.
– Luo Guanzhong

18.1 Introduction

Templates are one of the most interesting features of C++, which enable the programmers to apply the concept of **generic programming**. Templates are a fundamental idea of generic programming, where one can write the code that is independent of any particular data type. In general, templates are a blueprint for creating a **generic class** or a **function**. In other words, we can use templates to define functions as well as classes. Basically there are two types of templates: class templates and function templates. Templates can be parameterized by types, compile-time constants, and other templates. In C++, the templates are implemented by instantiation at compile time.

To describe the use of templates, let us consider a situation where we want to define two functions with same name AddTwo() that can add two integers and double numbers. Their function definitions look as follows:

```
int AddTwo(int p,  int q)
{
    return p+q;
}
double AddTwo(double x,  double y)
{
    return x+y;
}
```

As we can see in previous two function codes, the only change is the data type. AddTwo() function uses integers as parameters, and returns an integer after adding two numbers. AddTwo() function uses double as parameters, and returns a double after adding two double numbers. Program 18.1 shows the entire code of using these functions effectively.

```
// Program 18.1
// A program without templates
#include<iostream>
using namespace std;

int AddTwo(int p,  int q)
{
```

https://doi.org/10.1515/9783110593846-018

```
      return p+q;
}

double AddTwo(double x,  double y)
{
      return x+y;
}

int main()
{
      int a = 10;
      int b = 20;
      cout << "AddTwo(a, b): " << AddTwo(a, b) << endl;
      double c = 10.5;
      double d = 20.6;
      cout << "AddTwo(c, d): " << AddTwo(c, d) << endl;
      return 0;
}
```

The result of Program 18.1 is as follows:

```
      AddTwo(a, b): 30
      AddTwo(c, d): 31.1
```

However, the kinds of programs such as Program 18.1 have their own shortcomings. We have to repeat the function code for different data types, that is, if we have to add numbers of different data types, such as long, short, float, and so forth, we have to repeat the code again and again. Templates play an important role to deal with these problems. Now, let us consider Program 18.2, showing an example of using templates in C++, accomplishing the same task as shown in Program 18.1.

```
// Program 18.2
// A program with templates
#include<iostream>
using namespace std;

template<typename T>

T AddTwo(T  x, T  y)
{
      return x+y;
}

int main()
{
      int a = 10;
```

```
    int b = 20;
    cout << "AddTwo(a, b): " << AddTwo(a, b) << endl;
    double c = 10.5;
    double d = 20.6;
    cout << "AddTwo(c, d): " << AddTwo(c, d) << endl;
    return 0;
}
```

The result of Program 18.2 is as follows:

```
    AddTwo(a, b): 30
    AddTwo(c, d): 31.1
```

Program 18.1 shows a simple example, where AddTwo() function is defined as a template, and is used to add both integers and double numbers. It is clear from the program that there is only one function definition for AddTwo(), which makes it a generic function in this case, that is, it uses a generic data type as parameters, rather than specific data types. In order use a template, we first need to build a template definition. This can be done as follows:

```
    template<typename T>

    T AddTwo(T  x, T  y)
    {
        return x+y;
    }
```

Through the statement template<typename T> the template header tells the compiler that we are going to use templates in this program. In other words, the "template" keyword specifies a function as a template function. Writing <class T> or <typename T> after keyword "template" specifies that the function takes a generic type argument T. The uppercase letter T, could be any letter, however, it is a usual practice to use T. In this case, the symbol T is called **type parameter**. It is simply a place holder that is replaced by an actual type or class when a function is invoked.

18.2 Function template

In Section 18.1, we have introduced templates. There are two basic types of templates in C++: **function templates** and **class templates**. A function template is declared in the same way as an ordinary function is declared, except that it is preceded by the specification:

```
template<class T>
```

The general form of a template function definition is shown as follows:

```
template <class type> return-type function-name(parameter list)
{
    // body of function
}
```

Here, "type" is a placeholder name for a data type used by the function. The "type" parameter T may be used in place of ordinary types within the function definition. The word "class" is used to mean a class or primitive type. Program 18.2 shows an example of a function template. Template functions are addressed like ordinary functions. A template may have several type parameters as follows:

```
Template<class T, class X, class Y, class Z>
```

Function templates provide a generic solution for overloaded functions. Instead of writing many functions that share the same task, we can write one generic function by using templates. Program 18.3 shows another example of function template, where template functions is used to swap two integers, floating-point numbers, and two strings. As shown in Program 18.2, we have used typename keyword. Although it is a common practice to use "class" instead, both keywords carry the same meaning. Originally, the developers used class to specify types in templates to avoid introducing a new keyword. Some worried that this overloading of the keyword can lead to confusion. Hence, a new keyword typename to resolve syntactic ambiguity is introduced later, and decided to let it also be used to specify template types to reduce confusion; however, class kept its overloaded meaning for backward compatibility.

```
// Program 18.3
// A program with function template
#include<iostream>
using namespace std;

template<class T>

void swapTwo(T& x, T& y)
{
    T temp;
    temp = x;
    x = y;
    y = temp;
```

```
}

int main ()
{
    int a = 10, b = 20;
    float p = 30.5f,q = 40.8f;
    char *r = "Hello", *s = "world";

    // swapping integers
    cout << "Swapping Integers" << endl;
    cout << "a= " << a << " and b =" << b << endl;
    swapTwo(a,b);
    cout << "a= " << a << " and b =" << b << endl << endl;

    cout << "Swapping Floating Point Numbers" << endl;
    cout << "p= " << p << " and q =" << q << endl;
    swapTwo(p,q);
    cout << "p= " << p << " and q =" << q << endl <<endl;

    cout << "Swapping Strings" << endl;
    cout << "r= " << r << " and s =" << s << endl;
    swapTwo(r,s);
    cout << "r= " << r << " and s =" << s << endl;

    return 0;
}
```

The result of Program 18.3 is as follows:

```
Swapping Integers
a= 10 and b =20
a= 20 and b =10

Swapping Floating Point Numbers
p= 30.5 and q =40.8
p= 40.8 and q =30.5

Swapping Strings
r= Hello and s =world
r= world and s =Hello
```

A template function is used to construct a family of functions working in the same fashion. They are also known as **"parameterized"** or **"generic" functions**. Each template is a skeleton for a set of similar functions working on different types of data. A template becomes a real function when it is invoked or instantiated with a specified data type. We can replace many overloaded functions with a single template.

A template function may be preceded by any of the normal modifiers such as `inline`, `extern`, `static`, and so forth.

18.3 Class template

Class templates work in the same way as function templates, except that they generate classes instead of functions. They provide the users a good way to define a generic pattern for class definitions. A class template must contain at least one generic type field. The general form of a generic class declaration is shown here:

```
template <class type> class class-name
{
    ...
}
```

Here, type is the placeholder type name that must be specified when a class is instantiated. We can define more than one generic data types by using a comma-separated list. A class template, like a function template, may have several template parameters. Moreover, some of them can be of primitive types of parameters:

```
template <class T, int x, class Y> class A
{
    ...
}
```

Sometimes, class templates are also called **parameterized types**. The parameters of the primitive types must be constant. Program 18.4 shows an example of a class template.

```
// Program 18.4
// Example for Class Template
#include <iostream>
using namespace std;

template <class T>

class addTwo
{
    T x, y;
    public:
        addTwo (T a, T b)
        {
            x = a; y = b;
```

```
            }
            T getSum ()
            {
                T sum;
                sum = x+y;
                return sum;
            }
};

int main ()
{
    addTwo <int> ADD (10, 55);
    cout << "Sum = " << ADD.getSum() << endl;
    return 0;
}
```

The result of Program 18.4 is as follows:

```
        Sum = 65
```

It is important to note that the member functions of a class template themselves function templates with the same template header as their class. Hence, we can rewrite Program 18.4, as Program 18.5 that also produces the same result.

```
// Program 18.5
// Example for class template
#include <iostream>
using namespace std;

template <class T>

class addTwo
{
    T x, y;
    public:
        addTwo (T a, T b)
        {
            x = a; y = b;
        }
        T getSum ();
};

template <class T>
T addTwo<T>::getSum()
{
    T sum;
    sum = x+y;
    return sum;
```

```
}

int main ()
{
    addTwo <int> ADD (10, 55);
    cout << "Sum = " << ADD.getSum() << endl;
    return 0;
}
```

Now, let us consider following statements in Program 18.5.

```
template <class T>
T addTwo<T>::getsSum()
{
    T sum;
    sum = x+y;
    return sum;
}
```

In this part of code, T is used four times: (a) first one is the template parameter; (b) second T refers to the type returned by the function; (c) third T (the one between angle brackets) specifies that this function's template parameter is also the class template parameter; and (d) fourth T represents generic type of sum variable.

18.4 Standard template library

In C++, standard template library or STL provides a set of well-structured generic C++ components that work together in seamless ways. They contain a collection of classes and function templates. This includes helper class and function templates, container and iterator class templates, generic algorithms that operate over iterators, function objects, and adaptors. The C++ STL is a powerful set of C++ template classes that provides general-purpose classes and function templates that implement many popular and commonly used algorithms and data structures, such as vectors, lists, queues, and stacks. The C++ STL includes three well-structured core components: containers, algorithms, and iterators. Containers are used to manage collections of objects of a certain kind. There are several different types of containers, such as deque, list, vector, map, and so forth. Algorithms act on containers by providing the means by which initialization, sorting, searching, and transforming of the contents of containers are performed. Iterators are used to step through the elements of collections of objects. These collections may be containers or subsets of containers. Some of the standard templates in C++ are shown in Table 18.1.

In this chapter, we will elaborate on vector STL. Vectors are useful when we have an unknown sequence of items to store but we want to access them by their sequence

Table 18.1: Some of the standard templates in C++ and their details.

Library Name	Description
<vector>	A dynamic array
<list>	A randomly changing sequence of items
<stack>	A sequence of items with pop and push at one end only
<queue>	A Sequence of items with pop and push at opposite ends
<deque>	Double-ended queue with pop and push at both ends
<bitset>	A subset of a fixed and small set of items
<set>	An unordered collection of items
<map>	An collection of pairs of items indexed by the first one

numbers. To use STL vectors in a program, we have to include the statement: #include <vector>. Suppose that T is any type or class, say an int, a float, a struct, or a class, then vector<T> v; declares a new and empty vector called v. Vector STL provides many functions so that a programmer can use them when necessary. Table 18.2 shows some of vector functions and their details.

Table 18.2: Details of functions available in vector STL in C++.

Function Name	Description
v.empty()	Test to see if v is empty.
v.size()	Find the number of items in v.
v.push_back(t)	Push a t:T onto the end of v.
v.pop_back()	Pop the front of v off v.
v.front()	To get the front item of v.
v.front() = expression	To change the front item.
v.back()	To get the back item of v.
v.back() = expression	To change the back item.
v[i]	To access the ith item ($0 \leq i < size()$) without checking to see if it exists.
v.at(i)	To access the ith item safely.
v = v1	To assign a copy of v1 to v.

Program 18.6 shows an example of understanding vector STL in C++.

```
// Program 18.6
// A program with vector STL
#include <iostream>
```

```
#include <vector>
using namespace std;
int main()
{
    // Creating a vector V to store integers
    vector<int> V;
    int i;

    // Printing the initial size of V
    cout << "Vector size = " << V.size() << endl << endl;

    // Pushing 10 values into the vector V
    for(i = 0; i < 10; i++)
    {
        V.push_back(i);
    }

    // Displaying the extended size of vector V
    cout << "Extended vector size = " << V.size() << endl << endl;

    //Accessing 10 values from the vector
    for(i = 0; i < 10; i++)
    {
    cout << "Value of V [" << i << "] = " << V[i] << endl;
    }

    cout <<endl;
    // Use iterator to access the values
    vector<int>::iterator v = V.begin();
    while( v != V.end())
    {
    cout << "value of v = " << *v << endl;
    v++;
    }

    cout << endl << "Accessing the 5th item = " << V.at(4) << endl;
    cout << "Accessing the front item = " << V.front() << endl;
    cout << "Accessing the back item = " << V.back() << endl;
    return 0;
}
```

The result of Program 18.6 is as follows:

```
Vector size = 0

Extended vector size = 10
Value of V [0] = 0
Value of V [1] = 1
Value of V [2] = 2
```

```
Value of V [3] = 3
Value of V [4] = 4
Value of V [5] = 5
Value of V [6] = 6
Value of V [7] = 7
Value of V [8] = 8
Value of V [9] = 9

value of v = 0
value of v = 1
value of v = 2
value of v = 3
value of v = 4
value of v = 5
value of v = 6
value of v = 7
value of v = 8
value of v = 9

Accessing the 5th item = 4
Accessing the front item = 0
Accessing the back item = 9
```

18.5 Review questions

1. What is a template? What are the common types of templates?
2. Discuss function template with an example program.
3. Discuss class template with an example program.
4. List the advantages of templates in C++.
5. Write a note on standard template library in C++.
6. Write a program to demonstrate vector STL in C++.

Appendix A

List of C++ header files and library functions

Header files

Title	Description
cmath	Declares functions for mathematical operations
cstdlib	Defines general-purpose functions
iostream	Defines standard input and output stream objects
cstring	Defines functions to manipulate C-style strings and arrays
cctype	Declares functions to classify (and transform) individual characters
csignal	Handles signals
clocale	Supports localization-specific settings, such as date/time formatting
cwctype	Declares functions for classifying and transforming individual wide characters
cstdio	Includes C Standard input and output library
cwchar	Defines several functions to work with C wide string
cuchar	Performs conversion between multibyte characters and UTF-16 or UTF-32
csetjmp	Bypasses the normal function call and return discipline
cfenv	Accesses floating-point environment
ctime	Contains function definitions to work with date and time

<cmath>

Title	Description
pow()	Computes power of a number
llrint()	Rounds an argument by using current rounding mode
remainder()	Returns remainder of x/y
nan()	Returns a quiet NaN value
cosh()	Returns hyperbolic cosine of an angle
copysign()	Takes two arguments and returns a number with value of first and sign of second
fma()	Takes three arguments such as x, y and z, and returns x*y+z without losing precision
abs()	Returns an absolute value of an int/long argument
fabs()	Returns an absolute value of an float/double argument
fdim()	Returns positive difference between arguments
fmin()	Returns smallest between two given arguments
fmax()	Returns largest between two arguments passed
hypot()	Returns square root of sum of square of arguments
nexttoward()	Returns next value after x in direction of y, where y is always of type long double
nextafter()	Returns next value after x in direction of y
cbrt()	Computes cube root of a number
sqrt()	Computes square root of a number
remquo()	Returns remainder and stores quotient of x/y

https://doi.org/10.1515/9783110593846-019

logb()	Returns logarithm of	x	
log1p()	Returns natural logarithm of x+1
scalbln()	Scales x by FLT_RADIX to the power n
log2()	Returns base2 logarithm of a number
scalbn()	Scales x by FLT_RADIX to the power n
ilogb()	Returns integral part of logarithm of	x	
nearbyint()	Rounds an argument to an integral value by using current rounding mode
expm1()	Returns the exponential e raised to the power minus 1
ldexp()	Returns product of x and 2 raised to the power e
frexp()	Breaks float to its binary significant
exp2()	Returns base-2 exponential function of a number
exp()	Returns exponential (e) raised to a number
modf()	Breaks a number into an integral and a fractional part
log10()	Returns base-10 logarithm of a number
lrint()	Rounds an argument by using current rounding mode
rint()	Rounds an argument by using current rounding mode
llround()	Rounds an argument to its nearest long long integer value
lround()	Returns a long integer value nearest to an argument
round()	Returns an integral value nearest to an argument
trunc()	Truncates the decimal part of a number
log()	Returns natural logarithm of a number
atanh()	Returns arc hyperbolic tangent of a number
asinh()	Returns arc hyperbolic sine of a number
acosh()	Returns hyperbolic cosine of a number
fmod()	Computes floating point remainder of division
tanh()	Returns hyperbolic tangent of an angle
floor()	Returns floor value of a decimal number
ceil()	Return ceiling value of a number
sinh()	Returns hyperbolic sine of an angle
acos()	Returns inverse cosine of a number
atan2()	Returns inverse tangent of a coordinate
tan()	Returns tangent of an argument
atan()	Returns inverse tangent of a number
asin()	Returns inverse sine of a number
sin()	Returns sine of an argument
cos()	Returns cosine of an argument

<cstdlib>

Title	Description
calloc()	Allocates a block of memory and initializes it to zero
wcstombs()	Converts a wide character string to a multibyte sequence
mbstowcs()	Converts a multibyte character string to a wide character sequence
wctomb()	Converts a wide character to a multibyte character
mbtowc()	Converts a multibyte character to a wide character
mblen()	Determines the size of a multibyte character
lldiv()	Computes integral division of two long long integers

llabs()	Returns an absolute value of a long long integer data
ldiv()	Computes integral division of long integer numbers
labs()	Returns an absolute value of a long or a long integer number
abs()	Returns an absolute value of an integer
div()	Computes integral quotient and remainder of a number
qsort()	Sorts an array by using quick-sort algorithm
bsearch()	Performs binary search on a sorted array
_Exit()	Causes termination without cleanup tasks
quick_exit()	Causes termination without cleaning resources
getenv()	Returns a pointer to environment variable passed
at_quick_exit()	Registers a function and calls on quick termination
atexit()	Registers a function to be called on termination
realloc()	Reallocates a block of previously allocated memory
malloc()	Allocates a block of uninitialized memory
free()	Deallocates a block of memory
srand()	Seeds pseudo random number for rand()
strtoull()	Converts a string to an unsigned long long integer
strtoll()	Converts a string to a long long integer
atol()	Converts a string to an integer
strtol()	Converts a string to a number
atof()	Converts a string to a double
strtod()	Returns a string float to a double

\<iostream\>

Title	Description
wclog	Writes to log stream with wide character
wcerr	Prints to error stream as wide character type
wcout	Displays wide characters (Unicode) to screen
wcin	Accepts input in wide character type
clog	Used for streaming logs
cerr	Writes to error stream
cout	Displays output to output device, that is, monitor
cin	Accepts input from a user

\<cstring\>

Title	Description
strxfrm()	Transform a byte string into an implementation defined form
strcoll()	Compares two null terminated strings
strlen()	Returns the length of a given string
strerror()	Gives the description of a system error code
memset()	Copies a character to beginning of a string n times
strtok()	Splits a string based on a delimiter
strstr()	Finds the first occurrence of a substring in a string
strspn()	Gives the length of a maximum initial segment

strrchr()	Searches the last occurrence of a character in a string
strpbrk()	Searches the characters of one string in another string
strcspn()	Searches a string for characters in another string
strchr()	Searches the first occurrence of a character
memchr()	Searches an array for the first occurrence of a character
strncmp()	Compares two strings lexographically
strcmp()	Compares two strings
memcmp()	Compares two pointer objects
strncat()	Appends a string to the end of another string
strcat()	Appends a copy of string to the end of another string
strncpy()	Copies a character string from source to destination
strcpy()	Copies a character string from source to destination
memmove()	Copies a memory, even if there is overlapping blocks
memcpy()	Copies a block of memory from source to destination
strxfrm()	Transforms a byte string into an implementation defined form

\<cctype\>

Title	Description
toupper()	Converts a given character to uppercase
tolower()	Converts a given character to lowercase
isxdigit()	Checks if a given character is a hexadecimal character
isupper()	Check if a given character is uppercase or not
isspace()	Check if a given character is a whitespace character
ispunct()	Check if a given character is a punctuation character
isprint()	Check if a given character is printable or not
islower()	Checks if a given character is lowercase
isgraph()	Checks if a given character is graphic or not
isdigit()	Checks if a given character is a digit or not
iscntrl()	Checks if a given character is a control character
isblank()	Checks if a given character is a blank character
isalpha()	Checks if a given character is analphabet or not

\<csignal\>

Title	Description
raise()	Sends a signal to the program
signal()	Sets an error handler for a specified signal

\<clocale\>

Title	Description
localeconv()	Returns current locale formatting rules
setlocale()	Sets locale information for the current program

<cwctype>

Title	Description
iswdigit()	Checks if a given wide character is a digit or not
wctype()	Returns a wide character classification
wctrans()	Returns current transformation for a wide character
towctrans()	Transforms a given wide character
iswctype()	Checks if a given wide character has a certain property
towupper()	Converts a given wide character to uppercase
towlower()	Converts a given wide character to lowercase
iswxdigit()	Checks if a given wide character is a hexadecimal number
iswupper()	Checks if a given wide character is uppercase
iswspace()	Checks if a given wide character is a wide whitespace
iswpunct()	Checks if a given wide character is a punctuation
iswprint()	Checks if a given wide character can be printed
iswlower()	Checks if a given wide character is lowercase
iswgraph()	Checks if a wide character has a graphical representation
iswcntrl()	Checks if a given wide character is a control character
iswblank()	Checks if a given wide character is a blank character
iswalpha()	Checks if a given wide character is an alphabet
iswalnum()	Checks if a given wide character is an alphanumeric

<cstdio>

Title	Description
getc()	Reads next character from an input stream
fseek()	Sets a file position indicator for a given file stream
ungetc()	Pushes a previously read character back to the stream
vsscanf()	Reads data from a string buffer
vscanf()	Reads data from a stdin
vfscanf()	Reads data from a file stream
freopen()	Opens a new file with a stream associated to another
fflush()	Flushes any buffered data to the respective device
setvbuf()	Changes or specifies buffering mode and buffer size
perror()	Prints an error to stderr
ferror()	Checks for errors in a given stream
feof()	Checks if a file stream EOF has been reached or not
clearerr()	Resets error flags and EOF indicator for a stream
rewind()	Sets a file position to the beginning of a stream
ftell()	Returns the current position of a file pointer
fsetpos()	Sets a stream file pointer to a given position
fgetpos()	Gets a current file position
fwrite()	Writes a specified number of characters to a stream
fread()	Reads a specified number of characters from a stream
puts()	Writes a string to stdout
putchar()	Writes a character to stdout
putc()	Writes a character to a given output stream

gets()	Reads a line from stdin
getchar()	Reads the next character from stdin
fputs()	Writes a string to a file stream
fputc()	Writes a character to a given output stream
fgets()	Reads *n* number of characters from a file stream
fgetc()	Reads the next character from a given input stream
vsprintf()	Writes a formatted string to a string buffer
vsnprintf()	Writes a formatted string to a string buffer
vprintf()	Write formatted data from variable argument list to stdout
vfprintf()	Writes a formatted string to a file stream
sscanf()	Reads data from a string buffer
sprintf()	Writes a formatted string to a buffer
snprintf()	Writes a formatted string to a character string buffer
scanf	Reads data from stdin
printf()	Writes a formatted string to stdout
fscanf()	Reads data from a file stream
fprintf()	Writes a formatted string to a file stream
setbuf()	Sets the internal buffer to be used for an input or output operation
fopen()	Opens a specified file
fclose()	Closes a given file stream
tmpnam()	Generates a unique filename
tmpfile()	Creates a temporary file with an auto-generated name
rename()	Renames or moves a specified file
remove()	Deletes a specified file

<cwchar>

Title	Description
wcscoll()	Compares two null terminated wide strings
wcstoull()	Converts a wide string number to an unsigned long long
wcstoul()	Converts a wide string of a given base to an unsigned long
wcstoll()	Converts a wide string of a specified base to an integer
wcsftime()	Converts a given date and time to a wide character string
wmemset()	Copies a single wide character for a certain number of time
wmemmove()	Moves wide chars from source to destination
wmemcpy()	Copies a specified number of wide chars from source to destination
wmemcmp()	Compares wide chars of two wide strings
wmemchr()	Searches for the first occurrence of a wide character
wcsxfrm()	Transforms a wide string to a defined implementation
wcsstr()	Finds the first occurrence of a wide substring in a string
wcsspn()	Returns the length of a maximum initial segment
wcsrchr()	Searches the last occurrence of a wide character in a string
wcspbrk()	Searches for a set of wide character in a given wide string
wcsncpy()	Copies a specified number of wide characters
wcsncmp()	Compares a specified number of wide character of strings
wcsncat()	Appends a specified number of wide character to another string
wcslen()	Returns the length of a given wide string
wcscspn()	Returns a number of wide character before its first occurrence

wcscpy()	Copies a wide character string from a source to destination
wcscmp()	Compares two wide strings lexicographically
wcschr()	Searches for a wide character in a wide string
wcscat()	Appends a copy of a wide string to the end of another
wcsrtombs()	Converts a wide character sequence to a narrow multibyte character sequence
wctob()	Converts a wide character to a single-byte character
wcrtomb()	Converts a wide character to its narrow multibyte rep
mbsrtowcs()	Converts a narrow multibyte character sequence to a wide character sequence
mbsinit()	Describes an initial conversion state of mbstate_t obj
mbrtowc()	Converts a narrow multibyte character to a wide character
mbrlen()	Determines in bytes the size of a multibyte character
btowc()	Converts a character to its wide character
wcstok()	Returns the next token in a null terminated wide string
wcstold()	Converts a wide string float number to a long double
wcstol()	Converts a wide string float number to a long integer
wcstof()	Converts a wide string float number to a float
wcstod()	Converts a wide string float number to a double
wscanf()	Reads a wide character from stdin
wprintf()	Writes a formatted wide string to stdout
vwscanf()	Reads a wide character from stdin
vwprintf()	Writes a formatted wide string to stdout
vswscanf()	Reads a wide character string from wide string buffer
vswprintf()	Writes a formatted wide string to a wide string buffer
vfwscanf()	Reads a wide character string from a file stream
vfwprintf()	Writes a formatted wide string to a file stream
ungetwc()	Pushes a previously read wide character back to the stream
swscanf()	Reads a wide character from a wide string buffer
swprintf()	Writes a formatted wide string to a wide string buffer
putwchar()	Writes a wide character to stdout
putwc()	Writes a wide character to a given output stream
getwchar()	Reads the next wide character from stdin
getwc()	Reads the next wide character from input stream
fwscanf()	Reads a wide character from a file stream
fwprintf()	Writes a formatted wide string to a file stream
fwide()	Sets or queries the orientation of a given file stream
fputws()	Writes a wide string except a null wide character to output
fputwc()	Writes a wide character to a given output stream
fgetws()	Reads a specified number of wide characters from a stream
fgetwc()	Reads the next wide character from a given input stream

\<cuchar\>

Title	Description
mbrtoc32()	Converts a narrow multibyte character to a 32-bit character
mbrtoc16()	Converts a narrow multibyte character to a 16-bit character
c32rtomb()	Converts a 32-bit character to a narrow multibyte character
c16rtomb()	Converts a 16-bit character to a narrow multibyte character

<csetjmp>

Title	Description
longjmp() and setjmp()	Restores a previously saved environment

<cfenv>

Title	Description
fetestexcept()	Tests a floating-point exception
feupdateenv()	Updates a floating-point environment
feholdexcept()	Saves and clears floating-point status flags
fesetenv()	Sets a floating-point environment
fesetround()	Set a rounding direction
fegetenv()	Stores the status of a floating-point environment in an object
fegetround()	Gets a round direction mode
fesetexceptflag()	Sets a given floating-point exceptions to the environment
fegetexceptflag()	Gets floating-point exception flags
feraiseexcept()	Raises specified floating-point exceptions
feclearexcept()	Attempts to clear floating-point exception flags

<ctime>

Title	Description
strftime()	Converts a calendar time to a multibyte character string
mktime()	Converts a local calendar time to a time since epoch
localtime()	Converts a given time since epoch to local time
gmtime()	Converts a given time since epoch to UTC time
ctime()	Converts a time since epoch to character representation
asctime()	Converts a calendar time to a character representation
time()	Returns a current calendar time
difftime()	Computes the difference between two times in seconds
clock()	Returns time consumed by a processor to run a program

Appendix B

List of non-OOP C++ programming exercises

1. Input two numbers and work out their sum; average and sum of the squares of the numbers.
2. Write a program to read a number of degrees Celsius of "float" type, and print the equivalent temperature in degrees Fahrenheit as a "float." Print your results in the following form:
   100.0 degrees Celsius converts to 212.0 degrees Fahrenheit.
3. If an input is given as an integer number of seconds, print the equivalent time in hours, minutes, and seconds as output. Recommended output format should be as follows:
   7322 seconds is equivalent to 2 hours 2 minutes 2 seconds.
4. Write a program to print several lines (e.g., your name and address). You may use either several cout instructions, each with a newline character in it, or one cout with several newlines in the string.
5. Write a program to find a maximum of three numbers by using ternary operator.
6. Declare (globally) an enumerated-type rainbow that consists of the hues of red, blue, green, and purple colors. In the main function, declare a variable "color" to be of enumerated-type rainbow. Initialize the color variable to the constant blue. Then, assign the color variable the constant purple.
7. Design, develop, and execute a program in C++ to find and output all the roots of a given quadratic equation, for non-zero coefficients.
8. Write a C++ program to generate n Fibonacci numbers by using for loop.
9. Write a program that outputs a right-side triangle of height n and width 2n–1; the output for n = 6 would be:

```
         *
        ***
       *****
      *******
     *********
    ***********
```

10. Design, develop, and execute a program in C++ to implement Euclid's algorithm to find the GCD and LCM of two integers and to output the results along with the given integers.
11. Design, develop, and execute a program in C++ to reverse a given four-digit integer number and check whether it is a palindrome or not. Output the given number with a suitable message.
12. Design, develop, and execute a program in C++ to evaluate the given polynomial $f(x) = a_4x^4 + a_3x3 + a_2x^2 + a_1x + a_0$ for a given value of x and the coefficients by using Horner's method.

13. Write a program that prompts the user for a string, and prints its reverse without using library function(s).
14. Write a program that prompts the user for a sentence, and prints each word on its own line.
15. Write a function to calculate whether a number is a prime. Return 1 if it is prime, and 0 if it is not a prime.
16. Write a function to determine the number of prime numbers below n.
17. Write a function to find the square root of a number by using Newton's method.
18. Write a Program to find out the number of even and odd numbers in a given data series.
19. Design, develop, and execute a program in C++ to copy its input to its output, replacing each string of one or more blanks by a single blank.
20. Design, develop, and execute a program in C++ to input N integer numbers in ascending order into a single-dimensional array and perform a binary search for a given key integer number and report success or failure in the form of a suitable message.
21. Design, develop, and execute a program in C++ to input N integer numbers into a single-dimensional array, sort them in ascending order by using the bubble sort technique, and print both the given array and the sorted array with suitable headings.
22. Design, develop, and execute a program in C++ to read two matrices A (M × N) and B (P × Q), and compute the product of A and B, if the matrices are compatible for multiplication. The program must print the input matrices and the resultant matrix with suitable headings and formats, if the matrices are compatible for multiplication; otherwise, the program must print a suitable message. (For the purpose of demonstration, the array sizes M, N, P, and Q can all be less than or equal to 3.)
23. Define an anonymous union consisting of the variables a (int), b (float), and c (char). Assign this union the value 224.
24. Write a program with a function that calls function a that, in turn, calls function b that, in turn, calls function c.
25. Write a C++ program to demonstrate the Tower of Hanoi program by using recursion.
26. Write a C++ program to generate n Fibonacci numbers by using recursion.

Appendix C

List of C++ OOP programming exercises

1. Define a class student, with two data members (age and number) and two method members [readValues() and printValues()]. The readValues() method reads the data values from the keyboard, and printValues() method prints the values to the screen. Create an object (TOM) of type student, and understand the use of both class and objects in a program. (The complete program is written here for this purpose.)

```
//Program by Liu Shan
//Date: January 20,2018
//C++ Programming@ SDUST
#include<iostream>
using namespace std;

class student
{
    public:

            int age;
            int number;

    void readValues()
    {
        cout << "Enter age of student " << endl;
        cin >> age;
        cout << "Enter student number " << endl;
        cin >> number;
    }

    void printValues()
        {
            cout << "Student Age :" << age << endl;
            cout << "Student Number :" << number << endl;
        }
};
int main()
{
    student TOM;

    TOM.readValues();
    TOM.printValues();

    return 0;
}
```

2. Repeat the previous Programming Exercise 1, and make data members public, private, and protected. See the changes, and note down the errors during compilation, if any. Try for all combinations of access modifiers as follows: (a) make all data and method members public, (b) make all data and method members private, (c) make all data and method members protected, (d) make some members private and some public, (e) make some members private and some protected, and (f) make some members public and some protected.

3. Repeat Programming Exercise 1, and create two objects (TOM and JACK) of type student class, and test the code for readValues() and printValues()for both objects.

4. Use the scope resolution operator (::), and place the two methods (of Programming Exercise 1) outside of the class body. Then repeat the exercise as described in Programming Exercise 1.

5. Define a student class as in Programming Exercise 1, and define a subclass (of student) freshmen without any data members, as shown below. Create one object of type student and another object of type freshmen; test the program to understand single (public) inheritance.

```
class freshmen: public student
{

};
```

6. Repeat Programming Exercise 5, and test for single, protected inheritance, and single private inheritance. Note down the errors, if any.

7. Define a student class as in Programming Exercise 1, and define subclasses (of student) freshmen and sophomore without any data members. Create an object each of type student, freshmen, and sophomore to test the program to understand multiple subclasses.

```
class freshmen: public student
{

};

class sophomore: public student
{

};
```

8. Define one student class, as in Programming Exercise 1, and another teacher class. Define a subclass instructor derived from both student and teacher

classes without any data members. Create an object each of type student, teacher, and instructor to test the program and understand multiple inheritance. (Hint: See the following code.)

```
class teacher
{
    public:
        int courseno;
        int classno;

    void readCourse()
    {
        cout << "Enter Course Number " << endl;
        cin >> courseno;
        cout << "Enter Class Number " << endl;
        cin >> classno;
    }

    void printCourse()
    {
        cout << "Course Number :" << courseno << endl;
        cout << "Class Number :" << classno << endl;
    }
};
class instructor: public student ,  public teacher
{

};
```

9. Define a student class, as in Programming Exercise 1, and define a subclass (of student) freshmen, without any data members. Then define another subclass sdustfresh derived from freshmen, without any data members. Create an object of type student, freshmen, and sdustfresh to test the program to understand multilevel inheritance.

```
class freshmen: public student
{

};

class sdustfresh:  public freshmen
{

};
```

10. Define a student class, as in Programming Exercise 1, and define subclasses (of student) freshmen and sophomore without any data members. Create a new class geniusstudent derived from both freshmen and sophomore and create objects of type student, freshmen, sophomore, and geniusstudent to test the program to understand diamond inheritance. Note down the problem of diamond inheritance.

```
class freshmen: public student
{

};

class sophomore: public student
{

};

class geniusstudent: public freshmen, public sophomore
{

};
```

11. Repeat Programming Exercise 10 and use virtual keyword to solve the problem with diamond inheritance.

```
class freshmen: public virtual student
{

};

class sophomore: public virtual student
{

};

class geniusstudent: public freshmen, public sophomore
{

};
```

12. Repeat Programming Exercise 5 by adding some data and method members to subclass freshmen to understand single inheritance.

13. Repeat Programming Exercise 7 by adding some data and method members to subclasses freshmen and sophomore to understand multiple subclasses.

14. Repeat Programming Exercise 8 by adding some data and method members to class instructor to understand multiple inheritance.

15. Repeat Programming Exercise 9 by adding some data and method members to subclasses `freshmen` and `sdustfresh` multilevel inheritance.
16. Repeat Programming Exercises 10 and 11 by adding some data and method members to classes `freshmen`, `sophomore`, and `geniusstudent` to understand diamond inheritance.
17. Repeat Programming Exercise 1 by adding a default constructor, as follows, and test the program.

```
student()
{
    cout << "I am student constructor " << endl;
}
```

18. Repeat Programming Exercise 1 by adding a parameterized constructor, as follows, and test the program.

```
student(int value)
{
    cout << "I am student constructor Value "
    << value << endl;
}
```

19. Repeat Programming Exercise 1 by adding one default constructor and few parameterized constructors, and test the program.
20. Repeat Programming Exercise 1 by adding a destructor, as follows, and test the program.

```
~student()
{
    cout << "I am student destructor " << endl;
}
```

21. Repeat Programming Exercise 1 by adding a constructor and a destructor, and test the program.
22. Repeat Programming Exercise 5 by adding a default constructor to base class as well as to derived class, and test the program.
23. Repeat Programming Exercise 5 by adding a destructor to base class as well as to derived class, and test the program.
24. Repeat Programming Exercise 5 by adding a constructor and a destructor to base class as well as to derived class, and test the program.

Appendix D

Decimal - Binary - Octal - Hex – ASCII Conversion Chart

Decimal	Binary	Octal	Hex	ASCII	Decimal	Binary	Octal	Hex	ASCII	Decimal	Binary	Octal	Hex	ASCII	Decimal	Binary	Octal	Hex	ASCII
0	00000000	000	00	NUL	32	00100000	040	20	SP	64	01000000	100	40	@	96	01100000	140	60	`
1	00000001	001	01	SOH	33	00100001	041	21	!	65	01000001	101	41	A	97	01100001	141	61	a
2	00000010	002	02	STX	34	00100010	042	22	"	66	01000010	102	42	B	98	01100010	142	62	b
3	00000011	003	03	ETX	35	00100011	043	23	#	67	01000011	103	43	C	99	01100011	143	63	c
4	00000100	004	04	EOT	36	00100100	044	24	$	68	01000100	104	44	D	100	01100100	144	64	d
5	00000101	005	05	ENQ	37	00100101	045	25	%	69	01000101	105	45	E	101	01100101	145	65	e
6	00000110	006	06	ACK	38	00100110	046	26	&	70	01000110	106	46	F	102	01100110	146	66	f
7	00000111	007	07	BEL	39	00100111	047	27	'	71	01000111	107	47	G	103	01100111	147	67	g
8	00001000	010	08	BS	40	00101000	050	28	(	72	01001000	110	48	H	104	01101000	150	68	h
9	00001001	011	09	HT	41	00101001	051	29	)	73	01001001	111	49	I	105	01101001	151	69	i
10	00001010	012	0A	LF	42	00101010	052	2A	*	74	01001010	112	4A	J	106	01101010	152	6A	j
11	00001011	013	0B	VT	43	00101011	053	2B	+	75	01001011	113	4B	K	107	01101011	153	6B	k
12	00001100	014	0C	FF	44	00101100	054	2C	,	76	01001100	114	4C	L	108	01101100	154	6C	l
13	00001101	015	0D	CR	45	00101101	055	2D	-	77	01001101	115	4D	M	109	01101101	155	6D	m
14	00001110	016	0E	SO	46	00101110	056	2E	.	78	01001110	116	4E	N	110	01101110	156	6E	n
15	00001111	017	0F	SI	47	00101111	057	2F	/	79	01001111	117	4F	O	111	01101111	157	6F	o
16	00010000	020	10	DLE	48	00110000	060	30	0	80	01010000	120	50	P	112	01110000	160	70	p
17	00010001	021	11	DC1	49	00110001	061	31	1	81	01010001	121	51	Q	113	01110001	161	71	q
18	00010010	022	12	DC2	50	00110010	062	32	2	82	01010010	122	52	R	114	01110010	162	72	r
19	00010011	023	13	DC3	51	00110011	063	33	3	83	01010011	123	53	S	115	01110011	163	73	s
20	00010100	024	14	DC4	52	00110100	064	34	4	84	01010100	124	54	T	116	01110100	164	74	t
21	00010101	025	15	NAK	53	00110101	065	35	5	85	01010101	125	55	U	117	01110101	165	75	u
22	00010110	026	16	SYN	54	00110110	066	36	6	86	01010110	126	56	V	118	01110110	166	76	v
23	00010111	027	17	ETB	55	00110111	067	37	7	87	01010111	127	57	W	119	01110111	167	77	w
24	00011000	030	18	CAN	56	00111000	070	38	8	88	01011000	130	58	X	120	01111000	170	78	x
25	00011001	031	19	EM	57	00111001	071	39	9	89	01011001	131	59	Y	121	01111001	171	79	y
26	00011010	032	1A	SUB	58	00111010	072	3A	:	90	01011010	132	5A	Z	122	01111010	172	7A	z
27	00011011	033	1B	ESC	59	00111011	073	3B	;	91	01011011	133	5B	[	123	01111011	173	7B	{
28	00011100	034	1C	FS	60	00111100	074	3C	<	92	01011100	134	5C	\	124	01111100	174	7C	|
29	00011101	035	1D	GS	61	00111101	075	3D	=	93	01011101	135	5D	]	125	01111101	175	7D	}
30	00011110	036	1E	RS	62	00111110	076	3E	>	94	01011110	136	5E	^	126	01111110	176	7E	~
31	00011111	037	1F	US	63	00111111	077	3F	?	95	01011111	137	5F	_	127	01111111	177	7F	DEL

Appendix E

Bibliography

[1]   Bjarne Stroustrup, *The C++ Programming Language*, 4th Edition, Addison-Wesley, Pearson
       Education, 2013.
[2]   Bruce Eckel, *Thinking in C++, Introduction to Standard C++* (Vol. 1), 2nd Edition, New Jersey,
       Prentice Hall, March, 2000.
[3]   C++ Library Functions, available from: https://www.programiz.com/cpp-programming/library-
       function/.
[4]   Code::Blocks, available from: http://codeblocks.org.
[5]   Donald Weiman, Decimal-Binary-Octal-Hex-ASCII Conversion Chart,2012, available from:
       http://web.alfredstate.edu/faculty/weimandn/miscellaneous/ascii/ascii_index.html.
[6]   E. Balaguruswamy, *Object Oriented Programming with C++*, 4th Edition, Tata McGraw-Hill,
       2008.
[7]   Ivor Horton, *Beginning C++*, 4th Edition, Apress, November 2014.
[8]   Visual Studio 2017, available from: www.visualstudio.com.

Index

Abacus 1
Abstract class 312
Access modifiers 264
Access specifiers 255
Actual parameter 175
Addition 2
AI 6
ALGOL 6
Algorithm 2
Analysis 2
Analytical Engine 1
Application software 4
Argument 175
Arithmetic expression 71
Array of characters 168, 211
Array of pointers 152
Arrays of objects 261
Arrays of strings 143
Arrays of structures 215
Arrays 121
Assigned 49
Assignment operators 71
Associativity 81
Attribute 9
Automatic 64

Babbage, Charles 1
Backus, John 6
Base class 283
Bell laboratories 6
Binary code 6
Binary files 18
Binary operators 71
Binary search 155
Bitwise operators 71
Block scope 64
Bool 61
Boolean 52
Break 114
Bubble sort 159
Buffer 62, 239
Built-in functions 140
Built-in operator 13

C 13
Catch 229

char 49
Child Class 283
cin 17
Class 41
Class templates 315
Class variables 293
COBOL 6
Coding 3
Comments 15
Compiler 18
Compile-time 299
Compound assignment 82
Compound statement 93
Conditional operator 71
Const 57
Constants 57
Constructors 269
Continue 116
Copy constructor 278
cout 16
CPU 1

Data abstraction 11
Data hiding 255
Data members 256
Data types 47
Decision-making 85
Declarative 7
Decrement operations 110
Decrement operators 71
Default constructor 271
default 94
#define 57
Definiteness 2
Derived class 283
Destructor 280
Difference engine 1
Directive 15
Divide by zero 228
Documentation 3
Dot notation 206
double 49
do-while 101, 104
Dynamic binding 11
Dynamic polymorphism 299

https://doi.org/10.1515/9783110593846-020